Revelation Revolution

The Overlooked Message of the Apocalypse

GREG ALBRECHT

world PUBLISHING
SINCE 1928

Table of Contents

Acknowledgements

Only one popular notion about the Book of Revelation prevails in early twenty-first century Christendom, and fools who attempt to question the biblical integrity of that generally accepted worldview are not usually suffered gladly. My thanks therefore go to those who have assisted, motivated, and encouraged me to critically examine the prophetic status quo and walk on ground that many consider to be holy.

Solomon was right; of making many books there has been no end (Ec 12:12). There is no end of prophetic books about future events and the end times. Solomon was noted for his wisdom—he resisted the temptation, as far as I know, to author a book about the "end times message" of the Book of Revelation. I can hear you say, "How could he have, living 1,000 years before it was written?" My personal experience of walking down the same-old, same-old calf path of prophetic teaching for several decades leads me to conclude that Solomon would have done as good a job writing about the Book of Revelation having never seen it as some who have seen it. In all fairness, it doesn't appear that critical study of the Book of Revelation has always been a prerequisite for offering dogmatic opinion about what it means.

Books about the end times, the last days, and a "fast-approaching/soon-coming" end of the world, based upon one exclusive view of how to interpret the Book of Revelation, have littered the landscape of the days of our lives. Many have lost faith in God because of sensational interpretations about the Book of Revelation that have failed. When a specific interpretation of Revelation failed, those who believed it have often blamed God.

We North Americans have been, and continue to be, an easy mark for lurid, spine-tingling portrayals of future events said to be based on the Book of Revelation. We are people who trust in and believe the Bible—but in most cases we don't read it carefully. We let others do our biblical thinking for us. Our biblical illiteracy has turned us into fair game for those who have turned the Book of Revelation into an epic horror movie of biblical proportions. God has not failed us; soothsayers and prognosticators with "end times messages" have.

I would also be remiss in failing to acknowledge the many who contributed to the predictions I once believed. Interpretations of the Book of Revelation that have failed have in turn motivated me to return to this pivotal book, asking God to help me discover its real message. Were it not for my own experiences with failed predictions, and my personal ministry to many who have suffered enormous pain when bogus interpretations have failed, my view of the Book of Revelation would probably remain unchanged.

I thank those who work with me in Plain Truth Ministries, whose talents and efforts have contributed to this final product. Laura Urista has served in many ways, from proofreading and editing to other stages of production of the final manuscript. Her son, Tim, helped me locate and research a variety of resources that comprise some of the literature I consulted. My co-worker, good friend and "right hand man" Monte Wolverton worked with me on this manuscript for several years. Monte shares a religious journey similar to mine through the wilderness of bizarre and irresponsible interpretations of Revelation.

My wife, Karen, has been supportive of my interest in discovering the core meaning of Revelation, and I thank her for her patience as I searched for *Revelation Revolution.*

Words fail to express my appreciation for the faith and confidence expressed in me by World Publishing. Randy Elliott, you have become a good friend, taking the time to understand my vision for not only this book, but the work of Plain Truth Ministries. Frank Couch, you are an enormously gifted editor. It is an honor to be associated with you and learn from your knowledge and wisdom. Bruce Barbour has been the hands-on editor who has seen the manuscript through its final stages, and I am grateful for your expertise, Bruce. You took the book I thought was virtually complete, and through your graciously offered, insightful critique this "finished" product has been vastly improved.

Most importantly, I thank you, the reader. If you are reading these words, chances are you are searching for meaning; and I pray that the following pages will not disappoint you. As you read, may you come to know the Lamb of God in new and fresh ways. After all, *Revelation Revolution* is all about Him.

Frequently Used Terms and Phrases

Alpha and Omega—The first and last letters of the Greek alphabet, used in Revelation as a symbolic reference to God's eternity.

amillennialism—The belief that the thousand years used in the Book of Revelation should not be understood literally, but instead that it refers to a symbolic "long period of time"—specifically, the length of time between the first and second comings of Jesus Christ.

Antichrist—An enemy imposter, a philosophical or religious idea or leader that counterfeits and poses as Jesus Christ. While the biblical use of the term is confined to the letters of John (the human author of Revelation), the term is often used of the powers in Revelation that oppose the one true God.

Apocalypse—Specifically, the Book of Revelation—in common usage, colossal and staggering "acts of God" usually associated with the end of this age.

apocalyptic literature—A genre of literature (Revelation being an example) that presents scenes of the end of the world while offering hope and vindication to the oppressed.

Babylon—A metaphor, in the Book of Revelation, of human culture and religion that rejects and opposes the one true God.

beast—Referred to 36 times in the Book of Revelation, a representation of the combined political and religious powers that oppose Jesus Christ.

Christ-centered—A worldview and biblical interpretation that places Jesus Christ at the center of all reality.

Christological—Pertaining to Christ, His person and work.

dispensationalism—A method of biblical interpretation that divides history into different periods (dispensations), that requires a literal interpretation of Scripture and a premillennial view of eschatology.

end times—An era thought to be the last generation before the second coming of Jesus Christ, the last generation in earthly history.

eschatology—The study of last things, events surrounding the end of time as humans experience it.

futurism—An interpretive view of the Book of Revelation that sees the vast majority of its prophecies as being fulfilled in some future time, shortly before the second coming of Jesus Christ.

genre—A distinctive type of literature, a literary style.

gospel—The message of salvation offered to all who believe in Jesus.

grace—God's relationship with humanity, on the basis of His goodness, in spite of any merit on the part of humanity; undeserved and unmerited favor given to humans on the basis of God's goodness and generosity.

hermeneutics—The science and art of interpreting the Bible.

historicism—A viewpoint of the Book of Revelation that understands its message to be a prophetic record of history from the time of the early church to the end of the world. Prophetic fulfillment is thus seen as progressive.

idealism—An approach to understanding the Book of Revelation that sees Revelation as a spiritual message, with its fulfillment either in spiritual reality or in some historical events. The message of Revelation is thus understood as timeless, always relevant to Christians.

Jerusalem—The city of God; in the Book of Revelation, the symbolic antithesis of Babylon.

kingdom of God—The reign and rule of God, both internally within the hearts of humans as well as through external actions that God produces in those who trust in Him.

Lamb—A designation for Jesus Christ found 28 times in the Book of Revelation.

literalism—Interpretation of the Bible that takes the most obvious and concrete meanings to be the primary sense of any passage.

millennium—A symbolic term that has reference to a long period of time.

Millennium—A literal and exact one thousand year era, based upon one interpretation of the "thousand years" of Revelation 20:2-7.

postmillennialism—The belief that the second coming of Jesus Christ follows a millennial rule of His body, the church, which exemplifies the kingdom of God on earth.

prediction addiction—An emotional state of dependency, a need for regular doses of prophetic speculations about future events.

premillennialism—The belief that the second coming of Jesus Christ will precede His millennial, earthly rule.

preterism—An approach to the Book of Revelation that sees the fulfill-ment of the majority of its prophecies as having occurred not long after the author's time, in the distant past from our perspective.

rapture—The general biblical teaching concerning believers who are alive at the second coming being "caught up," ascending to meet Christ in the air.

Rapture—The specific, extra-biblical teaching about the rapture, in-cluding the supposition that Jesus will come for His saints first, sav-ing them from physical suffering during the tribulation, and then again with His saints (a third coming?).

religion—As opposed to authentic Christianity, the idea that good deeds will either save us, contribute to our salvation in some way, help to maintain our salvation, and/or produce a higher standing with God than we would otherwise enjoy.

tribulation—Biblical references to the suffering of God's people. The "great tribulation" (Matthew 24:41; Revelation 2:22; 7:14) is thought by some to be an unparalleled time of trouble shortly before the sec-ond coming. Some also believe that the church, true believers, will be saved from part or all of the great tribulation by a preliminary coming of Jesus, an event they speak of as the Rapture.

CHAPTER ONE

Beauty and the Beast

Have you seen those television programs with ordinary people like you and me bringing unheralded antiques and heirlooms to be appraised by experts? Most of the time the attic yields no surprise treasures, but occasionally an object of fine art once relegated to some dust-filled niche is converted from an overlooked ugly duckling into a highly regarded beautiful swan.

Suddenly an object that was thought to have little or no value is transformed into a priceless work of art. The parables of a treasure hidden in a field (Ma 13:45) and of a pearl of great price (Ma 13:45-46) illustrate how such a discovery can reveal the riches of the kingdom of heaven.

Almost 15 years ago, I found myself face to face with the spiritual riches of God's amazing grace—an unbelievable, almost too-good-to-be-true grace that I had never experienced. For more than three decades, my religious experience had devalued and diminished God's matchless grace, causing me to be oblivious to the true treasures hidden in the field of Holy Scripture, a field whose terrain I thought I knew so well.

The riches of God's grace revealed the futility and bankruptcy of what I came to call *Bad News Religion*. I eventually subjected all my religious convictions and values to the standard of God's grace, and in so doing my entire world was turned upside down.

William Temple, the Archbishop of Canterbury (1942-1944) once explained how human efforts often reverse the values of the kingdom of heaven. Temple said it is as though someone slipped into the department store of our lives during the night and reversed all the price tags. The next morning those things of real value that should carry expensive price tags are now regarded as cheap trinkets while virtually worthless items carry price tags that indicate they have enormous value.

My experiences as a captive in the swamps of religious tyranny and oppression, combined with an addiction to prophetic addiction cheapened the Book of Revelation, running it into the ground with misuse and abuse. I did not realize that legalistic prophecy-mongering took me on a predictable, same-old, same-old religious journey. Parroting what I had been taught about prophecy, I misunderstood, misinterpreted, misapplied—and missed the Book of Revelation! I knew only one way to understand its symbols and message. For me, the real message of Revelation was lost. God's grace turned Revelation right side up, and revalued this profound and meaningful book. God's grace engenders revolutions in our lives; God's grace is all about new life, new and fresh perspectives.

From my early years in elementary school, the so-called "end times message" of the Book of Revelation informed my entire view of human history as well as my own personal present and future. Many years later, I discovered this "end times message" interpretation of the Book of Revelation, which my family accepted without reservation, to be a teaching that had beguiled many others for well over a century. I learned that the layman's term "end times message" referred to eschatology, the study of last things. The theological roots of what my family believed to be esoteric knowledge about eschatology, based upon the Book of Revelation, went back to a man named John Nelson Darby (1800-1882). William Miller (1782-1849) was one of Darby's peers who came to similar conclusions about biblical prophecy (another layman's term for eschatology), eventually proclaiming, as a result of intricate calculations, the year 1843 as the date for the second coming of Jesus Christ. When the specific date selected in 1843 passed without divine cooperation, Miller and his followers set a new date in 1844. Eighteen forty-four became known as the "Great Disappointment"—destined to be but one of many failed predictions for the second coming.

Ellen G. White (1827-1915) was a follower of Miller and founded the Seventh Day Adventist Church in the aftermath of the Great Disappointment. White's teachings, as with so many others, were based on eschatological interpretations of the Book of Revelation—with such teachings always holding followers in suspense, as true believers in such teachings presume that apocalyptic events may break out at any moment. Common to virtually all prophetic teachers is some kind of assurance or promise for their followers of divine protection or immunity from the horrific "end times" events described in the Revelation.

By the 1870s, Darby's teachings became known as dispensationalism, a method of Bible interpretation that grew in popularity, not only in Adventism, but among fundamentalist Protestant churches of the time. While dispensationalism proposes much more than a particular view of eschatology, the popular impact of the prophetic implications of dispensationalism are significant. Toward the end of the nineteenth century prophecy conferences started to be a staple feature of Protestant fundamentalist churches in North America, with Cyrus Ingerson (C.I.) Scofield (1843-1921) emerging as a leading advocate of dispensationalism. Scofield eventually published his *Scofield Reference Bible* (1909), one of the first Bibles to have a human interpretation of the divinely inspired message of the Bible printed alongside biblical passages. Unfortunately, many who accepted the teachings of dispensationalism failed to adequately discriminate between Scofield's "inspired margins"—his interpretations that were printed in marginal notes—and the actual inspired Word of God.

Then came the twentieth century, a century filled with preachers and teachers who applied the prophetic "end times message" to the generation to which they ministered. Lewis Sperry Chafer (1871-1952) founded Dallas Theological Seminary in 1924, an educational institution that, among other contributions, attempted to give academic credibility to the eschatological ramifications of Darby's end times methodology. As the twentieth century unfolded, many continued to popularize the "end times message" of dispensationalism, with Hal Lindsey and Tim LaHaye being perhaps the two most well-known popular eschatological authors.

Hal Lindsey's best-selling books included *The Late Great Planet Earth* (1970), followed by *There's a New World Coming* (1973) and *The 1980's: Countdown to Armageddon.* Tim LaHaye followed in Lindsey's footsteps with his enormously popular *Left Behind* series. With his fictionalized messages about the end time, LaHaye distanced himself from the ongoing and obvious criticism that dispensational predictions had all failed. Once again, as with Scofield's marginal notes in his reference Bible, the vast majority of *Left Behind* readers took LaHaye's fictionalized narratives as gospel truth, failing to question the bankrupted methodology that generated his sensationalized books.

I grew up in this prophecy-saturated religious culture. Beginning in the second grade, I lived in constant apprehension and fear of an impending doomsday. My family and I believed that "the end" could come at any time; we were convinced that we always lived in a window of a "few short years" from the events surrounding the second coming. I did not treasure the message of Revelation, I feared it. The specific "end times" interpretation I was taught exercised enormous power over me and many others. Decades later God's grace completely changed my understanding of Revelation—from a book to be feared to a book to be treasured. God's grace helped me to find the authentic message and unique Messenger of Revelation and in the process to discover what it has to say about the real agenda of performance-based religion.

I was not alone in my experiences. In his book *The Jesus I Never Knew*, Philip Yancey shares his childhood experiences growing up in a church that sponsored annual prophecy conferences. Yancey relates that these conferences "revealed" that a ten nation European Common Market would fulfill the prophecy of the biblical beast with ten horns. "What sticks with me, though, is not so much the particulars of prophecy as their emotional effect on me. I grew up at once terrified and desperately hopeful."[1]

Today millions continue to be enslaved by "just-around-the-corner" interpretations of the Book of Revelation. Some live in fear within cultic groups where apocalyptic anxieties allow leaders to combine irresponsible prophecy teaching with authoritarian control, while others experience the rigors of prediction addiction (prophetic teaching that turns into a religious addiction) within churches that generally teach sound doctrine but corrupt and cheapen the gospel with irresponsible speculation. In either case Revelation is used by religion as a club to control and intimidate.

In my experience, the eschatological implications of the Book of Revelation were anything but good news; a far more accurate definition was that such convictions were my worst nightmare. In fact, when I was young, the shallow and illogical interpretations of this precious book often contributed to literal nightmares, causing reactions similar to those of horror movies.

The power of God's grace eventually dismantled my former understanding of Revelation. I came to see that Revelation was not about an out-of-control-beast I had to fear; rather it was all about the beauty of God's amazing grace and the sovereign power of the Lamb.

Why do I presume to write about the one book that many believe to be the most complex and controversial of all books of the Bible?

For many years my relationship with God was in large part dictated by what I was taught about the Book of Revelation. Wild and preposterous prophetic teaching pretending to be based upon the 22 chapters of Revelation in turn formed the pages and chapters of the story of most of my life. I was forever looking to future events and predicted dates that were misinterpretations drawn from Revelation. I was focused on a Jesus who would return, rather than the one who had already come and conquered on the cross: the risen Lord, the head of the church, who is always with His people. Millions of people still suffer from similar eschatological interpretations of the message of Revelation, and it is my prayer that God will use *Revelation Revolution* as one of His tools to rescue them.

I attended the school of prophetic hard knocks, not only experiencing what a twisted understanding of Revelation produced in my life, but also observing what that eschatological teaching did in the lives of tens of thousands of others. I now see that such prophetic teaching is much like a drug, providing an incredible rush while also being the source of the depression and disillusionment that inevitably results from unrealized and unfulfilled expectations.

God's grace intervened in my life and liberated me from the fear and bondage that is the product of religious manipulation of the Book of Revelation. By God's grace, I came to see that the views I had cherished, believed, and taught amounted to a sleazy religious carnival where prophecy pundits and pushers sell their prophetic potions.

Along with its equally seductive cousin of religious legalism, prediction addiction had been the language of my life, the drum beat of my religious soul. Prediction addiction is an obsession, a compulsion to continually seek exhilarating "fulfillments of Bible prophecy" in current events of the day. In my experience, the bondage of legalism combined with an addiction to prediction gave meaning and order to my world while at the same time being the perfect one-two punch religion needed to control me. Legalism told me what I had to do in order to earn God's love and the kingdom of heaven. Prophetic teaching assured me that people who did not do what I was convinced the Bible taught would experience the plagues of Revelation; and, on the other hand, if my works were acceptable to God, I would be saved from those plagues.

The two evil cousins of religious legalism and prediction addiction work hand in hand; where one flourishes the other cousin is surely to be found in the same general vicinity. They feed off of each other. They both lead to religious captivity, as religious legalism and prediction addiction eventually control those who buy into their premises and beliefs.

It is only fair to note that what I propose as a revolution to the popularly accepted understanding of the Book of Revelation should not be accepted without careful scrutiny and study. I don't propose a new legalism; but rather in these pages I will urge that we read the Book of Revelation for all its worth, reading it as it was written, reading it as it was intended, rather than accepting cultural adaptations and interpretations of its inspired message. I contend that the Book of Revelation has been cheapened, tarnished, twisted, and perverted by eschatological teachings, and that many have become addicted to the promises and drug-like rush of such prophetic teachings.

In my experience, both teaching and believing in an "end times" message of the Book of Revelation gave me an artificial high. I was persuaded that I knew what the future held: this esoteric knowledge felt like theological insider trading. I had eschatological "hot tips" that others needed to know. It turned out that all the promises were just fool's gold that glittered, but had no value.

God's grace patiently helped me to deconstruct bogus perceptions and slowly construct a new reality, the real message of Revelation. My reading, research, and study of this amazing book has taken me all over the biblical and theological map, considering the trail that others have blazed in coming to terms with the message God gave to John. By His grace God has mercifully opened my eyes to the real Revelation, a new (for me) Revelation that helped to explain my experiences in the school of religious hard knocks. In my case, *Revelation Revolution* emerged out of the ashes of the religious ghetto I had inhabited, a place where tragedy and heartache are the product of religion's pills and potions.

I offer *Revelation Revolution* 1) as a Christ-centered remedy to the sensationalism of prophetic teaching and 2) from a compelling sense of duty in an attempt to spare others the inevitable loss of faith in God that is invariably left behind in the wake of such flawed and failed teaching. I am grieved to see that the same old broken-beyond-repair methodology of prophetic teaching continues to tease and allure millions into its destructive clutches.

Breathtaking and lurid preaching about Revelation fills churches and crusades. Books written from such a perspective sell like hotcakes, and videos that predict the future based upon the Book of Revelation are successful because they cater to the human desire to be special and to know something others don't about the future. The seductive appeal of discovering the "true meaning" of prophetic minutia can blur and obscure the central truth of this critically important book.[2] This cheap and tawdry sensationalism is nothing more than fortune-telling and palm reading masquerading as "biblical teaching."

Sensational predictive preaching and teaching about the Book of Revelation is but one of the many tools used by legalistic religion to control its followers by keeping them ever vigilant and on edge about some eminent event , such as the Rapture.[3] In order to maintain its control, religion keeps moving the finish line as to "when" the prophecies will happen. The focus in such cases is almost exclusively on the future. By contrast, authentic Christianity proclaims the second coming, but always in the context of the freedom we now have in Christ, because He has already conquered on His cross and is now alive as the risen Lord.

Revelation Revolution is designed to open eyes, raise suspicion, comfort those who are or have been afflicted by prediction addiction and afflict those who are comfortable with dogmatic, specific, and literal interpretations and "fulfillments" of the message Jesus reveals in these last pages of the Bible.

The greatest revelation in my life has been that God's grace is sufficient for my life: all of it. The clash between God's grace and my long-term views of the Book of Revelation was an apocalyptic, titanic confrontation. My flawed ideas came crashing down like a house built upon sand (Ma 7:26-27). That's what Revelation had been for me, an accumulation of ideas, speculations, interpretations and predictions—a house of cards with no firm foundation. For over three decades the message of the Book of Revelation convinced me that I was in a never-ending race to be found faithful at the soon-coming second coming, and so my life on earth consisted of earning my own salvation by deeds. There was no doubt in my mind that if I didn't "get right" I would "get left." As long as I misunderstood the Book of Revelation, I accepted predictions and date setting as a part of my life; failed predictions would all simply be re-issued by extending the goal line to some even more future and far off date.

In my case religious legalism and prediction addiction teamed up as a lethal one-two religious punch. While they both may exist apart from one another, they are cousins in the sense that they are religious co-conspirators. They contribute to one another, leading to the same kind of religious captivity. I experienced the "combo platter" of religious legalism and prediction addiction; and while they go together like rice and beans, or hamburgers and french fries, they may be "served" as a la carte selections, independent of each other. Not everyone who is captivated or seduced by prediction addiction finds themselves in a church that authoritatively controls and manipulates. And there are many who are captives of religious legalism who do not believe in any of the eschatological notions of "end times" teaching.

Other than that Jesus Christ would return to this world, upset and looking for vengeance, Jesus did not have the leading role in the Revelation I was taught as a young man. And, amazingly, this "Christ-lite" view of Revelation was taught in His name—effectively diminishing and devaluing Him. This same watered down interpretation of Revelation is still being preached, taught, and published widely today, in the name of Jesus.

Political and historical events and people, past and future, had the lead roles in the Revelation I once knew, with Jesus far from center stage. The Jesus of the Revelation of my past was a far-off, future Jesus, not one who had already conquered on His cross and who was already reigning in my life and in the lives of those who trusted in Him. Seeing Revelation through the eyes of grace, with a Christ-centered filter, revolutionized this amazing book for me. It's my prayer that this same focus will do the same for you!

CHAPTER TWO

The Big Picture of God's Grace

Multi-headed monsters rising out of the ocean. Fire-breathing crea-tures destroying anything in their path. Giant demon-insects with tails de-livering a sting that kills with agonizing pain. Catastrophic acts of God: plagues, famine and earthquakes. With its strange and mystifying symbols, the bizarre images and doomsday scenarios ascribed to the Book of Revelation have been the raw material for a myriad of curious interpreta-tions and predictions throughout the centuries. No other book in the Bible inspires such shock and awe—not to mention mystery and misunder-standing—as does the Book of Revelation.

Revelation has served as a launching pad for many unbiblical teach-ings that have fizzled, but not before they have won the support of millions who have been Raptured into an outer-space world of sensational pro-phetic interpretations. Interpretations of this book have sent millions on a spiritual voyage into a deep space filled with alien ideas, speculations, con-spiracy theories, and endless predictions about the future.

Mention the Book of Revelation in a conversation, and even Christians will generally react in one of two extremes. Some think that Revelation has nothing of importance to offer. They see this book as archaic, grisly and grotesque first-century writing with no relevance for today. On the other hand, some Christians seem to think that Revelation (and any other part of the Bible that is related to it or used to interpret it) is the only part of the

Bible worth reading and studying. Many are virtual prophecy junkies, addicted to "updated interpretations" of Revelation, because they see this book as a handbook for predicting the end of the world, an outline of history written in advance. Many new books, fiction and non-fiction, proclaiming some new fulfillment of Revelation, are turned into best sellers by prophecy addicts who cannot live without their fix.

Getting high on Revelation is not a new religious drug of choice. Around the middle of the second century, based on his interpretation of Revelation, a newly baptized Christian named Montanus taught that he and his peers were living in the end times.

Montanus and his followers predicted that the new Jerusalem was about to descend upon the nearby village of Pepuza, in what is now Turkey. Montanus' influence spread rapidly and widely among Christians throughout the Roman world—almost as fast as sensational prophecy books based on the Book of Revelation disappear from bookstores today.

But, of course, the prophecy of Montanus failed. The new Jerusalem did not descend on that small village in Turkey. The end did not come about 1,850 years ago, as Montanus predicted. By misinterpreting Revelation, Montanus tarnished the book's reputation to the point that some Christians thought it shouldn't be part of the Bible.

The claims of Christian groups, from Montanus to the present, that Revelation pinpoints the events, personalities, and time period of "the end" have all failed. Within the last 100 years many prophetic pundits and speculators have offered predictions. Perhaps these erroneous and futile attempts are best summed up by the title of Edgar Whisenant's *88 Reasons Why the Rapture Will Be in 1988.* Whisenant's title is itself an obvious testimony to the failure of "end times" predictions. The last decades of the twentieth century has seen prophecy "experts" outdoing themselves, reading the Bible in one hand and the newspaper in the other, as they attempted to provide specific identities for world leaders, nations, and dates of events that would lead to the second coming.

The record of failed predictions should be a red flag for Christians, a caution against using Revelation as a predictive handbook. The fact that our religious landscape is littered with predictions and speculations about eschatology is itself a reason why you need to carefully consider this issue. Why have so many been so wrong so often? The view that you accept of the ordering of events before Christ comes need not affect your salvation, for eschatology isn't a core doctrine of Christianity. But your eschatological beliefs can stunt your Christian growth. Your beliefs about the future can affect your peace and happiness on this side of eternity. Your eschatological beliefs can affect what others think about you and the Christianity you exemplify. You need to carefully examine the *Revelation Revolution* and discover for yourself what the fascinating last book of the Bible is all about.

A Message of Hope

For almost 2,000 years, many have insisted on using the Book of Revelation in a way similar to a fortune-teller using a crystal ball. Many today use the Book of Revelation somewhat like a psychic, biblical prediction hotline. The track record of failed prophecies and bankrupt predictions suggests that a crystal ball might be more effective for those who wish to foretell the future accurately.[1]

Revelation was written during a time of extreme crisis and suffering for God's people. It served to remind them—and it serves to remind us now—that, in spite of persecution and pain, God is fully aware of what we are going through. Revelation proclaims *a message of hope.*

This Book of Revelation is also written to help Christians identify and understand a mortal enemy, an enemy which is often in disguise. The enemy in Revelation often comes as a wolf in sheep's clothing, as an enemy which counterfeits authentic Christianity. The Book of Revelation leaves no stone unturned in *exposing religious requirements, rituals, and regulations* as the relentless and irreconcilable enemy of Christianity.

Religion is the villain of Revelation, but paradoxically, religion has often succeeded in convincing its followers to focus on other themes and ideas from the text as they read this book. Revelation is an indictment of religion and all of its legalisms, yet legalistic religion uses this very book to promote its own agenda.

Popular and common usage of the word "religion" attaches a benign definition to it, having to do with service to and worship of God as expressed in a variety of practices and beliefs. A common denominator in most religious worship and practices is the idea that human relationship with God is directly tied to human performance. So upon further examination, religion usually teaches salvation as given by God based on human accomplishment.

By such a definition, Christianity is not a religion. Authentic, biblically based and Christ-centered Christianity teaches that Jesus Christ is the only source of our salvation. According to the gospel of Jesus Christ, we are saved by grace (Ep 2:8-10). Religion counters God's grace and denies the power and sufficiency of the cross of Christ by asserting the fundamental importance of human deeds and works. Religion assures its followers that their performance can, at the very least, gain them a higher standing with God than they would have otherwise enjoyed.

The gospel of Jesus Christ teaches that we are incapable of earning God's favor, because His perfection and righteousness is beyond the capacity of human effort or accomplishment. Religion is self-serving and manipulative because it offers a system and structure of behaviors and practices that promise divine blessing in return for human obedience and fidelity. Christianity is thus not a religion at all, but a way of life that is absolutely and diametrically opposed to religion and all of its potions and prescriptions.

The gospel of Jesus Christ is good news—it is a message of hope. Religion is inherently bad news for humans, for it offers slavery and subservience, a life of captivity and drudgery, an endless quest to somehow prove oneself worthy to the God that religion claims to represent. We will see that the Book of Revelation exposes performance-based religion, insisting that the Lamb of God is our Savior, and that trust in Him is the only stipulation on which God insists. The Book of Revelation announces a religious revolution!

The word *revelation* is translated from the Greek word *apokalupsis*, which means "unveiling," or "revealing." In English, *apocalypse* has come to mean disaster or appalling destruction. Yet the word originally referred to an unfolding or revealing of things that were not generally known. The purpose of the Book of Revelation is not to present a maze of puzzling images for some clever interpreter to unveil—specific details about future world events that can be unraveled if some human prognosticator provides the key—but rather to reveal the victory of Jesus Christ.

Revelation names its author as John, probably John the apostle, son of Zebedee, and close friend of Jesus. The book is a message from Jesus Christ to John to pass on to seven churches in Asia Minor, churches in cities located in what is today western Turkey, and from that original audience of seven churches to the body of Christ throughout all history.

Revelation was written to Christians who were suffering because of their faith.[2] Some were being persecuted, tortured, and even beheaded. This book had life and death meaning for its first hearers because it was written specifically to them. These believers desperately needed to be reminded that ultimate victory in this world belongs to those who pledge allegiance to Jesus Christ—not to the emperor in Rome or to any religious authority.

The early church started with Christians being excited about spreading the good news about Jesus Christ. These men and women of faith believed that the cross of Christ paid for the sins of all human beings, so believers could have eternal life through Him, and that Jesus would return soon to bring the kingdom of God on earth.

But the expectation of Jesus' imminent return turned into years, and then into decades. Persecution continued to take its toll. The hope of many Christians was primarily based upon a triumphant and powerful immediate second coming that would vindicate their suffering and perse-cution. Hope turned to disillusionment as the years and decades passed, and Jesus still did not return. Some Christians at that time may have won-dered if the real power and the real future were in the hands of earthly political and religious authorities like the emperor in Rome.

The Book of Revelation answers that question. The real ruler of all things is Jesus Christ, not evil oppressors. The Book of Revelation insists that the handwriting is on the wall for everyone and everything that op-poses God and His people. Though Christians may suffer and die, we are safe in God's hands; and in the end He will destroy all wickedness and bring all oppression to an end. Revelation is more than a book about the end of human history. The Book of Revelation not only looks forward to Jesus Christ's second coming, but it also dramatically insists that Christ has *al-ready* come and won the decisive victory.

Paul Minear comments about the critical importance of the victory Jesus won on His cross, "This was far more necessary to the survival of hope than was any detailed information about coming events."[3]

The Revelation Revolution

So, for the first readers of Revelation as well as for us today, this book encourages us to trust God with our lives as we await (1) the end of all earthly powers that destroy humanity and (2) entrance into the everlasting joy of the kingdom of God. Revelation is written to Christians who live in an often brutal world. Whether that world is the first century or the twenty-first century, whenever we as Christians find ourselves facing persecution or insurmountable obstacles, Revelation offers hope by reminding us that the battle belongs to the Lord.

At the end of Revelation's 22 chapters, a 22-round heavyweight cham-pionship bout between good and evil, the ultimate victory belongs to Jesus Christ. The forces of evil, whether they be governments or religions, will be vanquished once and for all.

But what if *you* aren't being physically persecuted or suffering hardship as you read these words? What if you are living in peace and security, living in a professing Christian country with freedom of religion and dozens of Christian churches in your city? Does the Book of Revelation have any meaning for you?

Is the Book of Revelation a "now" book or just a history book?

The relative peace and security that some of us in North America enjoy can be an illusion. The Book of Revelation stands as a warning, a stark reminder to us that Christ's kingdom is not of this world and that the forces of evil never cease to pervert and corrupt.

An authentic Christian worldview informed by the Book of Revelation includes the eyes-wide-open reality that people and events are complex, and that many shades of darkness and evil exist. Experience teaches each of us that while many humans may seem basically good, at the core of our being we are all flawed and imperfect. Our twenty-first century western culture is filled with those who do not know God. Some are actively searching for God, "seekers" in search of something in which they can believe. Others are agnostics, and do not know or perhaps even care what they believe.

The fact that people do not know Jesus Christ does not mean that they are necessarily any more immoral or permissive than followers of Jesus Christ. There are many atheists in our culture who have strong moral values and are good citizens. This human complexity and ambiguity is a part of the confusing moral maze of the days of our lives. Behavior is not the basis of our relationship with God; good deeds are not the key to our salvation. Jesus' sacrifice on His cross, for us, in our stead, did for us what we can never do for ourselves. We are all sinners, and apart from Jesus Christ we are not capable of compiling enough good deeds so that God will allow us into His kingdom of heaven on the strength of our behavior.

Performance-based religion opposes God's grace. God's grace is the enemy of religion, because grace means that legalistic religion loses its control over those it attempts to manipulate.

While it is a complex book to study, Revelation is a breath of fresh air. Revelation contains no ambiguity, no shades of gray. It is not hamstrung by political correctness. It minces no words in describing sin and evil. Revelation is clear about the evils of performance-based religion. The apocalyptic imagery of Revelation is inked in stark black and white. There is no middle ground. The people described in Revelation are either followers of Antichrist or followers of Christ. If you are not with Christ, you are part of the enemy camp.

Revelation calls us out of complacency and our illusions of peace and comfort. It calls Christians to overcome and conquer the world, not in some kind of political revolution or Holy War, but to conquer through Christ. Revelation itself is a revolution—the *Revelation revolution*—an absolute promise that victory over the evil in this world is available through the One who has already overcome the world on the cross. The *Revelation revolution* is spiritual, and as Paul's teaching in Romans 13 demonstrates, Christians overcome and conquer the world while they cooperate with and submit to government authority and order, even though the authority (especially the government of the original audience of this book, the Roman Empire of the first century) may be in opposition to God.

The Book of Revelation is for beleaguered Christians who are under siege, who need reassurance and not ambiguity. In the first-century world, virtually all governments and people were pagan. Christians were a tiny minority in the vast and hostile sea of polytheistic religions and philosophies of Rome. The reality of the world of the original recipients of the Revelation of Jesus Christ was, of course, a society completely unlike that of the same Roman Empire that converted to Christianity under Constantine two centuries later. It was a time long before Christian armies, civil governments, and missionaries won whole nations to Christ. Three primary themes permeated the thinking of early Christians: revelation, revolution, and restoration.[4] The original audience to whom Revelation was written lived long before the Protestant Reformation, which ultimately led to the hundreds of Christian denominations we now have and the freedom of religion that is enjoyed in many countries.

Though we do not live in precisely the same kind of society and culture as its original recipients, the Book of Revelation warns us not to be deceived. The freedom *of* religion that we may enjoy does not mean that we are free *from* religion and its oppression. The Book of Revelation is addressed to seven church congregations in Asia Minor who were painfully aware of religious tyranny.

The number seven often depicted completion to the ancients. To the original audience the use of the number seven suggested that the spiritual problems and emergencies facing these churches were to be considered representative of Christians throughout the Roman Empire. By extension, these problems can be seen as threats that Christians in all places and ages must confront.

The topic and theme of the Book of Revelation is Jesus Christ, not some geo-political, predictive timetable of future world events. The key to the Book of Revelation is its Christology, not its chronology. The *guiding interpretive principle* to be used in understanding Revelation is *"who,"* not *"when."* Minimize the importance of the *when;* maximize the importance of the *who.* Revelation teaches that our human future is not the primary issue, but the future of Revelation is *in* and *with* Christ. The future in Revelation is all about Jesus Christ and *His* future.[5]

Jesus, the Lamb of Revelation, the Messenger of the message, told His disciples that the timing of his second coming was not only not a priority but also that no human being would know the date of it (see Ma 24:36, 42, 44, 50; 25:13). Jesus came to save us, not to turn us into prophecy fanatics. The gospel of Jesus Christ is all about Jesus; He is the divine *who* of the story. We can lose sight of the *who* if we focus on the *when.*

Jacques Ellul observes, "the Apocalypse is not a book in itself, it is a book in relation to Jesus Christ. It cannot be interpreted for itself (or for ourselves) but as clarifying an unknown visage of this Jesus. It cannot be separated from *his person*. It has no meaning apart from that."[6]

Who are the primary characters in this book? Jesus is at center stage in the drama of Revelation. He is the "good guy" of the story while legalistic religion is the corrupt and depraved "bad guy." All sound and balanced interpretations of the meaning of Revelation must revolve around the crucified Lamb who brings history, death and the grave, time and eternity under His rule. Jesus is the key to unlock the meaning of Revelation.

Linguistic Style of Revelation

It is critically important to realize that the Book of Revelation is not written in a straight-forward style easily understood by the twenty-first century western mind. Revelation is written in a literary style called *apocalyptic*. Apocalyptic literature explains why the righteous suffer while placing an emphasis on God's ultimate vindication of the righteous.[7] The apocalyptic writing style uses poetic language, metaphorical messages, and figurative images and symbols to convey its message. Some images that are used are known—common animals for example. Other images described in the visions given to John that form the text of Revelation are nightmarish beasts, unknown to any biologist or zoologist. No book of the Bible contains more images and symbols than the Book of Revelation; it's a book filled with cosmic symbols.

The characters and events that are symbolized by images in the Book of Revelation are real but not literally real. Characters and events are portrayed in images, because no literal description could convey the profound meaning that the Lamb of God reveals. Theologian George Eldon Ladd says that the apocalyptic symbols of Revelation are "not meant to be photographs of objective facts; they are often symbolic representations of almost unimaginable spiritual realities."[8]

The symbols and images of Revelation are physical symbols of spiritual realities, and in the Book of Revelation the greatest reality is *spiritual*, with the physical and earthly reality being but a shadow of the greater and deeper heavenly reality.[9]

The symbols, figures, numbers, and colors in apocalyptic writing were not intended to be taken literally. Because of their culture and familiarity with apocalyptic literature, the original readers of Revelation would have had a better sense of how to interpret these symbols than we do. The Messenger of Revelation inspired the human author, John, to use the literary style of apocalyptic because it was familiar to the original audience. The Messenger used the apocalyptic style, with all of its images and symbols, because the original audience would understand. He didn't use it in order to hide or confuse the meaning so that twentieth and twenty-first century Christians would eventually need to decode its "true" meaning. Thus, the Book of Revelation cannot be read and understood the way we read and understand popular twenty-first century literature (but that doesn't stop literalists from giving it the old college try!). The practice of placing a premium on literal meanings can actually block the intended message.[10]

The failure to recognize and understand the symbols and apocalyptic images of Revelation as they were given to the original readers is a major pitfall that confronts us as we read and study in this century.[11] While the literary genre in which the book was written is not common for us, we can and should learn from the much publicized, failed attempts of those who have done their level best to impose literalism upon this symbolic book.[12]

One of the features of apocalyptic writing is its use of contrasting and comparing images and entities, such as:

- life and death
- light and darkness
- war and peace
- the old covenant nation of Israel contrasted with the church, the new covenant people of God
- angels and demons
- the Lamb and the beast
- those who bear the mark of the beast and those who have the seal of God

- the bride and the whore
- heaven and earth
- Jerusalem, the city of God; and Babylon, the city of man

Revelation is thus a book of extremes. As we explore this fascinating book, we are taken from the bottomless pit of sin and despair to the ecstasy of the new heavens. Suffering and misery give way to heavenly serenity and peace. The earth is depicted as polluted and besmirched only to be reformed and rejuvenated as God brings His heaven to a new earth.

Revelation differs from other apocalyptic writing, notably extra-biblical Jewish apocalyptic writing that was popular at that time, in that it places the hinge of history as being the cross of Christ, the Lamb of God who takes away the sin of the world. For the Jews, the key to apocalyptic writing was the future return of Messiah and His physical intervention in all of their sufferings, with an emphasis on physical deliverance. The Book of Revelation is Christian apocalyptic, with the suffering of the Savior, as well as those who follow Him, being central to the history of the body of Christ on earth.

While there is no doubt that the second coming is a prominent feature of the Book of Revelation, it is not the theme. The theme is not primarily about future fulfillments of prophecy. Instead, the Book of Revelation is centered in the past as well as the present. The past watershed event is the cross of Christ, with the present reality being the risen Lord who is ever alive and ever present with Christians who encounter the real problems of life in the flesh.

Apocalyptic writing is filled with images of violence and war, with woes, with judgment and battles occupying much of its message. The Book of Revelation is a grand spiritual epic that transcends any one historical time period (with the one exception being the seven churches, and even these churches, rooted in history, serve as recurring examples that have ongoing fulfillments). Even though many generations and cultures have attempted to plant their flag in this book and claim it as being written primarily for their time, *no one historical time period owns the Book of Revelation.* As William Sanford LaSor notes: "one of the principles of apocalyptic prophecy is to use names and symbols without intending historical accuracy."[13] Perhaps no culture has attempted to co-opt Revelation as its own story more than twentieth and twenty-first century America.

A Portrait of Grace

Jesus did not give this revelation to the apostle John as a precise chronological sequence of future world events. Jesus paints this portrait of God's grace in word pictures on a cosmic canvas, always contrasting Christ-centered Christianity with any and all forms of religious legalism. The Babylon of religious rituals and rites is Antichrist, the enemy of all who believe in and accept Jesus Christ alone as their Savior, Lord, and King.

In order to properly understand this revelation of God's grace, we must step back and get the big picture. To fully grasp this revelation we must admire the word picture inspired by Jesus at a distance. If we get too close, as many do, and try to attach precise historical detail and significance to every brush stroke in this painting, we may well miss the forest for the trees. Many miss the message of God's grace that Jesus reveals in the Book of Revelation because nitpicking legalistic religion diverts them with endless detail-obsessed detours; and consequently many spend a lifetime studying the Book of Revelation without ever seeing the big picture.

Have you ever seen the mesh screens that archaeologists use? They look like four two by four's with a screen across the bottom much like the window screens used to keep flies and mosquitoes on the outside of your house. Archaeologists construct mesh screens to allow dirt and silt to escape while capturing ancient artifacts. Their treasures remain after they have separated the unwanted debris from the treasures they have designed their filters and screens to capture.

This process is not unlike the process we all unconsciously use in understanding the Bible, particularly and especially the Book of Revelation.

When we first begin to read the Bible, we are often encouraged and taught to use an interpretative method to sift the words and concepts of Holy Scripture so that we will "find" what those who teach us want us to find. Some methodologies for studying the Bible are similar to the physical mesh screens of archaeologists; they attempt to predetermine the object of our search.

The obvious flaw in this process is that the pattern and plan of a methodology interprets the data so that the outcome is predetermined. *The conclusion is thus predetermined by the presumptions that inform the process.* The conclusion of study has been subjectively preordained; now all that remains is to filter the data to fit that conclusion.

This isn't good science, and it certainly isn't good Bible study. One important objective for any student of the Bible is to discover and isolate what he or she has been taught about the Bible and to question those *a priori* conclusions. Even if the conclusions that are questioned are eventually retained, it does not hurt to lay them aside to see if the facts will support and confirm what the text of the Bible says.

Most of what we believe about the Bible has come from trusted sources: parents, teachers, pastors, congregations, and denominations. Most of us have been given one perspective and one perspective alone, and we often find ourselves woefully unaware of the mesh screens and grids that are taught in other Christian faith traditions. No book of the Bible offers a better illustration of how these preconceived religious presuppositions work than the Book of Revelation.

Performance-based religion, often in the guise of Christianity, imparts tunnel vision, focusing on details and ignoring the big picture. Religion that flourishes within Christendom frequently entices us with the seductive and enticing claim that, if we follow its clues and directions, we will know something that no one else does. When it comes to understanding the Book of Revelation, many of us are drunk on the intoxicating wine of denominational teaching that claims to give unique and sectarian ideas about what this apocalyptic book means. Legalistic religion can lead to narrow and provincial ideas, which in turn may direct our study of the Bible into a quest to validate our specific brand of religious values and beliefs. With such a mentality millions "study" the Bible but rarely question the status quo of their personal beliefs. They continue to believe what they have always believed. Involved studies of the Book of Revelation thus come to the predictable conclusion that what was already known and believed continues to be true. *Sacred cows are often contented cows.*

Richard Jeske observes, "The book of Revelation asks us where our priorities are and whether in the church, our church, Christ is present or absent. Is the name proclaimed by our church its own name or the name of the state or a name not bound by the institutions of this world?"[14]

Religion, even in the name of Christ, can be a pied piper leading us away from the big picture. As far as the Book of Revelation goes, much of Christendom would prefer that we fixate on the *when* of events and historical personalities, rather than on the w*ho* of the book. The w*ho* is the big picture, and the big picture of God's grace is an image that legalistic religion does not want us to see, and for good reason. God's grace clearly reveals performance-based religion to be our enemy and the Antichrist an oppressor. Jesus Christ, constantly referred to as the Lamb of God in Revelation, is our Savior, our Liberator, who gives us freedom from religious legalism.

Four Grids/Screens/Methods of Understanding Revelation

Over the centuries Christian scholars, authors, priests, and pastors have attempted to blaze new interpretive trails to discover, mine, and sift the treasures contained in the Book of Revelation. Most of these ideas and methods can be summarized within *four foundational methods*. What you have been taught about the Book of Revelation is almost certainly some permutation or modification of one or more of these views. Each of these perspectives claims to be based in Scripture. Each one has strengths and weaknesses, is now believed, and has been believed by millions of Christians throughout history.

There's no reason for Christians to condemn each other merely because they take a different view of the Book of Revelation than do others. On the other hand, while each of the four views that follow have a biblical rationale, extreme allegiance to any interpretive screen or grid can distort the gospel of Jesus Christ.

The primary flaw in all of these methodologies is that each one places a premium on attempting to answer the *when* of Revelation (***idealism*** can be an exception). While the *when* is definitely an issue, it is not *the* issue. As Revelation is read and studied, *when* is generally the wrong question to ask and leads to wrong answers. The primary characters in Revelation are Jesus and religion. Jesus is the Message, the Subject, the Object, and the Goal of Revelation. In this 22-round heavyweight championship bout between good and evil, Jesus stands in one corner, while opposing Him in the other is oppressive religion, the villain and antagonist. Legalistic religion, as opposed to authentic Christianity, is the "bad guy" of Revelation—at all times and for all generations.

The first method of interpreting the Book of Revelation is *preterism*. The Latin word *praeter* means "past." Preterists believe that most of the prophecies in the Book of Revelation were fulfilled during the time of the Roman Empire.

Preterism can mean two extremely different things:

1) A belief that the text is not inspired prophecy but is rather a fanciful description of certain historical events.
2) A belief that the prophecies of the book are divinely inspired and were fulfilled mostly in the first or second generations after Christ.

The first type of preterist is theologically liberal, not accepting Scripture as divinely inspired; and while such a person accepts the historical reality of some events in the text, he or she believes John's apocalyptic visions were never fulfilled and never will be. They see apparently time-specific events written about in the Book of Revelation as being in the past and merely being reported about by the human author, John.

The second type of preterist can be theologically conservative, accepting the Bible as the inspired Word of God. Conservative or classical preterists believe that much of Revelation was fulfilled in the fall of Jerusalem in A.D. 70, and certainly no later than the further destruction of Jerusalem that followed in A.D. 135. They point to passages such as Revelation 1:1, which say that the message of Revelation must "soon take place." They also point to Jesus' Olivet Discourse (Ma 24) as primarily being fulfilled with the fall of Jerusalem to the Romans in A.D. 70. Classical preterists, who accept the Bible as the inspired Word of God, insist on an early date for the writing of the Book of Revelation—a few years before the fall of Jerusalem in A.D. 70. By taking this position, their view is that many of the apocalyptic events described in the Book of Revelation were fulfilled in the horrific events surrounding the fall of Jerusalem.

Some preterists do not believe that all the Book of Revelation has already been fulfilled. Some believe the last chapters of Revelation, with visions of new heavens and a new earth, are either to be fulfilled at some point in the future or are to be taken symbolically.

The second method of interpreting the Book of Revelation is *historicism.* Historicists believe that the prophecies of Revelation have been fulfilled throughout history and are still being fulfilled today. For historicists the images of Revelation refer to the entire history of Christianity.

Historicism isn't as popular today as it once was, but most of the great Bible commentators from a century or more ago were historicists. Many of the great leaders of the Reformation were historicists: Wycliffe, Knox, Tyndale, Luther, Calvin, and Zwingli, for example.

Historicists teach that Revelation is a kind of survey of church history with historical events symbolically portrayed. The test for historicists has been to line up the actual events in history with the details in the text. This challenge for historicists includes being flexible enough to revise their interpretations in light of ongoing world events, and it means being flexible enough to be wrong over and over again.

For example, most Protestant historicists of the past believed that the Antichrist of Revelation referred to the Pope and the Roman Catholic Church, the two witnesses were Luther and Calvin, with the triumph of Protestantism over Catholicism being the ultimate victory promised by Revelation.

Critics point out that historicism has not kept up with history much past the fourteenth century and that it is Eurocentric, not recognizing more recent and significant developments in the church in other parts of the world. Historicists can miss the big picture of God's grace while they attempt to retrofit history into the text.

The third method of interpreting the Book of Revelation is *futurism*. Futurism is the view held by many contemporary North American evangelical pastors and teachers. Ironically, many of its current advocates would be shocked to find that modern futurism originated in 1585 with Francisco Ribeira, a Spanish Jesuit priest, for the purpose of refuting the anti-Catholic historicist views of the Protestant reformers.

The most popular version of futurism today is *dispensationalism,* an interpretive grid which has only been around since the 1830s when J.N. Darby began teaching his ideas of a secret rapture of the church followed by the "great tribulation" and the Millennium—the thousand-year rule of Christ and the saints. The teachings of dispensational futurism have come to be known as the "end-times message" of biblical prophecy and specifically the Book of Revelation.

Dispensational futurists believe in a literal view of the Book of Revelation. From the 1830s until the present, each new generation of dispensationalists has projected chapters four through twenty-two of Revelation into a future time, often future dates on the calendar that occur within, or just after, their lifetime. Since their presupposition is that the events depicted in chapters four through twenty-two haven't happened yet, it's relatively easy for dispensational futurists to claim the vast majority of the Book of Revelation should be taken literally. Since the time of Darby, virtually every new generation of dispensationalists seems to offer revised, breathtaking insights about things they believe will happen in a "few short years"; and they always find a curious and often rapt audience, some of whom will eventually become virtually addicted to illogical and irresponsible predictions.

When futurists insist upon a literal interpretation of Revelation, they not only ignore the style of writing Jesus inspired John to use, but they can also unwittingly twist and distort the meaning given and inspired by the divine Author and Artist.

Many futurists disregard the literary style that God has inspired to convey His Revelation, and in the process they can conveniently avoid having their "this-is-going-to-happen-in-the-near-future" approach tested by actual historic events. Since they believe they will be "Raptured" before the bulk of Revelation is fulfilled, dispensationalists can make all sorts of predictions with the confidence that they will not be around on earth to be accountable for any inaccuracies in their predictions. Heavenly accountability for earth-bound failed predictions remains a real possibility, of course.

While a Eurocentric perspective is a valid criticism of the shortcomings of historicism, a similar criticism of futurism must be noted. Popular teaching of futurism, especially that of dispensationalism, has flourished for almost two hundred years in North America. The focus of this teaching, during this time, has centered on North American interests. The past 75 years have seen horrific tragedies in Europe, Asia, and Africa that have failed to be classified as the great tribulation by North American centered dispensational teaching. In spite of Lenin, Stalin, Hitler, Pol Pot, Mao Tse-Tung, Idi Amin, Sadam Hussein and their ilk, popular dispensational teaching usually did not identify the horrors they produced as being precursors of the tribulation. Are we to conclude that the Book of Revelation was written only for North Americans who live in the "end times," a time period that presumably stretches from the early 1800s until the second coming of Jesus Christ?

The fourth method of interpreting the book of Revelation is *idealism*. Idealists believe that most prophecies in the Book of Revelation portray an ongoing cosmic conflict of spiritual realities. Idealism is also called the spiritual, triumphant, or symbolic interpretation.

Idealists look for lessons or principles that are symbolically depicted in Revelation. The idealist interpretation takes into account the apocalyptic style of Revelation, and sees the central theme as the triumph of good over evil, Christ over Satan. While other approaches may take certain passages as chronological, idealists take these as recurring realities in history, as part of God's sovereign plan for humankind.

Of course, the advantage of this view is that there is no need to match events described in the book to historical or future events. It is the one view that minimizes the "when" factor in prophecy. The disadvantage of an exclusively idealist perspective is that the Book of Revelation seems to predict specific historical and future events.

Preterism, historicism, futurism, idealism—four ways that Christians have interpreted the Book of Revelation over the centuries. But incredibly, many Christians today are not aware of these four views. They are only aware of the futurist interpretation that their pastor or favorite televangelist or favorite prophecy writer teaches. Some Christians think there is only one way to understand this book, and the most popular approach today is the belief that Revelation is talking about the "end times" for today. Even more disturbing is the fact that some futurists claim that theirs is the only correct understanding and label other understandings as inferior or even non-Christian merely because they interpret the Book of Revelation differently.

Although scholars and teachers may identify themselves with one of these distinct methods for interpreting the Book of Revelation, in practice they may use various combinations of the four. Someone may call him or herself a preterist, believing that the majority of the prophecies in Revelation have already been fulfilled; but when it comes to the last few chapters, they may either be a futurist or an idealist. Or some may call themselves ideal-ists but believe that certain passages have a literal fulfillment in time.

These four basic interpretations are not a call to arms; they are not a reason for us to declare war on those who favor a differing view. There is some value in each of these views, but attempting to fit Revelation into one humanly devised time-bound interpretive mold is missing the boat. This author contends that what many appear to have missed is Revelation's em-phasis on God's timeless, eternal grace, as compared to time-bound hu-man religion-ism and church-ianity. *God's grace is centered in the divine who rather than in the human when.*

When Revelation was first written, the original audience and readers had a far better understanding of its symbols and literary style than we do today. In addition, the original audience was intimately aware of the power of religion that warred against the Lamb of God. But as time went by, Christianity moved away from a Christ-centered interpretation that indict-ed religion as the enemy of the Lamb of God. The message of the Book of Revelation, with all of its symbols and images, was marginalized and slow-ly spiritualized away.

In the centuries before the Reformation, the religion of Christendom, part of the villain of Revelation, buried the message and the Messenger un-der mountains of preterism, historicism, and early views of futurism. Idealism remained somewhat aloof from the perils of imposing a calendar upon Revelation; but while it refused to place "when" as the priority in in-terpreting Revelation, it did not single out legalistic religion as the enemy of the Lamb of God. Thus all four methods eventually diminished the mes-sage. The Christ-centered foundation of Revelation was forgotten in favor of esoteric and earth-centered, time-defined insights.

These ideas and methodologies even survived the rigorous examina-tion of the Reformation until the seventeenth century. At that time it be-came clear to many that Christianity understood and taught Revelation as a mysterious and mystical book that held little relevance for their lives.

They saw the mistake of over-spiritualizing Revelation (idealism), and could clearly see the shortcomings of preterism and historicism. We humans are creatures of extremes, and popular views of the Book of Revelation are a case in point.

While futurism had been a minority view during much of the history of Christendom, biblical passages had never been subjected to a detailed chronological analysis until John Nelson Darby (1800-1882; for more about Darby see chapter seven, "The Rapture—Religion's Fear Factor"). Darby contrived a new methodology to right the wrongs of what he saw as unsatisfying and mystical interpretations of Revelation as well as biblical prophecy in general.

Dispensationalism, a subset of futurism, was born, and the Book of Revelation was retooled and reinvented for the industrial age of the new American marketplace of capitalism. Darby proved to be a man for his times, at least in terms of marketing, for his ideas came on the scene just as impersonal machines and scientific inquiry started to threaten, challenge, and upset many Christians. The dispensationalism of John Darby rolled out a new, born-again Book of Revelation that offered pragmatic answers for Christians who were dealing with the impact of the enlightenment and of technology. Dispensationalism scratched a sociological itch and filled the new hunger for meaning and relevance.

Dispensationalism lifted the Book of Revelation from the muck and mire of one ditch and quickly deposited it into another equally spiritually dysfunctional ditch. Dispensationalism dumped what it saw as useless and meaningless spiritualizing of Revelation (idealism), outmoded historical fulfillments of prophecies (historicism and preterism), and substituted its equally disastrous methodology—over-literalizing the message of Revelation and, in the process, largely ignoring the historical context and culture, the literary genre and symbols.

Extreme interpretations of each of these four views have conveniently enabled performance-based religion and all of its legalisms to escape the incriminating message of Revelation relatively unscathed. Beyond that, these perspectives have enabled oppressive religion to thrive even in the face of the very message and Messenger that indict the legalisms of Christendom.

A Christ-Centered Perspective

God's grace can help remove multiple layers of misinterpretation so that we might see Jesus, giving us a Christ-centered understanding of this incredible book. God's grace enables us to see Jesus standing at the center of Revelation, and it is only by God's grace that Revelation can be saved from misunderstanding and manipulative, oppressive teaching. I do not claim to have mastered any of the four popular interpretations of Revelation, but my studies, teaching, and preaching compel me to reject any of the four as the sole and sufficient methodology for understanding Revelation. None of the four adequately and appropriately name Jesus as the most important element, subject, and topic. The emphasis of the four methods we have briefly considered is *when*. After weighing the issues, I believe there is *a fifth way, **a Christ-centered perspective*** of Revelation, based solely upon God's grace. The **Christ-centered perspective** is primarily concerned with the *who* of Revelation.

God, through what we call the Incarnation, came into our world in the person of Jesus. Jesus came into our time-bound world from eternity. The dilemma that the Incarnation presents for our human minds is that Jesus remained divine while becoming human. He still inhabited boundless eternity, but he also inhabited the limitations of our world and what it means to be human. He came *into* time. He was born, lived, died on the cross, and was resurrected. He is now risen; He's still *in time* as well as being *outside* of it. The Book of Revelation is from Him and about Him. This is a message *from* Jesus, who lives both with us and *in* eternity, about the relationship we can have *with* Him.

It is impossible to fully comprehend Revelation by reducing its message to our space and time. There is no question that there are some passages that have a human chronological perspective, but even those passages must be understood with a Christ-centered perspective. The time of Revelation is time calculated according to the Incarnation of Jesus Christ. All specific dates are time computed and measured by the "standard mean time" of the kingdom age ushered in when Jesus entered our world. Thus, we must have a Christo-centric focus as we read and study Revelation and avoid attempts to shoehorn its eternal perspective into our world. Our experience of time, our sense of past, present, and future can distort both the message and Messenger of Revelation. Jesus, the eternal Son of God, is the focal point of Revelation, not the days and times of our lives. Jesus does enter into our days and times, but he does so in ways that are difficult to measure with human instruments and tools like clocks, calendars, newspapers and history books.

A Christ-centered perspective of Revelation demands that we lay aside cherished notions we have been taught about this book or at the very least subject them to scrutiny. While blame for Christian preoccupation with detailed predictions, speculations, and the *when* of Revelation must be laid at the door of all four popular methodologies that have been used to interpret this book, dispensational futurism is the primary culprit. This is not to say that there is not a *when* element in the book, a "was, is and is to come" element. But we must never forget that the *when* of Revelation is subservient to the *who.*

The Lamb of God is not only the divine *who* of Revelation, He is also the *when* of Revelation. In Revelation 1:4, 8, we read about Jesus "who is and who was and who is to come." The Book of Revelation is not primarily a revelation of or about human time, whether that time is past, present, or future. It is first and foremost the "revelation of Jesus Christ" (Re 1:1).

A careful study of Revelation seems to clearly reveal to this author that the bodily second coming of Jesus Christ to this earth is a future event, yet to happen. But in the meantime, the risen Lord is with us, even while we often find ourselves engulfed by speculative predictions that obsess about specific events and times. Such an emphasis on the Book of Revelation does not center on the divine character of this book, and can even lead us away from Him. One cannot genuinely look to the past, present, or future without first coming to Christ, who embodies eternity.

Revelation is no easy book to study. It is complex and challenging. It can be a spiritual minefield for new Christians, or for those who do not have the resources and background to adequately understand the book. It can be especially troublesome for those who want simple black and white answers. Such individuals are probably at the highest risk of buying into extreme and destructive interpretations that are usually dogmatic viewpoints presented as the one and only way to understand what Revelation "really means."

The "fifth way" of understanding the Book of Revelation is centered in Jesus Christ. The fifth way is simply Christology above chronology!

What's your view of the Book of Revelation? Have you unquestioningly accepted just one of the four primary viewpoints to the exclusion of others? While there is some value in any of the four commonly accepted interpretations of the Book of Revelation, perhaps you have unknowingly accepted and believe some unsound ideas and interpretations. Most importantly, *where* is your primary emphasis when you read Revelation—on the *when* or the *who*? While each of the four views that attempt to place the events of the Book of Revelation into human chronology and time have some validity, the primary issue is not *when* but *who*.

Join me in considering a fifth way to understand Revelation, the Christ-centered perspective that will shed new light on this timeless message. In the *The Revelation Revolution* we will always consider Christ before chronology and calendars. Prepare to take another look at this amazing book.

CHAPTER THREE

The Human and Divine Authors

[1] The revelation of Jesus Christ, which God gave him to show his servants what must soon take place; he made it known by sending his angel to his servant John, [2] who testified to the word of God and to the testimony of Jesus Christ, even to all that he saw.

[3] Blessed is the one who reads aloud the words of the prophecy, and blessed are those who hear and who keep what is written in it; for the time is near.

[4] John to the seven churches that are in Asia:

Grace to you and peace from him who is and who was and who is to come, and from the seven spirits who are before his throne, [5] and from Jesus Christ, the faithful witness, the firstborn of the dead, and the ruler of the kings of the earth.

To him who loves us and freed us from our sins by his blood, [6] and made us to be a kingdom, priests serving his God and Father, to him be glory and dominion for ever and ever. Amen.

[7] Look! He is coming with the clouds;
every eye will see him,

even those who pierced him;

and on his account all the tribes of the earth will wail.

So it is to be. Amen.

[8] "I am the Alpha and the Omega," says the Lord God, who is and who was and who is to come, the Almighty.

[9] I, John, your brother who share with you in Jesus the persecution and the kingdom and the patient endurance, was on the island called Patmos because of the word of God and the testimony of Jesus. [10] I was in the spirit on the Lord's Day, and I heard behind me a loud voice like a trumpet [11] saying, "Write in a book what you see and send it to the seven churches, to Ephesus, to Smyrna, to Pergamum, to Thyatira, to Sardis, to Philadelphia, and to Laodicea."

[12] Then I turned to see whose voice it was that spoke to me, and on turning I saw seven golden lamp stands, [13] and in the midst of the lamp stands I saw one like the Son of Man, clothed with a long robe and with a golden sash across his chest. [14] His head and his hair were white as white wool, white as snow; his eyes were like a flame of fire, [15] his feet were like burnished bronze, refined as in a furnace, and his voice was like the sound of many waters. [16] In his right hand he held seven stars, and from his mouth came a sharp, two-edged sword, and his face was like the sun shining with full force.

[17] When I saw him, I fell at his feet as though dead. But he placed his right hand on me, saying, "Do not be afraid; I am the first and the last, [18] and the living one. I was dead, and see, I am alive forever and ever; and I have the keys of Death and of Hades. [19] Now write what you have seen, what is, and what is to take place after this. [20]

As for the mystery of the seven stars that you saw in my
right hand, and the seven golden lamp stands: the seven
stars are the angels of the seven churches, and the seven
lamp stands are the seven churches."

Revelation 1:1-20

The apostle John was nearing the end of his life. In an attempt to limit
his influence and inhibit the growth of the early church, political authorities exiled John to the island of Patmos, an island penal colony southwest
of Ephesus off the coast of what is now the nation of Turkey. Tradition has it
that he was being held in a cave, apart from the populated settlements on
the small island of some sixteen square miles. The Roman authorities, who
were trying to isolate him from the growing Christian movement, had no
idea what a powerful effect his writings would eventually have on the
church and the world.

Scholars are divided as to when John wrote Revelation. Some assign it
an earlier date, during the reign of Nero, about A.D. 60, before the fall of
Jerusalem. Others give it a later date, about A.D. 95, during the rule of
Domitian. Both emperors launched empire-wide campaigns against
Christians. While the Book of Revelation may have been written under the
reign of either emperor, the preponderance of evidence seems to place it in
the last decade of the first century. We can safely conclude that the exact
date of the book of Revelation is not nearly as important as having a Christ-
centered perspective when reading it.

John addresses this book as a letter to seven churches in the Roman
province of Asia (not the continent of Asia). The seven churches in seven
cities are addressed in the same order a traveler would encounter these cities on the road from the first church, Ephesus, to the last, Laodicea. By selecting seven churches—the number of completion—God seems to be using these churches as representative of the church for all time.[1]

The entire first chapter and the last passage of Revelation 22:7-21 serve as bookends to this dramatic and epic 22 chapter message. The number seven is prominent throughout Revelation, with the remainder of the book including:

1) Seven letters to seven churches (chapters 2-4)
2) Seven seals (chapters 5-7)
3) Seven trumpets (chapters 8--11:18)
4) Seven visions of conflict (chapters 12-14)
5) Seven bowls of wrath (chapters 15-16)
6) Seven messages of judgment (chapters 17--19:10)
7) Seven visions leading to the new heavens and new earth (chapters 19:11--22:6)

The first verse of Revelation informs us that this book is the revelation of Jesus Christ. Jesus is both the one who reveals the message as well as being the message itself. John is the human author, but Jesus is the Messenger and He is the message. He is both subject and object of this revelation.[2] John's vision of the Book of Revelation begins with Christ and so should ours.

This book is not primarily the revelation of past history, neither preterism nor historicism, nor is it primarily the revelation of future events yet to take place, which is how futurism interprets Revelation. The Book of Revelation is not time bound or time specific. Nor is this book primarily about spiritualized Christian principles and ideas, the idealistic view of Revelation. The Messenger of Revelation is not merely the one who will one day return on a white horse to conquer, but He is revealed as the Lamb of God who has already conquered on His cross, and who lives His resurrected life in those who accept Him and believe in Him.

At the same time, the first verse informs us that the revelation of Jesus Christ was given "to show his servants what must soon take place." The third verse ends with the phrase "the time is near." Similarly, no exact expressions of urgency are found in 2:16; 3:11; 22:6,7,12, 20. But the "soon" of verse one and the "near" of verse three are not specifically defined. This "soon" and "near" are actually speaking more about God's time than they are about ours; after all, for the Lord one day is like a thousand years and a thousand years are like a day (2 Pe 3:8). The Book of Revelation, in keeping with the gospel of Jesus Christ, does not primarily concern itself with days, months and years as measured humanly, but is measured as we experience time between the generation in which we live and the second coming.

The Divine Author

The Book of Revelation is the "revelation of Jesus Christ"—not primarily about our time and space, not primarily about world events yet to take place in world history, nor a history of events that have taken place. Neither is it a book filled with dire threats and warnings about the consequences of failure to perform religious rituals and regulations, thereby pleasing and appeasing God and convincing Him that we are qualified to be Raptured and escape the great tribulation.

The Book of Revelation is not primarily about when specific human leaders of religions or governments will rule and "fulfill" a precise prophecy. The Book of Revelation consistently and boldly warns about the enticements and power of religion. It's not about elaborate timelines and charts predicting the future of world empires and global military conflicts; it's about Jesus Christ, who is the Messenger and the message. Again, Christology is above chronology! *Who* more than *when*!

Verse three is the first of seven passages in Revelation that promise a blessing: seven beatitudes or declarations that begin with the word "blessed." The other six beatitudes of Revelation are found in verses 14:13; 16:15; 19:9; 20:6; 22:7, and 22:14. Revelation is the only book in the Bible that includes a special blessing for its readers. This first of seven beatitudes includes three instructions for those who would be blessed: 1) read, 2) hear, and 3) keep the words of this prophecy. Verse three tells us that those who read, hear, and keep Revelation are blessed, blessed because they are with Christ, blessed because they are on His side, blessed because by God's grace they have escaped the slavery of human religion with all of its legalism and regulations. The goal and purpose in this Book of Revelation is for

Christians to be sealed by Jesus Christ, the Lamb of God, sealed from religionism and religionists.

Verses five and six introduce "Jesus Christ, the faithful witness, the firstborn of the dead, and the ruler of the kings of the earth. To him who loves us and freed us from our sins by his blood, and made us to be a kingdom."

Here is the gospel in miniature! Revelation begins with a summary of the gospel and an emphasis on the message and Messenger of Revelation. "The firstborn of the dead" reminds us that Jesus is the risen Lord who has overcome death and the grave. "The ruler of the kings of the earth" boldly claims Jesus' preeminence and sovereignty over all earthly powers and introduces a critically important theme and repetition of Revelation.

The exodus of the nation of Israel from Egypt and the blood of the Passover lamb is another recurring theme of Revelation and is alluded to in the attribution "To him who loves us and freed us from our sins by his blood" (v. 5). The inclusive cross of Christ, which abolished dividing walls of hostility between the old covenant people of God and the rest of the world (Ep 2:14-18) enables all Christians to be a kingdom, regardless of racial, religious, or creedal claims of exclusivity. The New Testament church is the body of Christ, God's children who, in Revelation, encounter the world of pain and suffering at the hands of both secular and "sacred" foes.

Verse seven, "Look! He is coming with the clouds" introduces another ongoing theme and variation of Revelation: the second coming. The words are reassuring and comforting to those who are suffering and are a warning that authoritarian religions and their henchpersons are living on borrowed time.

The defining event in the salvation history of the Old Testament people of God was their deliverance from the slavery and oppression they experienced in Egypt. To this day, this watershed miraculous intervention of God in human history is central to the religion of Judaism. When God spoke to Moses, giving him a commission to lead his people out of religious bondage, the enslaved peoples of Israel didn't know the one true God. They knew the gods of Egypt, but they had forgotten the God of Abraham, Isaac, and

Jacob. God instructed Moses to tell them that I AM WHO I AM (Ex 3:14) would deliver them from the pharaoh of Egypt.

The Book of Revelation is a similar call to leave the religions of Babylon in favor of the Promised Land, the new heavens and new earth, a spiritual destination that flows with milk and honey. The God of the Exodus, I AM WHO I AM, is the Lamb of God who introduces Himself, in verse eight, to those in Babylonian bondage. The God of the Exodus and the God of Revelation is "the same yesterday and today and forever" (He 13:8). In Exodus 3:14, He introduces Himself as I AM WHO I AM. In the first chapter of Revelation, He identifies Himself as "'I am the Alpha and the Omega' says the Lord God, who is and who was and who is to come, the Almighty" (v. 8).

Using the first and last letters of the Greek alphabet, God tells us that He is the beginning and the end, the first and the last, the starter and the finisher, the creator and the judge. He is eternal, with no beginning and no end, "who is and who was and who is to come." Here is the Messenger who reveals Himself to be the message, the Messenger who conquered on the cross (past tense), who is now alive as the risen Lord (present tense) and will return to this earth a second time (future tense). *Is, was,* and *is to come.*

In verse ten we read, "I was in the Spirit on the Lord's Day, and I heard behind me a loud voice like a trumpet." The Lord's Day refers to the first day of the week, the day on which Christians commemorate the resurrection of Jesus from the dead. The term should not be confused with "Day of the Lord," which is a different grammatical construction in Greek and refers to God's wrath and judgment.

The resurrection of our Lord on Easter Sunday, or Resurrection Sunday as some prefer, was the spiritual benchmark for the new Christian church that emerged out of theological and cultural Judaism. The early church soon came to see that the Jewish Sabbath did not provide the context or Christ-centered focus of their faith. The resurrection of Jesus did, hence the Lord's Day. So while this reference to the Lord's Day may be the first day of the week, it is also, far more significantly, a testimony to the Lord's resurrection. He is risen, He is alive. "He is and was and is to come."

The early church recognized the centrality of the cross and the empty tomb as the bedrock of their belief. They were aware of Jesus' promise to return in the future, but their focus on the future did not obscure their worship of what the Lamb of God had done and what He was doing. An unwarranted emphasis on the future will always detract from and blur the twin foundation stones of Christianity: what Jesus has done on the cross and what He is now doing in the lives of those in whom He lives His resurrected life. Theologian Jurgen Moltmann succinctly notes that "Christian hope is resurrection hope."[3]

Verses 12-20 focus on the divine Author, the risen Lord, who is later introduced as the Lamb of God. The placement of this vision at the beginning of the book provides further emphasis for its Christ-centered perspective. His glorified appearance given here is the only biblical description of His immortal eminence and serves to place human mortality in dramatic contrast as Revelation details religious attempts to devalue and replace Jesus, whose "face was like the sun shining with full force." We are given an insight into the glory and majesty of eternity, providing a stark contrast with the limitations of our flesh and the world to which we are limited.

Here is the Christ-centered perspective; it is only by seeing Jesus as He really is that we can understand our world as it really is. We must not evaluate God according to our world, for in so doing we diminish Him. This is part of the force behind the Second Commandment of the old covenant, when Israel was commanded not to make images of God. Nothing we can create can begin to capture the essence of God; all human depictions devalue and corrupt Him. Many popular attempts at "end times prophecy" turn God into something and someone He is not. They result from having the theological cart before the horse. Our theology needs to be informed by who God is, not by our limited human insights, exaggerated sense of the value of our spiritual contributions, or by preoccupation with the future.

Jesus provides this spectacular picture of His glory, majesty, and power. The only other biblical description of the divine glory of the second person of the Trinity is provided in Daniel 10:5-6, which also happens to be a passage written by God's inspiration in an apocalyptic style. Speaking of Daniel and Revelation, many have engaged in hermeneutical gymnastics attempting to harmonize the messages of these two books. While there are many references in the Book of Revelation to symbols and passages within the Old Testament, an understanding of Revelation does not depend upon a precise correlation with Old Testament prophecies. The Old Testament does not determine our understanding of Revelation so much as our Christ-centered perspective does.

The seven gold lampstands (v. 12), which are identified as the seven churches (v. 20), provide an introductory reference to the importance of the number seven in Revelation. The seven stars (v. 16) are the seven angels of the seven churches (v. 20) to whom each one of the seven messages is given in chapters two and three.

As this first chapter concludes, the Christ-centered perspective reminds us that Jesus is "the first and the last" (v. 17), the "living one" who was dead and is now "alive forever and ever" (v. 18). These references to the eternity and immortality of the uncreated eternal Son of God join earlier references in this chapter "from him who is and who was and who is to come (v. 4) and "who is and who was and who is to come, the Almighty" (v. 8) to emphasize that while Jesus voluntarily became flesh and "lived among us" (Jo 1:14) "The Most High does not dwell in houses made by human hands" (Acts 7:48).

To ensure Christians that the human, Antichrist kingdoms of civil and religious governments of humanity are ultimately powerless before the one they oppose, Jesus tells John that "I have the keys of Death and of Hades" (v. 18). The risen Lord is Lord of all and holds the keys that unlock the graves of those whose physical lives are taken by secular or religious powers. Jesus is alive "in the midst" (v. 13) of the seven lampstands, the universal body of believers. Jesus Christ is with us "always, to the end of the age" (Ma 28:20).

CHAPTER FOUR

Messages From the Messenger

Bob and Mary really don't know what to do about church. Bob's parents were members of a church when he was born, and they took him to their church, sometimes against his will, until he was 16. A fleeting smile crosses Bob's face as he remembers that he was 16 when he "successfully negotiated his release" from his parents' church.

He also remembers attending, as a child, all his church activities—crusades, fairs, revivals, conventions, seminars, vacation Bible schools, and camps—and he does have fond memories of some of these experiences. But when he evaluates his total experience at the end of it all, he feels that control was the main objective of his parent's church.

Bob speaks about the steady spiritual diet he was served at home and at church: guilt and manipulation lavishly ladled upon a bed of rules and regulations. Sermon after sermon, week after week, and year after year— the same old thing. Bob feels he was never good enough for his parents, never good enough for his pastor and his church, and he became convinced that he would never be good enough for God.

When Bob and Mary visit his parents, sometimes he will give in and attend his old church with his parents, but he can hardly stand it. Bob can't talk religion with his parents, because it always ends up in a spiritual free-for-all. Some people call Bob "unchurched" while others call him a "seeker." Bob considers himself a Christian, but he doesn't know if he will ever be able to go back to regular attendance at any church.

Bob and Mary were burned out with their parents' hell fire and brimstone, our-way-or-the-highway, get-right or get-left, no-nonsense church. It's one unforgettable shared experience for Bob and Mary; they both endured religious boot camp together. They went to the same church in their hometown. In fact, they first became aware of each other at a summer Bible camp. In spite of the best efforts of vigilant counselors and chaperones, Bob and Mary fell in love. But that's about the only thing of any lasting value they believe their church gave them—each other.

Trying to Find God at Church

So Bob and Mary were conflicted when they decided to take their preschool age kids to a church and carefully did their homework before they even visited one. They compare their efforts to find a healthy church, after their negative religious experience, to be somewhat like being damaged and hurt in a romantic relationship, or even a marriage. Their trust in God was violated by the church of their youth, and they didn't want their children to have the same experience.

Bob and Mary eventually selected a traditional, mainline church that averaged about 200 people in attendance every Sunday. It seemed safe. It was a respectable church to attend, good for business and social contacts. They never felt particularly close to God there, but at least they didn't feel manipulated by a pastor who dangled the congregation's feet over the coals of hell every Sunday. When Bob and Mary's children grew to be teenagers, they announced they didn't want to go to church anymore; and in a few months the entire family drifted away from this church. In some ways Bob and Mary felt it was time to move on, because they were already concerned that this church was far too progressive, socially active, and lenient about lifestyles they did not believe to be biblically acceptable.

A few years later one of Mary's friends at work invited her to church. It had been several years since Bob and Mary had set foot in any church. They felt like "some church" wouldn't hurt them, so off they trudged with little idea of the kind of church they would visit. Bob and Mary had no idea that this kind of church existed. They knew about the white-washed, conservative, straight-laced, rule-happy, uptight church of their youth; and they had experienced the far more progressive, liberal mainline church they took their kids to when the kids were still at home.

The church they were invited to had one major mission; everything was all about spiritual warfare. The church was, and still is according to Mary's friend at work, convinced they need to "map" demon strongholds, identify demons by name, and even take trips to those geographical places to command the demons to leave the affected/infected area. Bob and Mary found all of this bizarre and illogical. As soon as they could politely leave worship services, they rushed home, found their Bibles in an old bookcase, and tried in vain to find biblical rationale for this spiritual warfare, which seemed to them to be superstition and witchcraft in the name of Christ. Mary thanked her friend at work for the invitation and told her that the church culture of spiritual warfare wasn't a good fit for them.

A few years later a relative who lived in the same metro area invited Bob and Mary to his mega-church, but after a few months they once again became disenchanted. It was a prosperity gospel church. This church spent most of the time telling its members that God wanted them to be healthy and wealthy, but as Bob and Mary checked out the hundreds of cars in the parking lot it seemed that the only ones getting rich were the pastor and his staff. Bob and Mary now refer to this church as the Jesus mall, a huge group of people convinced that Jesus will fill their shopping bags with physical stuff.

After bailing out of this think-and-grow-rich church, Bob and Mary started to feel like religious failures or at the very least like religious skeptics and cynics. Mary's mother kept saying that they were too critical, finding something wrong with every church they visited; and Mary started to think that her mother might be right. Mary's mother finally convinced them that they needed a spiritual shot in the arm.

They saw an advertisement for a church that sponsored revivals, so they decided that such a church might give them the spiritual kick-start they needed. The next weekend Bob and Mary found themselves in a church they now jokingly refer to as the "Heebie-Jeebie Church." As Bob and Mary looked for a seat, people were running up and down the aisles. They stepped over two people who seemed to have passed out in the aisle, except their arms and legs occasionally twitched. Bob and Mary were later told that these people had been "slain in the spirit." In the middle of the service a few people started to laugh uncontrollably, even though the pastor didn't say anything Bob and Mary found remotely humorous. They later found out that such an activity is called "holy laughter." A few of the people transitioned directly from hilarious laughter to barking like a dog. Bob and Mary left before the collection.

After that little "shot in the arm" Bob and Mary gave up on what they called organized religion for several years. They studied the Bible and decided to not give up searching, but they agreed to confine their church visits to the more traditional churches as well as evangelical community churches. They are now attending every six to eight weeks. It seems to them that the church they occasionally attend is on the right track with its teaching, and that it is not involved in some wild theological or experiential goose chase. It is a church that insists upon grace over human works, and that emphasis comforts them. But they have been burned so often they don't know if they can commit to becoming members.

The Seven Churches—Timeless Portraits

The twentieth and twenty-first centuries are not unique. Our generation is not the first time humans have become disillusioned with human imperfection in the name of God. The seven churches of Revelation form a snapshot of early Christian congregations that were either weak, sick, or were in good health.

Each of the seven churches of Revelation battles with the influence of corrupt religious practices on the authentic gospel of Jesus Christ. These seven churches are rooted in time, more than 1,900 years ago; but they are also a cross-section of the kinds of problems that have plagued the body of Christ from the beginning. There are hundreds of millions of people who are just like Bob and Mary. Their spiritual condition and attitude is in large part a product of religious misrepresentation of the gospel of Jesus Christ.

Surveys constantly report that many North Americans have had negative experiences with one or more churches. Welcome to the churches of Revelation, timeless portraits of the ongoing conflict between religion and authentic Christianity!

God's amazing grace is one of the most important lessons taught by Jesus' messages to the seven churches. It's a theme that is consistent throughout the Book of Revelation. Grace is the bottom line of Christianity. If grace is not present, it doesn't matter how old your church is, how correct and accurate its doctrines are, how educated your pastor is, or whether all of the bankers in town attend or not. If grace is not present, it doesn't matter how many great videos the pastor shows to spice up his sermon, how great and entertaining the music might be or how pumped up you feel when church is over. In Jesus' messages to the seven churches, grace is the bedrock issue that separates the sheep of His flock from the goats who advocate religious externalism.

In His messages to these seven churches Jesus, for some reason, omits any reference to *how many* people attend church, *how many* people are saved, or *how much* money is donated and collected. Jesus does not seem to be interested in the architecture or furnishings of the edifice in which His people gather for worship. As we study these seven churches, it becomes abundantly clear that Jesus does not measure spiritual success by statistics and size. Jesus' fundamental and essential focus in every message is about new life in Him, given by God's grace.

As we study these seven churches of Revelation, we will follow a cardinal rule of biblical interpretation: to read and understand the Scripture the way it was intended for its original readers and hearers in its original context and historical setting. What did the message mean to them? Once we understand that, we can consider what it means to us in the twenty-first century.

Of course the initial recipients are not the only and certainly not the largest audience Jesus was addressing. The Book of Revelation is fixed in history as is its original audience, but it is not confined to that original setting. The message of Revelation springs from its origins in the past to have significance and relevance for Christians of all ages.[1] The seven churches existed historically, but they also exist within the many denominational and theological permutations of Christianity today.

Some Bible teachers speculate that these seven actual churches in seven cities of Asia Minor also represent different chronological eras of the historical body of Christ. This idea is yet another attempt to impose a human chronological interpretation upon the timeless messages given in the second and third chapters of Revelation.[2] These seven churches represent different characteristics of Christians and churches not only during John's time but at any time. These messages are not limited by time and space; they are not confined to one geographical city, nor are they restricted to some presumed historical era.

Chapters two and three of Revelation reveal the message the Messenger gave to His human servant, John, to write down for the seven churches. Each message to each church begins with Jesus saying "I know." (2:2, 9, 13, 19; 3:1, 8, and 3:15). There is no question that Jesus is fully aware of all situations and difficulties facing His church. His message to each church is about the specific and particular problems and challenges faced by those individuals.

In verse seven of chapter 2, John writes: "Let anyone who has an ear listen to what the Spirit is saying to the churches." Some wonder if the Book of Revelation has anything relevant to say to Christians. Here is a warning that applies to all Christians in every age. Each one of us is told to listen to what the Spirit says to *all seven* churches.

In the next two chapters God describes these seven different churches.

Each church is called to change and repent: to remember, to conquer, and to be faithful. The initial audience that was being addressed lived in a society that was overwhelmed by religion. Their culture included a pantheon of gods. Temples to the gods existed in all cities along with temples of Roman emperor worship. There were local cults based upon every conceivable appeal—superstitions, special insight and knowledge, appeals to the flesh—you name it. For Christians at that time, the Jewish synagogue was another religion; it represented the old covenant Jewish Christians were called out of and to which they must not revert. Many in these seven churches were doing what Paul had chastised the Galatians for doing, trying to combine God's grace with religious requirements.

The Call to Conquer

Each of the seven churches is encouraged to conquer (2:7, 11, 17, 26; 3:5, 12, and 3:21). No church is exempt from the call to conquer. But *how* will these churches conquer and *what* specifically are they asked to conquer?

These passages that encourage each of the seven churches to conquer are often used, without regard to the immediate context or indeed to the overall theme of the book of Revelation, to cajole Christians into trying harder to eradicate sinful habits from their lives. But preaching that simply uses these passages as proof-texts for works-righteousness and performance-based religion is a contradiction of the grace-based gospel of Jesus Christ.

If you are a Christian, you will conquer. You will do many of the biblically correct things and avoid doing many of the biblically incorrect behaviors. But you will not conquer because of your own spiritual strength or your own hard work. As Christians, we are enabled and empowered to conquer by the new life that Christ lives in us.

What are we called upon to conquer? We are, of course, able to conquer and overcome many challenges and obstacles because of Christ. Because of Christ in us, "the hope of glory" (Col 1:27), we "are more than conquerors through him who loved us" (Ro 8:37). We are saved *by* grace *for* works; and, consequently, being saved means that "we are what he has made us, created in Christ Jesus for good works" (Ep 2:10). While Christ leads us to overcome many adversities, a more important objective and goal, according to the context of chapters two and three of Revelation, is conquering the perversion and corruption of religious legalism that brings us into bondage.

How do Christians conquer? The New Testament is filled with paradoxes, reversals of humanistic values and what we often call "common sense."

- Those who attempt to save their lives will lose them, while those who are willing to lose their lives in the cause of Christ will be granted eternal life (Ma 16:25).
- We often spend our lives accumulating and storing up treasures on earth, but in the end, only those treasures that are stored in heaven will endure (Ma 6:19-20).
- God's power is made perfect in human weakness (2 Co 12:9).
- Entrance into God's kingdom of heaven is not by merit, deed or worth, but by God's grace (Ep 2:4-10).
- God's kingdom does not necessarily belong to those who achieve human greatness, status and success, but to those who voluntarily humble themselves in a life of service to others (Ma 18:1-4; 20:25-28).
- Christians walk by faith, not by sight (2 Co 5:7).
- Though Jesus was rich, He became poor so that through His poverty we might become rich (2 Co 8:9).

One of the great gospel reversals is the way Christians conquer. Apart from God, the way humans conquer is by brute force. Darwin called it the survival of the fittest. In Christ, we survive and thrive because of Jesus. According to the Bible, only Jesus is qualified to conquer sin. The foundation and power of Christian conquering lies in the life, death, and resurrection of Jesus Christ. The final enemy of humanity is death and the grave, and the Lamb of God conquered death and the grave by and through His own death. The Christian doctrine of atonement teaches the Jesus conquered sin and all of its evil by taking it on Himself.

Those who believe in Jesus and trust in Him, and in whom Jesus lives His resurrected life, have this victory over sin and death. But we live in the flesh, and all of our lives in this fleshly body we are hounded by sinful human nature. It is in our own death that we finally realize the full and final release from our own flesh. This is the final conquest that we achieve. Death for a Christian is not the end; it is a victory that sets the stage for a new reality and dimension of eternity.

The call of Christ is a call to conquer, a call to conquer by accepting the victory won by Christ on His cross, a call from that point on to yield our bodies as living sacrifices (Ro 12:1; 2 Co 4:16). The call to conquer means giving priority to God's kingdom over the kingdom of humanity; and thus, finally through death we experience the final victory over our own flesh.

All of these churches of Revelation, both in the first century and throughout all time, are called to conquer by coming *out* of religious externalism with all of its potions and prescriptions, rites and regulations, ceremonies and conventions. They are called on to resist the religious beast and worship the Lamb of God. They are called on to be the bride of Christ rather than to play the religious harlot. The seven churches are called on to live in the Christ-centered new Jerusalem of grace, mercy, and peace rather than in the Babylon of human-centered religious legalism, spiritual pride and denominationalism, competition, lust, greed, and materialism.

The Old Testament nation of Israel was called out of the pagan religious bondage of Egypt. The churches of Revelation are called to "come out of her my people" (18:4), called to come out of any and all Babylons where human actions, deeds, and accomplishments are glorified; and instead they are directed to look to the sufficiency of Jesus Christ, who has done, is doing, and will do all that is necessary for their salvation.[3] He is, was, and is to come. Jesus is the Messenger and the message of the Book of Revelation. Through Him we can become "more than conquerors" (Ro 8:37). The seven churches are reminded: *Jesus saves, religious legalism enslaves.*

Ephesus

¹ 'To the angel of the church in Ephesus write: These are the words of him who holds the seven stars in his right hand, who walks among the seven golden lamp stands:

² 'I know your works, your toil and your patient endurance. I know that you cannot tolerate evildoers; you have tested those who claim to be apostles but are not, and have found them to be false. ³ I also know that you are enduring patiently and bearing up for the sake of my name, and that you have not grown weary. ⁴ But I have this against you, that you have abandoned the love you had at first. ⁵ Remember then from what you have fallen; repent, and do the works you did at first. If not, I will come to you and remove your lamp stand from its place, unless you repent. ⁶ Yet this is to your credit: you hate the works of the Nicolaitans, which I also hate. ⁷ Let anyone who has an ear listen to what the Spirit is saying to the churches. To everyone who conquers, I will give permission to eat from the tree of life that is in the paradise of God.

Revelation 2:1-7

The first church Jesus addresses is Ephesus, and it may have been in the most important city of these seven cities. It was a bustling seaport and home to one of the seven wonders of the ancient world. The city of Ephesus was economically dependent upon the temple of Diana. Diana (her Greek name was Artemis) was the goddess of fertility, often illustrated as having many breasts. In the nineteenth chapter of the Book of Acts an Ephesian silversmith named Demetrius was so upset about what Paul's preaching would do to his pocketbook that he started a riot that caused Paul to leave the city. Religion seems to have had the city of Ephesus in a stranglehold.

In the twentieth chapter of Acts, Paul warned the elders of the church in Ephesus about heresy and persecution that would come to that church. In verses 29 and 30, Paul warned, "after I have gone, savage wolves will come in among you, not sparing the flock. Some even from your own group will come distorting the truth in order to entice the disciples to follow them."

In His message to Ephesus, Jesus has many positive things to say. These Christians are patient and persevering. They can spot heretics a mile away; they don't tolerate false apostles or the heretical "Nicolaitans." In the letter to the church of Pergamum (v. 15) the teaching of the Nicolaitans is compared to that of Balaam, who preached a politically correct message of appeasement, compromise, and sensual pleasure.

The Ephesians saw through the seductive appeal of the Nicolaitans, yet although the church at Ephesus stood for doctrinal purity, their genuine Christian love seems to have disappeared:"you have abandoned the love you had at first" (v. 4).

What love was it that the Ephesians had abandoned? The context does not elaborate. Many preachers have traditionally used this passage to hammer Christians into submission to a host of congregational and denominational rules and regulations, teaching that human efforts and performance will recapture the first love that has been abandoned. Such an interpretation is itself the very kind of distortion that Paul reminded the Ephesian elders against (Acts 20:30).

The first love of Christians is our romance with God's grace. The love we have at first involves our deep, heartfelt admiration and appreciation for Jesus, who died for us in our stead. The love we have at first includes our trust and faith in the Lamb of God who took our place, substituting for us. This initial love comes from the realization of the depth of our own sin, and the corresponding and opposite love of God for us that is without measure.

"The Ephesians apparently abandoned their first love, leaving their grace-based relationship with God in favor of a relationship with an institutional church, a church that had exacting and rigorous doctrine, a church that was correct, morally, theologically and intellectually impervious to error."[4]

This first of the seven churches of Revelation is the only one of these churches to which another New Testament letter was written. In the Book of Ephesians, Paul offers a prayer to them and to all Christians in which God's love is central.

> [16] I pray that, according to the riches of his glory, he may grant that you may be strengthened in your inner being with power through his Spirit, [17] and that Christ may dwell in your hearts through faith, as you are being rooted and grounded in love. [18] I pray that you may have the power to comprehend, with all the saints, what is the breadth and length and height and depth, [19] and to know the love of Christ that surpasses knowledge, so that you may be filled with all the fullness of God.
> *Ephesians 3:16-19*

It is possible that our zeal for biblically correct doctrinal beliefs and teachings can morph into a desire to position ourselves as being right, true, and accurate, coupled with a fanatical fervency to brand all who do not measure up as substandard. Such a process can turn the grace of God into a mean-spirited religion, a religious club with entrance requirements we could not pass if we were not already members ourselves.[5] Today there are churches who seem to be consumed with their desire to be holy, but in so doing they often become self-centered and self-righteous and may actually lose their first love. Love is, after all, the hallmark of authentic Christianity (Jo 13:35). Religion can cause us to set aside the love that God gives us in favor of judgment and condemnation. Perhaps in their zeal to protect the gospel, some of the Ephesians had become religiously motivated rather than grace driven. Perhaps they abandoned their first love as they hunted heretics (Re 2:2).

Are you careful about correct, biblically based doctrine? You should be. But being on guard for doctrinal errors can lead to what is called heresy-hunting and that kind of thing can lead you deep into the woods of legalistic religion. While the desire for doctrinal purity and fidelity is a right and proper cause, it can lead to hyper-criticism, even inquisitions. Everyone can become a suspect. Zeal for academic truth can suppress God's love. The desire to be correct breeds self-righteous pride, spiritual arrogance, and religious superiority. What begins as a desire to protect and preserve the gospel of Jesus Christ can lead to a self-righteous inbred world where we huddle together in Christian communes, dedicating ourselves to the careful pursuit of religious legalism that we are convinced will make God happy and will make us better than outsiders. These religious legalisms also will encourage us to judge the hell out of the rest of the world.

Smyrna

> [8] "And to the angel of the church in Smyrna write: These are the words of the first and the last, who was dead and came to life:
>
> [9] "I know your affliction and your poverty, even though you are rich. I know the slander on the part of those who say that they are Jews and are not, but are a synagogue of Satan. [10] Do not fear what you are about to suffer. Beware, the devil is about to throw some of you into prison so that you may be tested, and for ten days you will have affliction. Be faithful until death, and I will give you the crown of life. [11] Let anyone who has an ear listen to what the Spirit is saying to the churches. Whoever conquers will not be harmed by the second death."
>
> *Revelation 2:8-11*

Like Ephesus, Smyrna was a seaport, a beautiful and prosperous city located in present-day Turkey; but the city was so overwhelmed and controlled by religion it was difficult for Christians to live and make a living.

Christians in Smyrna endured all sorts of hardships, many of which were at the hands of religion. Jesus lets them know that He recognized everything they'd endured, the severe persecution and even imprisonment for their faith.

Jesus reminds these embattled Christians in Smyrna that He "is the first and the last, who was dead and came to life" (3:8), reminiscent of the self-identification Jesus provided John in the vision recorded in the first chapter (1:17-18).

The church in Smyrna was under incredible pressure to give in to Roman emperor worship. They were also exposed to the idolatry of the many gods of religion and the dogmatic assurances of Jewish legalism. Many Christians in Smyrna were impoverished, probably because pagan religion boycotted them and would not let them compete or earn a living. Followers of Jesus Christ insist that Jesus is Lord. The Roman emperor was not god, nor was any religious or governmental human leader at any time in history god. Christians who lived then knew and, those who now live in such conditions, know the incredible pressure to conform that can be imposed by religious oppression.

Jesus mentions persecution, suffering, and death as the lot of the church in Smyrna. This persecution was the result of their steadfast faith in the one who died and came to life again. He mentions a specific foe, "those who say that they are Jews and are not, but are a synagogue of Satan" (v. 9). There is no reason to see a veiled encouragement for anti-Semitism in this statement, but there is every reason to understand it as a warning about toxic religion. At that time in the Roman Empire, the Jews were protected as a bona fide religion, whereas Christians were not. Roman imperial law recognized Judaism, but Christianity was an illegal religion.

Earlier in the first century, Christianity was viewed both by Rome as well as by many Jews as a sect or dissident offshoot of Judaism. Jewish leaders in Corinth accused the apostle Paul of "persuading people to worship God in ways that are contrary to the law" (Acts 18:13). Gallio, the proconsul of Achaia, heard this charge and decided that the dispute was not about Roman law, but about Jewish law; and he would not interfere in what he perceived as an in-house squabble about the Jewish religion.

While it is true that all of the early Christians were Jews culturally and racially, it is also true that these Christian Jews were no longer accepted, even in the early days of Christianity, by their fellow Jews (the opposite dynamic was also true; some Jewish Christians, in their zeal to leave Judaism behind, rejected their own blood relatives who did not convert to Christianity). The early church struggled with God's grace versus the law of the old covenant, with the implications of God's grace causing the Jewish synagogue to see a clear demarcation between themselves and Christianity, even though Roman judges like Gallio did not.

By the time of the writing of the Book of Revelation, some 40 years after the ruling made by Gallio, the gap between the faith and practice of Judaism and that of Christianity had become far more pronounced. Thus the Christians in Smyrna were under intense persecution "by those who say that they are Jews and are not." Jesus is saying that even though these Jews in Smyrna claimed to be Abraham's children (Jo 8:31-41) they rejected the foundation and basis of Abraham's faith in God. Abraham was justified by grace (Ro 4:1-3, 16-25), not by works of the law. This passage suggests that a true Jew would be one who accepted the finished and complete work of Messiah, our Lord and Savior who Himself was a Jew, who did for us what the law could never do.

Much has been made of the persecution of *ten days* (v. 10) in an attempt to impose an unwarranted chronological grid or framework upon Revelation. There is no known record of a persecution of such duration, but of course that does not mean such a time did not happen. Not to be deterred, some who insist on imposing strict literalism on the text of Revelation suggest that these ten days should be understood as 10 Roman emperors who persecuted Christianity (and lists of ten emperors who seem to have done so are then compiled as "proof") or that there were 10 historical eras of persecution (accompanied by another stampede to the history books to "find" evidence to support the imposed methodology). We don't know precisely what or when these ten days were, are, or will be.

Pergamum

> [12] "And to the angel of the church in Pergamum write: These are the words of him who has the sharp two-edged sword:
>
> [13] "I know where you are living, where Satan's throne is. Yet you are holding fast to my name, and you did not deny your faith in me even in the days of Antipas my witness, my faithful one, who was killed among you, where Satan lives. [14] But I have a few things against you: you have some there who hold to the teaching of Balaam, who taught Balak to put a stumbling block before the people of Israel, so that they would eat food sacrificed to idols and practice fornication. [15] So you also have some who hold to the teaching of the Nicolaitans. [16] Repent then. If not, I will come to you soon and make war against them with the sword of my mouth. [17] Let anyone who has an ear listen to what the Spirit is saying to the churches. To everyone who conquers I will give some of the hidden manna, and I will give a white stone, and on the white stone is written a new name that no one knows except the one who receives it."
>
> *Revelation 2:12-17*

The third church receiving a letter from Jesus is Pergamum, the capital of the province of Asia, a city built on a hill, towering over the valley below.

Once again, religion played a central role in the daily life of the citizens of Pergamum. The temple of Zeus was probably the most impressive of all of the temples in Pergamum. It was so impressive that archaeologists unearthed remains of the temple and shipped it to the Berlin Museum. Almost 40 years ago, as a college student, I remember traveling to what was then East Berlin to see those remains in the Berlin Museum.

Many other shrines and altars were part of the landscape in Pergamum, with the temple of the Greek god of healing, Aesculapius, being one of the most prominent. People came to this temple looking for healing, claiming that Aesculapius was their savior. The insignia used by the temple—a serpent entwined around a staff—is used by medical physicians to this day. Religion in many forms so overwhelmed life in Pergamum that Christianity found itself in an alien, hostile atmosphere.

Another source of pride in Pergamum was the library. The library of Pergamum was second in size and fame only to the library in Alexandria, Egypt, and was, of course, a source of intellectual smugness and vanity.

To this city and to its church Jesus reassuringly says, "I know where you are living, where Satan's throne is" (v. 13). The city of Pergamum united civil government with religious power and, combined with its intellectual pride, created a spiritual environment that was a diabolical challenge for Christians. The intercourse that civil government has with religion and the control religion is therefore able to exert over the secular world is an ongoing theme in the Book of Revelation. Jesus commends those who have remained true to His name in the face of such powerful forces; but He also says, "I have a few things against you" (v. 14), charging them first with holding to the teaching of Balaam and then, in verse 15, with the teaching of the Nicolaitans.

In the Old Testament (Nu 25) Balaam manipulated Israel after being offered riches and power by Balak to destroy Israel. He tempted the men of Israel with Moabite women, causing them to engage in sexual immorality, thus paving the way for compromise with paganism. Balaam encouraged immorality by playing both sides against each other. He was a politician who tried to exist in the middle of the road by appeasing and compromising. Because accommodation and compromise is the teaching of Balaam, we can safely assume religion in Pergamum encouraged Christians to compromise rather than obey Jesus Christ.

Accommodation and compromise is alive and well today, with its popular contemporary permutation being the cult of tolerance. Our western world worships at the throne of tolerance, where the decree goes forth that everyone may do as they please and not be accountable to anyone; for we must tolerate all behavior and practice. The gospel of Jesus Christ commands that we love our neighbor, but that does not include tolerating false religion and sin. Modern Nicolaitans attempt to brainwash us, often in the name of God, into thinking that love means tolerating behavior that leads to misery and heartache.

No one has been able to discover the exact identity of the Nicolaitans and what they practiced and preached. Understanding the context that was present in Pergamum, we can surmise the kind of teaching to which Jesus was opposed. One must be careful with word studies, forming a dogmatic conclusion from the simple reduction of a word to its root meaning. Having offered that disclaimer, Nicolaitan is an interesting word, using the well known Greek word in our western world "nike" (the shoe company with its swoosh symbol), which means "to conquer and be victorious" along with "laos," which means people.

If the very word Nicolaitan defines one of the products of legalistic religion as conquering people—chewing them up, spitting them out, consuming, using and abusing them—then it would be symbolic of all religion opposed to authentic Christianity. Religion, apart from God's grace, eats people alive. It overwhelms them. It masters them. It does not seek to serve humans, but it seeks the servitude of humans. The word Nicolaitan itself may well be a fitting metaphor for oppressive religion.

That description and definition is of course in direct contrast to Jesus, who did not come to be served but to serve. Jesus did not come to this earth to start another religion. Human beings have always had, and continue to have, too much religion. We don't need more religion; we need more Jesus.

The church in Pergamum had suffered persecution; some had been martyred and remained faithful to God in the face of death. But many others had apparently tried to have it both ways, maintaining their Christianity while bowing to the dictates of religious legalism. The words of Elijah on Mt. Carmel, as he confronted the priests of Baal, echo across human history, "If the Lord is God, follow him; but if Baal, then follow him" (1 Ki 18:21).

In the early days of the New Testament church, Peter and the other apostles were charged by religious leaders who were "filled with jealousy" (Acts 5:17) with illegally preaching the gospel. Peter and the apostles were placed in jail, released by an angel, and returned to the streets of Jerusalem, boldly preaching the gospel. When they were called to answer, "Peter and the apostles answered, 'We must obey God rather than any human authority!'" (Acts 5:29).

Jesus warns all of us, as we deal with challenges and temptations, to remain true to the gospel of Jesus Christ, to the clear, main, and plain teachings of the Bible, and to repent of whatever compromises we may be allowing in our lives.

Jesus concludes His letter to the church in Pergamum with a promise to give "hidden manna and a white stone" (v. 17) to those who conquer. Here is another Old Testament figure, the manna that sustained the children of Israel for 40 years in the wilderness. Jesus used the metaphor of bread to speak of Himself, the true Bread from heaven. "Whoever comes to me will never be hungry, and whoever believes in me will never be thirsty" (Jo 6:35). The white stone appears to be a metaphor referring to a judicial practice of a judge handing the accused a verdict stone, which in cases of acquittal, was a white stone. Christians, though they may be condemned by secular or religious sources of this world, are justified in the supreme court of heaven.

CHAPTER FIVE

The Battle Belongs to the Lord

Jesus Christ founded His universal church, available to all, offering a personal relationship with God. His church is based on relationship, not the rituals, rites, and regulations of religion. But many of the first Christians wanted to legalize His teachings, and almost 2,000 years later some who assume they are Jesus' disciples continue marching to the drumbeat of legalism. Some of the pagans who heard of the newly formed Christian church wanted to turn it into a philosophy, and their efforts continue to this day. The Romans determined to institutionalize the church, and today a party spirit of denominationalism pervades Christendom with competing cries of exclusive truth claims echoing across the Christian world.

But one of the greatest insults and perversions of the body of Christ is less than 300 years old. When the gospel came to America, it met the forces of capitalism and free enterprise. Many citizens of these United States have done their best to turn the gospel of Jesus Christ into a business.

Today, in twenty-first century America, God is in the process of being repackaged and reinvented. We Americans don't have time for theology, doctrine, expository preaching, or Bible study because our attention span is limited to snappy 28-second television commercials filled with special effects. We are used to brief television programs that present solutions for anything from crime and obesity to financial problems and sexual dysfunctions. We want our God presented, explained, and "served" to us in

67

practical, easy to understand, bite-sized portions.

Courtesy of the American entrepreneurial spirit, God is now available in microwave versions. We don't need to wait for one hour while our spiritual food is prepared in the oven. Now it is 60 seconds in the microwave, and we have God where we want Him. Twenty-first century America has morphed God into bumper sticker messages and feeling based multi-sensory experiences that are called worship services.

Truth? We Americans don't want to critically examine issues; we want someone to prepackage and shrink wrap our thinking for us, so that there is little mental chewing involved in digesting the final product. What zeal we have for right and wrong often fades as complexities demand intellectual attention, and we find ourselves shifting our allegiance to whatever is quick and easy. Many would rather read Christian fiction and Christian fantasy than Christian teaching. One of the seminal contributions to Christian literature from the blockbuster "Left Behind" series has been the merging of Christian fact and fiction. Many readers are either unable to discern the difference or simply don't care. Is it any wonder that the Book of Revelation has come to be warped and twisted into a disaster movie?

Truth? In our culture of fast spiritual food, many critically important themes of the Book of Revelation have been diminished and devalued in a rush to over-literalize its message and force political paradigms and personalities into the text. Topics of eternal significance are continuously stressed in the Book of Revelation, such as God's grace and God's judgment against religious and political oppression and evil. The triumphal rule of Jesus and His eventual victory over all religious imposters, who create a Babylon of religious confusion in our world, are pushed aside by attempts to impose human time on this timeless message.

Truth? We want Jesus to come now, in our generation! And there are plenty of prophecy teachers who are quick to realize a financial profit by giving people what they want. As a result, Revelation's Christ-centered focus is at best blurred and, beyond that, sometimes lost in the fog and smoke of sensational, lurid distortions of its message.

Truth? Entertain me and make me feel good. If the truth happens to accompany feel-good entertainment, that's great. If not, it may be too much trouble for us to pursue truth from the friendly confines of our couch or recliner. Given our cultural reality, the Book of Revelation is not an easy read, and as a result, it is often distorted and "dumbed down."

Truth? Remember, the Book of Revelation is a message from the divine Author, Jesus Christ, to the human author, the apostle John. Revelation is not predigested spiritual fast food ready to be nuked in a religious microwave. Properly read and understood, Jesus' message to you will cause you to think, and it may rock your spiritual boat.

As I've said, Revelation begins with letters to seven churches located in seven cities in the area that is modern Turkey. These letters provide vital insight and direction into the focus of the remainder of this gospel-centered book. Once we leave chapter three of the Book of Revelation, there is a major shift in language. We begin to read of strange symbols, mysterious numbers, and frightening beasts given to John in nightmare-like visions. But the theme remains the same, the same theme found in the letters to the seven churches in chapters two and three. The battle of Revelation is between the sacred and the profane, between Christ and Antichrist, between performance-based religion and the gospel of Jesus Christ. The battle is ongoing, but Revelation continually assures us that the battle belongs to the Lord.

In our chapter four, we took an in-depth look at the first three churches of the seven churches of Revelation; now we're ready to consider the final four. We have already considered Ephesus, Smyrna, and Pergamum; and we will now we turn our attention to Thyatira, Sardis, Philadelphia, and Laodecia.

Thyatira

> [18] "And to the angel of the church in Thyatira write: These are the words of the Son of God, who has eyes like a

flame of fire, and whose feet are like burnished bronze:

[19] "I know your works—your love, faith, service, and patient endurance. I know that your last works are greater than the first. [20] But I have this against you: you tolerate that woman Jezebel, who calls herself a prophet and is teaching and beguiling my servants to practice fornication and to eat food sacrificed to idols. [21] I gave her time to repent, but she refuses to repent of her fornication. [22] Beware, I am throwing her on a bed, and those who commit adultery with her I am throwing into great distress, unless they repent of her doings; [23] and I will strike her children dead. And all the churches will know that I am the one who searches minds and hearts, and I will give to each of you as your works deserve. [24] But to the rest of you in Thyatira, who do not hold this teaching, who have not learned what some call 'the deep things of Satan,' to you I say, I do not lay on you any other burden; [25] only hold fast to what you have until I come. [26] To everyone who conquers and continues to do my works to the end,

[27] "I will give authority over the nations;

to rule them with an iron rod,

as when clay pots are shattered—

[28] even as I also received authority from my Father. To the one who conquers I will also give the morning star. [29] Let anyone who has an ear listen to what the Spirit is saying to the churches."

Revelation 2:18-29

Thyatira was a manufacturing and trade center, the smallest of the seven cities of the seven churches. Many of the citizens of Thyatira were working-class, blue-collar people. One of the many trades in Thyatira was the garment industry and a dye that was unique to this region was used to color some of these garments.

When Paul went to the area of Macedonia, just across the Aegean Sea from Thyatira, the first person who was converted to Christianity was a woman named Lydia. Lydia was from Thyatira, in Acts 16:14 we read that she was a "dealer in purple cloth." Perhaps she imported these fabrics from her hometown of Thyatira.

Unique forms of religion flourished in Thyatira, many of them connected with trade unions. Each craft and type of labor had a guild or union, and most of them identified themselves with a pagan deity. They had meetings, feasts, and banquets that included religious observances, like sacrificing the meat of an animal to a god.

For many in Thyatira, it may be that work was not only their god (as for many today), but their workplace and union were directly associated with gods. Christians in Thyatira were challenged in their work place by deeply entrenched religious superstition that was part of everyday life in Thyatira.

Some in the church at Thyatira had apparently allowed a false teacher named "Jezebel" to lead them away from God into idolatry and sexual immorality. Jesus commended this church for its love, faith, service, and perseverance; but he also corrected them because they tolerated the woman, Jezebel, who called herself a prophetess.

Was this woman's literal name Jezebel, or was it a generic name that described her and the kind of religion she promoted? In the Old Testament, Jezebel was the wife of wicked King Ahab (I Ki 16:31). She was an evil person who opposed God and killed His prophets (2 Ki 9:7, 37). Her name, to this day, is proverbial for an evil, scheming, wicked woman. You won't find many mothers and fathers naming their little baby girl "Jezebel."

The Jezebel of Thyatira was evil and diabolical, just like her Old Testament namesake. She encouraged permissiveness, promiscuity, and pleasure. While this particular religion may have pandered to the desires of the flesh, giving people what they wanted in return for their compliance to the dictates of religion, the Old Testament Jezebel was primarily guilty of leading Israel into idolatry: false religion. This Jezebel attracted a religious following, captivating them and eventually ensnaring them like a spider enticing prey into its web.

Solomon tells us, "What has been is what will be, and what has been done is what will be done; there is nothing new under the sun" (Ec 1:9). The Jezebel of Thyatira continues to be reincarnated in many religious systems today. Some, under the guise and cover of Christianity, propose that any behavior that is designated as loving by humans is acceptable and must be allowed and tolerated. Some who think of themselves as Christians say that the supreme morality is tolerance of others' views and behaviors, even if such practices are condemned in the new covenant given to us by the blood of the Lamb.

The message of the gospel is that slaves of human lust need the one true God. We need His forgiveness and His rescue. We need a new life, so that we may leave the old habits and addictions behind. Unfortunately, some who are looking for a way out of their empty lives of addiction and pain find a religion that uses the name of Jesus Christ, counterfeits His teachings, offering a different gospel that sounds good, seems reasonable and rational, says all of the politically correct feel-good things, and does not disturb the status quo of sinful behavior.

Feeling good is not the basis of Christianity. Seeming right is not the foundation of Christ-centered faith. In His message to Thyatira and to our world today, Jesus pulls no punches. He says, "I gave her time to repent, but she refuses to repent of her fornication. Beware, I am throwing her on a bed, and those who commit adultery with her I am throwing into great distress, unless they repent of her doings" (vv. 21-22).

Many people today turn to unbiblical religious teachings for quick fixes, to make them rich, to give them miraculous healing, asking their chosen religion to validate their desires in the name of God. Religiosity can become a convenient way to justify our own lust, pride, and vanity. Our twenty-first century is awash with authors, preachers, pastors, and prophets who in God's name cater only to feelings and felt needs while ignoring the deep needs of our souls.

We human beings often don't actually need what we want; but that fact is ignored by religion as it attempts to deceive, beguile, and seduce us. *Legalistic religion will sell you anything you want,* as long as you sign on the bottom line, promising to pay its price.

In His message to Thyatira, Jesus is telling us that the fine print in the contracts of unbiblical religions is severe. In the end oppressive religion will own us, hook, line, and sinker. We may begin thinking that the god of religion is marching to our tune, but in the end unbiblical religion will herd us along in a death march of oppression and bondage.

Some religion attracts us with fluffy promises and attractive assurances that we don't need to repent of our behavior or addictions as long as we have love. But our human ideas about love are not always true. We desperately need God's love, a love that exists at another dimension beyond human love. God *does* want us to come to Him, to change our lives, to accept Jesus Christ, and He *does* accept us just the way we are. But our journey with God doesn't end with "just the way we are." The "way we are" is only the starting place. God then demonstrates His love for us, from that point on, by leading us to become the way He is; and that means an end to the way we are or were. When we accept Jesus, He lives His resurrected life in us. He turns our defeat into victory. Though we are failures, He transforms us into conquerors (v. 26). "We are more than conquerors through him who loved us" (Ro 8:37).

Jesus promises the morning star (v. 28) to those who conquer. He is promising us nothing less than Himself, and the new Jerusalem He brings, "I am the root and the descendent of David, the bright morning star" (22:16).

Sardis

> [1] "And to the angel of the church in Sardis write: These are the words of him who has the seven spirits of God and the seven stars:
>
> "I know your works; you have a name for being alive, but you are dead. [2] Wake up, and strengthen what remains

and is at the point of death, for I have not found your works perfect in the sight of my God. ³ Remember then what you received and heard; obey it, and repent. If you do not wake up, I will come like a thief, and you will not know at what hour I will come to you. ⁴ Yet you have still a few people in Sardis who have not soiled their clothes; they will walk with me, dressed in white, for they are worthy. ⁵ If you conquer, you will be clothed like them in white robes, and I will not blot your name out of the book of life; I will confess your name before my Father and before his angels. ⁶ Let anyone who has an ear listen to what the Spirit is saying to the churches."

Revelation 3:1-6

At the time Jesus revealed His letter to the church in Sardis to John, the city of Sardis was a city in decline. Five hundred years before, Sardis had been great; but at the time Revelation was written, the citizens of Sardis were living in the past.

W.M. Ramsay, in his *The Letters to the Seven Churches of Asia*, says, "The letter to the Sardian church breathes the spirit of death, of appearance without reality, promise without performance, outward show of strength betrayed by want of watchfulness and careless confidence."[1]

Jesus tells the church in Sardis "you have a name of being alive, but you are dead" (v. 1). Reputations and appearances that are humanly discerned may not accurately reveal internal spiritual reality. The church at Sardis played the Christian game. They were nominal Christians. They were spiritual zombies going through the motions, performing all of the right religious duties, ceremonies, and behaviors at the right times, showing up at the right places, wearing the right clothing, mouthing the right words; but they were dead. This church was a church in a dead spiritual state, a Christian church in name only. Many have followed in its footsteps, using the name of Jesus but denying the gospel He proclaimed.

Outward appearances, things that look and seem good externally, combined with unseen internal disease and decay are products of religion apart from the Lamb of God. Religious legalism with all of its demands is like a spiritual vampire that sucks away our spiritual life. The resurrected, living Jesus Christ, the slain Lamb of God, who was dead but is now alive, is the only source that makes us truly alive.

Remember what Jesus said of the religion of the Pharisees? They were whitewashed tombs, beautiful on the outside but on the inside filled with dead bones and uncleanness (Ma 23:27). They appeared righteous and obedient externally, but internally they were filled with arrogance and corruption (Ma 23:28).

The message to Sardis includes Jesus' advice to "Wake up" (v. 2). The message to us today is clear: membership in a church, attendance at a church, sitting in a chair or a pew, being seen in the right place at the right time, paying all of our religious "union dues" means nothing if we do not have a personal relationship with God. Many people deceive themselves, thinking that their relationship with a church will save them. Jesus tells us otherwise. Nominal Christians are dead. We are either alive in Christ or we are dead; there is no middle ground.

The letter to Sardis is a warning against complacency and compromise that spans the ages. The letter to Sardis warns us of the dangers of:

- Living in the past, when our congregation or denomination was in its glory days when we were "important." Jesus tells us to "wake up."
- Compromising with our culture so that the culture in which we live overcomes the church, rather than the opposite.
- Appeasing opponents of Christianity by assuring them that all roads lead to heaven, and that it does not matter whether you accept God's grace or attempt to make your own way into God's kingdom of heaven via the stipulations of religion.

Jesus tells the church at Sardis that a few of them "have not soiled their clothes" (2:4). One of the industries in Sardis was wool; and, of course, there were many references in the Old Testament that Christians would have understood as being metaphors for the clothing Jesus supplies those who accept Him. Perhaps one that Jesus had in mind was Isaiah 1:18, "though your sins are like scarlet, they shall be like snow; though they are red like crimson, they shall become like wool."

Paul tells us to "put away" the old self (Ep 4:22) and "clothe yourselves with the new self, created according to the likeness of God in true righteousness and holiness" (Ep 4:24). This word picture suggests that we take off pseudo-spiritual clothing we humans manufacture and put on clothing provided by God's grace.

The purity of the garments of Christ's righteousness that are given to us by God's grace can be soiled by religious compromise and accommodation. Religion can use all of the right words and phrases, giving lip service to Jesus Christ, while insisting on its own performance-oriented agenda.

Philadelphia

> 7 "And to the angel of the church in Philadelphia write:
> These are the words of the holy one, the true one,
> who has the key of David,
> who opens and no one will shut,
> who shuts and no one opens:
> 8 "I know your works. Look, I have set before you an open door, which no one is able to shut. I know that you have but little power, and yet you have kept my word and have not denied my name. 9 I will make those of the synagogue of Satan who say that they are Jews and are not, but are lying—I will make them come and bow down before your feet, and they will learn that I have loved you. 10 Because you have kept my word of patient endurance, I will keep you from the hour of trial that is coming on the whole

world to test the inhabitants of the earth. 11 I am coming soon; hold fast to what you have, so that no one may seize your crown. 12 If you conquer, I will make you a pillar in the temple of my God; you will never go out of it. I will write on you the name of my God, and the name of the city of my God, the new Jerusalem that comes down from my God out of heaven, and my own new name. 13 Let anyone who has an ear listen to what the Spirit is saying to the churches."

Revelation 3:7-13

The region around the city of Philadelphia experienced frequent earthquakes, and for that reason may have had a small population. Jesus says that Philadelphian Christians "have but little power, and yet you have kept my word and have not denied my name" (v. 8). In spite of pressure and persecution, the Christians in Philadelphia were much like their city. Earthquakes and calamities helped to make the church in Philadelphia aware of its need for God, and that it could never be righteous enough by its own power to attain God's kingdom of heaven.

Jesus assures the church in Philadelphia that He has "the key of David" (v. 7). A key signifies power and authority. The one who has the key controls the entry and the exit. The same human author to whom Jesus, the divine Author, gave this Revelation was inspired to write in his Gospel that Jesus is the gate to eternal life (Jo 10:7, 9). Jesus is the only one who can open up the way, show us the way, lead us, direct, and guide us.

Unbiblical religion, in all of its permutations, including many religions that call themselves Christian, usually sets up little kingdoms and empires. But legalistic kingdoms of religion are kingdoms of misery, suffering, and hell. They are kingdoms where humans are never free, where humans are forever slaves, never good enough, forever on the treadmill of legalism trying to perform at a high enough standard to achieve the impossible goal of human perfection.

Religion yearns to be considered the gate to eternal life. Legalistic religion wants you to believe that it has the key of David so that it, not Jesus, will control who will come in and go out. Such religion wants us to believe that it has the authority to control access to God's eternal kingdom.[2] But Jesus is the head of the church, He is the door, He alone has the key. Don't allow any human being to convince you that they, or their movement, group or church, will decide your eternal destiny.

Jesus tells Philadelphia, and all of us, all Christians whenever and wherever they live, that He has given us "an open door, which no one is able to shut." (v. 8). Jesus is the way, the truth, and the life. Through His death on the cross the Lamb of God opened the way to the holy place depicted by the tabernacle and temple of the old covenant. No one is more powerful than Jesus. No human can shut you out of God's kingdom of heaven.

Jesus says "those of the synagogue of Satan who say that they are Jews and are not, but are lying—I will make them come and bow down before your feet, and they will learn that I have loved you" (v. 9). Once again, as He did in His message to the church in Smyrna (2:9), Jesus has harsh words for anyone who claims the heritage of faith through Abraham but does not accept justification by faith alone, as did Abraham (Ro 5:1-17). Those "who say that they are Jews and are not" is a commentary on the Jews who had rejected their Messiah. This condemnation is similar to the curse that Paul explains is on those who, in the name of Christ, attempt to earn their salvation by obedience to some or all of the old covenant (Ga 3:10, 13).

Apparently, the Christians in Philadelphia were few in number and not an impressive group. They were not a mega-church with 600 people in the choir and 78 different ministries, with a parking lot for 10,000 cars.

Philadelphian Christians didn't have much physical, financial, or political clout. Philadelphian Christians did not boast the impressive members and followers that religion covets. It wasn't their size, prestige, magnificent sanctuary, breathtaking outreach programs, or number of books their pastor had authored for which Jesus commends this small church. This church didn't have money or power, but they did have Jesus, who has the key of David, who opened a door that no one else can, a door that no human or group can shut.

Jesus tells them, and us, "hold fast to what you have" (v. 11). To the naked eye, this group from Philadelphia doesn't have much. But they have Jesus, and that means they have everything. They have Jesus who Ephesians 1:23 says is the "fullness of him who fills all in all." Don't surrender what you have been given by God's grace!

Don't let some fast-talking, smooth-tongued religious con artist come along and deceive you into thinking that having Jesus is good, but not enough; that you need more than Jesus to be saved. Performance-based religion bombards us with the message that we need to do more, work harder, try harder, give more, do more, volunteer and serve more, and pray more if we expect to "make it." Hold fast to the cross of Christ, to the resurrected Lord of your life who is all that you need. He is the door. He has the key of David. Don't let religion take you hostage; don't give in to clever sounding arguments and attractive ideas that will make you their slave. Hold fast to Jesus; He is all you need.[3]

Jesus promises to keep Philadelphian Christians "from the hour of trial that is coming on the whole world to test the inhabitants of the earth" (v. 10). Here is an excellent illustration of how the four popular interpretive methodologies used to understand the *when* of Revelation (see chapter one) yield completely different conclusions.

The *preterist* suggests that this hour of trial was the destruction of Jerusalem in A.D. 69-70. They, of course, believe the Book of Revelation was written before this time, and that "the inhabitants of the earth" were represented by the whole world of Judaism to which this passage applied. Some *historicists* attempt to find and identify specific times of trial through history that would have been particularly difficult times of trial for Christians. Some *futurists* see verse 10 as some yet future calamity, perhaps one and the same as the great tribulation or "the great ordeal" (Re 7:14). The *idealist* view would generally see this "hour of trial" as beyond any chronological or geographical limitations.

Regardless of the exact time and *when* of this trial, Revelation continually maintains that the source of the "hour of trial" is Babylon the Great, a religious system bearing the name of an ancient city that stands in opposition to the Lamb of God. Jesus promises, in verse 12, that those who keep His word and do not deny His name, conquering religious opposition that stands against Christianity, will bear the name of the city of God, the new Jerusalem.[4] The battle belongs to the Lord. With apologies to novelist Charles Dickens, Revelation is, in many ways, a *Tale of Two Cities*.

Laodicea

[14] "And to the angel of the church in Laodicea write: The words of the Amen, the faithful and true witness, the origin of God's creation:

[15] "I know your works; you are neither cold nor hot. I wish that you were either cold or hot. [16] So, because you are lukewarm, and neither cold nor hot, I am about to spit you out of my mouth. [17] For you say, 'I am rich, I have prospered, and I need nothing.' You do not realize that you are wretched, pitiable, poor, blind, and naked. [18] Therefore I counsel you to buy from me gold refined by fire so that you may be rich; and white robes to clothe you and to keep the shame of your nakedness from being seen; and salve to anoint your eyes so that you may see. [19] I reprove and discipline those whom I love. Be earnest, therefore, and repent. [20] Listen! I am standing at the door, knocking; if you hear my voice and open the door, I will come in to you and eat with you, and you with me. [21] To the one who conquers I will give a place with me on my throne, just as I myself conquered and sat down with my Father on his throne. [22] Let anyone who has an ear listen to what the Spirit is saying to the churches."

Revelation 3:14-22

The city of Laodicea considered itself to be self-sufficient, in need of nothing.[5] Laodicea was the banking center of that area, so wealthy in fact that when an earthquake struck that region about 30 years or so before the message of Revelation was given by Jesus to John, the city of Laodicea declined any financial assistance from the Roman Empire. They didn't need any help. They preferred to take care of themselves.

But Jesus said they were actually "wretched, pitiable, poor, blind, and naked" (v. 17), a severe commentary about their pride in being physically self-sufficient.[6] This is the only church about which Jesus has nothing positive to say. Laodicea manufactured a world famous eye salve, and they were known for their textile industry. They, the city corporately and many of its citizens, were financially independent. But Jesus is saying, in effect, "You only think you have it all. It only appears as if you need nothing. You have all the external stuff you think you need to take care of yourselves, but I am telling you that you are actually spiritually poor, spiritually blind, and spiritually naked."

There was one thing about which the Laodecians could complain. Their water supply had to come by aqueduct, and by the time the water arrived in Laodecia, it was neither cold nor hot, but lukewarm. In nearby Colossae the water was cold, pure, and delicious; but by the time it arrived in Laodecia it had become lukewarm. In Hieropolos, another town close to Laodecia, citizens enjoyed therapeutic, hot mineral springs, but these waters also became lukewarm as they made the journey to Laodecia. Laodecia was neither cold nor hot. Jesus found Laodecia wanting. He said that their spiritual condition was like their drinking water; therefore, He was about to spit them out of His mouth. The Laodecians exemplified one of the products of unbiblical religious traditions. Religious legalism assures us that all is well. Performance-based religion tells us that if the outward physical signs are vital, if we have all of our religious ducks lined up, then we will pass our religious checkup with flying colors. But Jesus tells Laodecian Christians that they are deceived. In spite of their eye salve, the Laodecians fail to see that their true standing with God is not based upon externals.

Laodecians are deceived into thinking that compliance with outward religious regulations gains them positive standing with God. They think that they are wearing robes of righteousness, but in reality Jesus tells them that they are naked.

Like the emperor in the story "The Emperor's New Clothes," Laodiceans strut their spiritual stuff, but they are actually naked. There is only one "place" to find true spiritual clothing, only one source for white robes of righteousness. If Jesus does not clothe us, and if we do not accept His garments on His terms, we are spiritually naked, regardless of what we might think or what some religious authority might assure us. Later on, when we consider the nineteenth chapter of Revelation, we will find that the bride of Christ wears righteous clothing *given* to her by Jesus (19:8). Her righteousness is *not earned* by her work, but it is given to her as a gift.

Jesus tells people who are proud of the eye salve they produced that they have need of the eye salve that will anoint their eyes so they will no longer be spiritually blind. Jesus' ministry was and continues to be all about spiritual eyesight. He gives us eyes to see; He heals our spiritual blindness; He helps us see from God's perspective. He rescues us from the blindness that is caused by the Babylon of religious confusion that enslaves our world.

Physical wealth often gives a false sense of security.[7] Physical wealth often gives those that possess it (or, rather, are often possessed by it) the illusion that their material riches impart some spiritual superiority as well. The Laodecians seem impressed with their own abilities and resources, and they seem blinded to the fact that Jesus Christ is the source of all spiritual wealth. He alone, by and through His cross and resurrection, is the way for us to be given the riches of God's grace. Grace is the only way that we might please God. Grace is the only way that we can be reconciled to God. Grace is the only means of salvation.

Religion hates grace, because God's grace will eventually put it out of business. The good news of the Book of Revelation is that Jesus Christ has already won the victory, and eventually He will permanently close the doors of and to religion. Jesus will eventually destroy unbiblical religion—with all of its do's and don'ts, all of its controls, all of its superstition and mumbo jumbo, all of its passwords and secret knowledge, all of its voodoo (however that voodoo might be dressed up and disguised), all of its legalism, all of its ceremonies, and all of its priests, pills, potions, and philosophies.

Jesus again comments on the debilitating impact of performance-based religion upon authentic Christianity, "Listen! I am standing at the door, knocking; if you hear my voice and open the door, I will come in to you and eat with you, and you with me" (v. 20). Many fail to fully appreciate this passage as preachers and artists depict Jesus knocking at the door of the heart of unsaved sinners. Sometimes the passage is used to demonstrate that Jesus knocks at the door of the Christian's conscience, reminding us to do or not do a particular behavior.

Jesus is saying that He is standing at the door of His own church trying to get in! What a commentary! Jesus is knocking on the door of a church that believes He is already in their midst; but in reality He is locked out, requesting to be allowed to enter into a community that is self-satisfied, assured that they are Christian, people who believe they need nothing (v. 17).

Jesus gives good news to the churches of Revelation, to the church, the body of Christ, down through time, and to you and me today. Good news! Jesus is alive; He is the Messenger and the message! To those who open the doors of their religious institutions, to those who are willing to consider that they may need to set aside cherished traditions and precious practices in order to invite Him in, Jesus says, "I will come in to you and eat with you, and you with me" (v. 20). We can conquer the grip of oppressive religion through Christ and sit with Him on His throne (v. 21).

CHAPTER SIX

The First Six Seals

One evening I was driving home and, as many commuters do in metro areas, I turned on news radio to find out about the condition of the freeway ahead. Hearing about a monstrous traffic jam, I decided to attempt the rest of my commute home on surface streets. Driving in an area I rarely visit, I stopped at a traffic light and was greeted by a message on a billboard just across the intersection. "Jesus is coming back to judge the world."

I thought, "Well, yes He is, but isn't He primarily coming back because He loves us?" If His primary mission is to return and punish us, why should He bother? This world is a complete mess, and if He just wants us all to be paid in full for our sins, then why not just let things continue as they are? It seems to me we humans need to be saved from the hell we have created. That famous passage in John 3:16 tells us that God loved the world so much that He sent His Son. It seems to me that religion tries to convince us that God loved us when He sent Jesus the first time, but the reason for the second coming is because He has finally lost His patience with us. I'm not buying that religious message, for it has little to do with the gospel of Jesus Christ. John 3:17 tells us, "Indeed, God did not send the Son into the world to condemn the world, but in order that the world might be saved through him."

Of course, Jesus is coming both because He loves us and in order to judge the world humans have created. Jesus is coming back to judge the world, but what impression about God does that billboard give? I was intrigued about this billboard and wondered if there were other such messages that claimed to speak for God. A little research uncovered the fact that two of the most popular religious messages on billboards across the

United States are statements attributed to a direct quote from God: 1) "Don't make me come down there," and 2) "You think it's hot here?" (usually found in the south and in sunbelt states).

Legalistic religion is selling us a bill of goods. Performance-based religion is convincing us that God is angry, and of course that's easy for us to believe because we already believe God has every reason to be angry with us. We know that Jesus Christ is justified in coming back to this world, wiping us all out, and starting all over again. We don't need any proof of that. Unbiblical religion convinces us that God is upset and that Jesus will return once He finally loses His patience. Religious legalism, of course, tells us that there is a way out and, in return for our compliance, offers us a way to get out of town so we don't have to be on this earth when Jesus comes back.

Jesus is coming, in love, to judge the world's religions. He is coming to conquer and obliterate religion and all of its devices that lead humans away from God.

Tens of millions of Christians misunderstand the nature of God, with an out-of-focus interpretation of the Book of Revelation contributing to their misunderstanding. Millions are missing the point of this eternally significant last book of the Bible. Here's the book that puts the capstone on God's special, written revelation to humanity, completing the gospel of Jesus Christ. But instead of coming away from reading and studying the Book of Revelation with God's intended message of faith and encouragement, many come away with a feeling of anxiety and fear. Fear of the "end times." Fear of the unknown. Fear of the beast. Fear of being deceived by the Antichrist. Fear of the horrible plagues and disasters described in the Book of Revelation. Fear of not being ready for the Rapture and being "left behind." Fear of the judgment and wrath of God.

The real message of the Book of Revelation actually fills us with faith and courage as well as arming us with an understanding and awareness of the pitfalls that face us as Christians. Once again, we are following a cardinal rule of biblical and literary interpretation, reading and understanding the Scripture the way it was intended for its original readers and hearers, the way it was written, in its original context and historical setting nearly 2,000 years ago. Once we understand the original message, we can begin to understand what it also means for us today in the twenty-first century.

It is impossible for any portion of the Bible, including Revelation, to have a meaning for us today that does not spring from its original meaning. As we understand the Bible, and the Book of Revelation, we must first establish what the message meant to the original readers and listeners, and then base our understanding upon that conclusion.

Many Christians are missing the point of Revelation because they're reading it as though it were a newspaper, with verses lined up with and seemingly corresponding to an event in today's news, or the news they've been told will almost certainly be printed in the newspaper next month or next year.

Reading the Book of Revelation as if it were an advance copy of next week's or next month's newspaper has resulted in many people losing faith in God when world events don't work out the way they were told they would. Whose fault is that? Is it God's fault, or the bogus interpretation and fatally flawed methodology used when they first read this critically important book?

Not only does reading Revelation like a newspaper completely misrepresent and misinterpret God, it gives non-Christians just the excuse they are looking for to resist and deny the claims of the Bible. For those who are running away from God, the unending parade of silly and superstitious speculations and predictions gives them a reason to label all Christians as people who don't have a brain in their head or at least one that they are using.

Some Christians decline to study the Book of Revelation for themselves and, in turn, surrender their brains to some dynamic Bible teacher and interpreter. That's exactly what I did, for several decades. I was like a parrot in a cage. As long as I remained in a religious cage, listening to endless repetition of the same terms and phrases, I was only capable of reiterating, reciting, and repeating what I heard. No thinking was necessary, or desired, on my part. But Jesus has no desire to control, brainwash, or clone us. He loves us, and offers us a relationship, based upon independent thought and choice on our part.

In our last chapter, we completed our survey of the seven churches of Revelation and the profound teaching conveyed in the messages Jesus gave not only to them, but also to us. We saw that these messages are not mysterious messages, which have to be decoded and deciphered, but they are clear, cogent, coherent, Christ-centered messages with timeless teaching for Christians of all ages.

Worship His Majesty

[1] After this I looked, and there in heaven a door stood open! And the first voice, which I had heard speaking to me like a trumpet, said, "Come up here, and I will show you what must take place after this." [2] At once I was in the spirit, and there in heaven stood a throne, with one seated on the throne! [3] And the one seated there looks like jasper and cornelian, and around the throne is a rainbow that looks like an emerald. [4] Around the throne are twenty-four thrones, and seated on the thrones are twenty-four elders, dressed in white robes, with golden crowns on their heads. [5] Coming from the throne are flashes of lightning, and rumblings and peals of thunder, and in front of the throne burn seven flaming torches, which are the seven spirits of God; [6] and in front of the throne there is something like a sea of glass, like crystal.

Around the throne, and on each side of the throne, are four living creatures, full of eyes in front and behind: [7] the first living creature like a lion, the second living creature like an ox, the third living creature with a face like a human face, and the fourth living creature like a flying eagle. [8] And the four living creatures, each of them with six wings, are full of eyes all around and inside. Day and night without ceasing they sing,

"Holy, holy, holy,

the Lord God the Almighty,

who was and is and is to come."

[9] And whenever the living creatures give glory and honor and thanks to the one who is seated on the throne, who lives for ever and ever, [10] the twenty-four elders fall before the one who is seated on the throne and worship the one who lives for ever and ever; they cast their crowns before the throne, singing,

[11] "You are worthy, our Lord and God,

to receive glory and honor and power,

for you created all things,

and by your will they existed and were created."

Revelation 4:1-11

Chapter four abruptly shifts the scene and setting from letters written to churches located in first-century cities of Asia to the eternal throne room of God. Between the end of chapter three and the beginning of chapter four, the program notes call for the lights to dim as the stage crew sets an entirely different stage. Our attention is moved from struggling churches and imperfect humans, who are confined to the limitations of time and space, to a glimpse of perfection and holiness, of splendor and glory beyond our wildest imaginations, of the eternity that God inhabits. It's as if this passage is here to remind us once again that Revelation is not primarily about *when*, but about *who*. Jesus is the divine *who* of Revelation.

We are encouraged to direct our attention from the earthly realm of sin and tyranny and lift our eyes to the majesty of God and His throne. Chapter four paints a word picture of the worship and praise that is continually given to God, who is the only hope for humans who on this side of eternity endure corrupt political and religious regimes.

John conveys the vision that Jesus gave Him, a vivid and graphic description of God's throne, with all of the spectacular sights and sounds:

- surrounded by 24 other thrones, with "flashes of lightning, and rumblings and peals of thunder" (v. 5) coming from God's throne;

- with 24 elders who represent the people of God on earth, offering praises to the sovereign God of time and eternity (v. 4, 10-11);[1] and

- with four living creatures who never stop saying "Holy, holy, holy, the Lord God the Almighty, who was and is and is to come" (v. 8). These four angelic beings draw upon heavenly images previously revealed in Isaiah 6 and Ezekiel 1, perhaps each one representing the highest and most impressive of its created earthly species. These four angelic beings echo the description of the eternal essence of God in 1:4, 8.

Here is a powerful picture of the majesty of God that shows God is infinitely more powerful than all human governments, than all imperfect attempts on the part of humans to represent Him, than all of the forces of evil to deny Him. John can only convey this majesty, might, and power in metaphorical terms of brilliance because the glory of God is beyond human language and comprehension.[2] While chapters two and three convey imperfections and blemishes that exist within the seven first-century churches as typical of the history of Christianity, chapter four whisks us from the problems to the solution, from sin to holiness and eternal, absolute perfection.

There is nothing in chapter four that would lead us to conclude that the message revealed by the Messenger will provide newspaper-like accounts of future events. Rather, chapter four provides a stark contrast with the all too human realities of life on earth, even within the body of Christ as described in chapters two and three. Chapter four directs our focus to heaven, to the throne room of God, which may be the primary stage setting for the entire Revelation, where we find hope in the heavenly, divine absolutes of perfection, righteousness, and holiness.

This change of scenery and setting provides a guide for Christians at all times. As we find ourselves engulfed by the sin and corruption of our world, and even of its religious organizations and institutions, God provides hope and inspiration through a vision that reminds us, in spite of all that we endure on earth, the heavenly reality is that God is our creator and Jesus is our redeemer. It is Jesus through whom "all the fullness of God was pleased to dwell, and through him God was pleased to reconcile to himself all things, whether on earth or in heaven, by making peace through the blood of his cross" (Col 1:19-20).

The shift in focus from earthly religious imperfection in chapters two and three to heavenly perfection in chapter four redirects our horizontal vision preoccupied with the here and now to the vertical dimension of eternity in heaven above. Paul encourages us: "So if you have been raised with Christ, seek the things that are above, where Christ is, seated at the right hand of God. Set your minds on things that are above, not on things that are on earth, for you have died, and your life is hidden with Christ in God" (Col 3:1-3).

We Really Aren't Worthy, But Jesus Is!

¹ Then I saw in the right hand of the one seated on the throne a scroll written on the inside and on the back, sealed with seven seals; ² and I saw a mighty angel proclaiming with a loud voice, "Who is worthy to open the scroll and break its seals?" ³ And no one in heaven or on earth or under the earth was able to open the scroll or to look into it. ⁴ And I began to weep bitterly because no one was found worthy to open the scroll or to look into it. ⁵ Then one of the elders said to me, "Do not weep. See, the Lion of the tribe of Judah, the Root of David, has conquered, so that he can open the scroll and its seven seals."

⁶ Then I saw between the throne and the four living creatures and among the elders a Lamb standing as if it had been slaughtered, having seven horns and seven eyes, which are

the seven spirits of God sent out into all the earth. [7] He went and took the scroll from the right hand of the one who was seated on the throne. [8] When he had taken the scroll, the four living creatures and the twenty-four elders fell before the Lamb, each holding a harp and golden bowls full of incense, which are the prayers of the saints. [9] They sing a new song:

"You are worthy to take the scroll

and to open its seals,

for you were slaughtered and by your blood you ransomed for God

saints from every tribe and language and people and nation;

[10] you have made them to be a kingdom and priests

serving our God,

and they will reign on earth."

[11] Then I looked, and I heard the voice of many angels surrounding the throne and the living creatures and the elders; they numbered myriads of myriads and thousands of thousands, [12] singing with full voice,

"Worthy is the Lamb that was slaughtered

to receive power and wealth and wisdom and might

and honor and glory and blessing!"

[13] Then I heard every creature in heaven and on earth and under the earth and in the sea, and all that is in them, singing,

"To the one seated on the throne and to the Lamb

be blessing and honor and glory and might

forever and ever!"

[14] And the four living creatures said, "Amen!" And the elders fell down and worshiped.

Revelation 5:1-14

First-century readers recognized the scroll that John saw (v. 1) as an ancient will. John saw a scroll with writing on both sides and sealed with seven seals. The giving of wills was customarily witnessed by seven people, who would then affix their seals to the document. Only those who were legally qualified to open and read the scroll, the will, were entitled to do so. Only the heir of the deceased was entitled to break the seal, read the will, and execute the instructions written in it. This scroll in the hand of God represents the will and purpose of God for all humanity and in particular for those who have accepted Jesus Christ. This scroll sealed with seven seals represents the inheritance of the saints, the kingdom of heaven, given as a gift by God's grace, because of the death of the Son of God, the Lamb of God.[3]

Only one person is qualified to take this heavenly document and open its seals and reveal the purposes of God. That divine person is none other than the one who is revealing this book to John, who is both the Messenger of this book and the central character of the story. Jesus is the Author, the theme, and premise of this story.

We meet Jesus initially in chapter one, the "Alpha and Omega" (1:8), "the faithful witness, the firstborn of the dead, the ruler of the kings of the earth" (1:5), "who is and who was and who is to come, the Almighty" (1:8). He is the "first and the last" (1:17), "the living one … who was dead and is alive forever and ever" (1:18). He holds the "keys of death and of Hades" (1:18) and "the key of David" (3:7).

Ultimate authority lies with Jesus Christ, not with a human king, emperor, dictator, president, or prime minister; not with a pastor, a bishop, an apostle, a cardinal, a pope, a right reverend, a prophecy preacher, or charismatic religious leader. All humans are accountable to Jesus; we are all equal before Him; all of us must appear before Him. No human achievement—neither riches, nor property by right of birth, nor royalty, nor religious title, nor human accomplishment in terms of wealth or wisdom, degrees, certificates, awards, titles or honors—gives us heavenly privileges.

The financial equity we have in our house, how much property we own, how much money we have in stocks, bonds, and banks—none of that means anything before Jesus. Religious deeds we have performed, religious traditions we have faithfully adhered to, careful ceremonial observance to gain righteous standing before God—none of that gains us an advantage before the Master. He alone is the measure of judgment, the standard of achievement, the goal and purpose of life itself. Jesus is the will of God; He is the heir of the scroll. He has bought and purchased all humankind with His blood and rightfully owns all of us, of every tribe, language, people, and nation.

John asks who is worthy to open the scroll (Re 5:2), and the answer is given, "See, the Lion of the tribe of Judah, the Root of David, has conquered, so that he can open the scroll and its seven seals" (v. 5). Here is one of the great paradoxes that the new covenant in the blood of Christ insists upon, Jesus conquers through His death, His ignominy, and His humiliation.

In the Gospels, Jesus says those who are in His kingdom will be servants. God's kingdom reverses human values; those things that are deemed to be of ultimate value in our human lives are often trivial in God's view. The things that God esteems highly, on the other hand, are often overlooked and minimized by humans. The new covenant tells us, enigmatically, that when we are weak God makes us strong. It tells us that God does not reward our obedience to Him in this life with health and wealth, but rather the new covenant is a covenant that includes adversity and service. Christians are called to take up their own cross and follow Jesus.

It is in death and in His miraculous resurrection from the grave that Jesus overcomes and conquers the world. The one who was dead is now alive and remains so forever and ever. He is the Lamb of God, and He is worthy of praise, reverence, and worship. Chapter five is filled with inspiring words of praise, reverence, and worship that have become known to us in some of the most inspirational Christ-centered music: traditional, conservative, and classical, and in contemporary praise and worship music. The whole host of heaven, thousands upon thousands, and ten thousand times ten thousand, joined by every creature in heaven and on earth, sing, "Worthy is the Lamb!"

A Lion Becomes a Lamb

Here is a great mystery of the book of Revelation, and of the gospel of Jesus Christ: in order to conquer, a lion becomes a lamb.[4] The Lion of Judah is a conqueror. Conquerors in our world win. They rule. They are heroes. They are successes. We humans are attracted by lions. We thrill at the power of a lion's deep and commanding roar. Lions are the king of the jungle and we are impressed. We want to have that kind of power and respect.

Religion tells us that if we follow its dictates and march to the beat of its drums we too can have power and respect. Some even say we can "claim" health and wealth from God. If we jump through religious hoops, some in Christendom assure us we will qualify to be in a special Rapture. We, they say, will be physically saved while others suffer, because we have followed religious rites, rules, and regulations. We will have special spiritual blessings because we do more stuff; and performance-based religion tells us that doing more stuff makes God happy. If we bow down to the gods of religious oppression, then in turn unbiblical religion promises to make us into a conquering lion.

There's one sure way to tell that you're listening to or reading about legalistic religion. When someone starts telling you about physical success, wealth and health, when you start reading and hearing about how superior, how much better, how much more truth and how much more understanding you will have if you are in a specific church, congregation, or movement—if you hear that kind of stuff, hide the women and children! Lock the doors, bring in the dog, and hang on to your wallet. Religious oppressors and overlords are on the prowl.

Religious legalism says it will reward you for your obedience. You will become great, powerful, and blessed. The emphasis of performance-based religion is on us. However, authentic Christianity says that Jesus is the Lion of Judah; but in order to conquer all, to win the victory that no one else could win, to do what no one could do, He became a Lamb. He became the slain Lamb. The Lion conquers all by voluntarily becoming the Lamb of God, sacrificed in our stead.

The scene described in verse 6 depicts a lamb that has just been slaughtered, a grisly sight. John expects to see the Lion of Judah, but it is as if the Lion of Judah has morphed into the Lamb of God. It's one of the great reversals of the kingdom. What we expect and admire, the power in which we trust, is very often replaced by the exact opposite.

This is a great mystery, a profound paradox, and it illustrates a major difference between authentic Christianity and religion. Unbiblical religion says, "You need help, do what we say and you will have power." Jesus says, "Come to me, all you that are weary and are carrying heavy burdens, and I will give you rest" (Ma 11:28). Jesus tells us that all human power, including our own, is irrelevant to His eternal purposes. He is the Lion of Judah who became the Lamb of God. And in so doing He won the victory over death and the grave, and He will give us that same victory if we trust in Him and follow Him.

Once again, here is the point, theme, and message of the Book of Revelation. The fifth chapter is one of the watershed chapters of this book, for it insists that the message is all about Jesus.[5] This is the good news of the gospel. The real story of Revelation is the divine *who*, not some physically ascertained and decoded *when*. The message of Revelation is not some spiritual recipe about how we can decrypt and decode ancient prophecies so that we can save our physical necks or any other part of our anatomies from pain and suffering.

The gospel is that Jesus Christ is the very center, focus, and core of our faith; and He alone is worthy of our worship, attention, and time.[6] The central message of the Book of Revelation has nothing to do with deciphering literal interpretations of colors, numbers, beasts, and symbols, but in being centered in the Lamb of God.

The Four Horsemen

[1] Then I saw the Lamb open one of the seven seals,
and I heard one of the four living creatures call out, as
with a voice of thunder, "Come!" [2] I looked, and there was

a white horse! Its rider had a bow; a crown was given to him, and he came out conquering and to conquer.

³ When he opened the second seal, I heard the second living creature call out, "Come!" ⁴ And out came another horse, bright red; its rider was permitted to take peace from the earth, so that people would slaughter one another; and he was given a great sword.

⁵When he opened the third seal, I heard the third living creature call out, "Come!" I looked, and there was a black horse! Its rider held a pair of scales in his hand, ⁶ and I heard what seemed to be a voice in the midst of the four living creatures saying, "A quart of wheat for a day's pay, and three quarts of barley for a day's pay, but do not damage the olive oil and the wine!"

⁷When he opened the fourth seal, I heard the voice of the fourth living creature call out, "Come!" ⁸ I looked and there was a pale green horse! Its rider's name was Death, and Hades followed with him; they were given authority over a fourth of the earth, to kill with sword, famine, and pestilence, and by the wild animals of the earth.

⁹When he opened the fifth seal, I saw under the altar the souls of those who had been slaughtered for the word of God and for the testimony they had given; ¹⁰ they cried out with a loud voice, "Sovereign Lord, holy and true, how long will it be before you judge and avenge our blood on the inhabitants of the earth?" ¹¹ They were each given a white robe and told to rest a little longer, until the number would be complete both of their fellow-servants and of their brothers and sisters, who were soon to be killed as they themselves had been killed.

¹²When he opened the sixth seal, I looked, and there

came a great earthquake; the sun became black as sackcloth, the full moon became like blood, [13] and the stars of the sky fell to the earth as the fig tree drops its winter fruit when shaken by a gale. [14] The sky vanished like a scroll rolling itself up, and every mountain and island was removed from its place. [15] Then the kings of the earth and the magnates and the generals and the rich and the powerful, and everyone, slave and free, hid in the caves and among the rocks of the mountains, [16] calling to the mountains and rocks, "Fall on us and hide us from the face of the one seated on the throne and from the wrath of the Lamb; [17] for the great day of their wrath has come, and who is able to stand?"

Revelation 6:1-17

Chapter six begins with Jesus Christ, the Lamb of God, starting to open the seals in the scroll He has received from God the Father. The breaking of each seal doesn't gradually open the book (the seals are all on the outside of the scroll), the scroll cannot be opened until the last seal is opened.

But as Jesus opens each seal something happens. The first four seals, which have become known as the Four Horsemen of the Apocalypse, are opened here in the sixth chapter. They are similar to another vision of four horses in the sixth chapter of the Old Testament Book of Zechariah, and the original readers who were familiar with the Old Testament would have immediately thought of those four horses (Ze 1:8; 6:1-3). In both cases, in Zechariah and here in Revelation, the four horses are symbolic tools and agents of God's avenging judgment.

These four horses and their riders do not represent any particular historical figure of any specific era, but instead they depict chaos, terror, and destruction whenever it may be unleashed. They bring incredible suffering to humanity: misery and pain that is allowed by God but caused primarily by the evil that humans inflict upon themselves.

These first four seals, the Four Horsemen of the Apocalypse, illustrate the product of all human effort, religious and irreligious. There is no doubt that much of the suffering introduced by the Four Horsemen is physical, but we should also consider the emotional and spiritual pain and abuse they leave in their wake.

The White Horse

The first horse is the white horse of conquest. The most probable meaning and interpretation of this horse is that it represents human governments and religion that promise rewards to their subjects in return for obedience and worship. Remember, we have just been told in chapter five that Jesus alone is worthy of worship. And here is the white horse that goes out and conquers.

This white horse can't be Jesus, because the Lamb of God in chapter five conquered through His own death, not through terrorizing others. He did not crucify anyone; He was crucified. He did not intimidate, attempt to control, or browbeat people with fear. The Lamb of God entered the city of Jerusalem in the last week of His life on a donkey, coming to be sacrificed as the Lamb of God for you, me, and every other human who has ever or will ever live. Another paradox. He was on a donkey, not a white horse. He was showing that His kingdom was not of this world; His kingdom does not rely on weapons, on ritual, on fear, on group think, on brainwashing, on mob rule, on deception, or any other kind of human enticement or expression of power.

This white horse represents the combined efforts of government and religion, even if a sword, a tank, or a fighter aircraft must be used to enforce its will. It also represents religious legalism, which subjugates and conquers people through whatever means necessary. In Matthew chapter ten, Jesus warned the disciples about religious oppression and persecution, about being flogged (v. 17), arrested (v. 19), betrayed (v. 21), hated (v. 22), and persecuted (v. 23). But Jesus said, "Do not fear those who kill the body but cannot kill the soul; rather fear him who can destroy both soul and body in hell" (Ma 10:28).

This white horse is the power and spirit of deception—of the use of superstition, ignorance and fear by religion and religious leaders—to control, manipulate, and enslave. It is the spirit of Antichrist of whom John had already written in his first epistle (1 Jo 4:3) as the false Christ who was at that time already in the world.[7]

Here is a warning for all Christians; the way of the cross is not easy. There are false Christs who deceive many. There are many who counterfeit Christianity, many who fleece the flock rather than feed the flock. Remember, this is a white horse, the Antichrist, who deliberately looks and sounds like Christ, who appropriates His name, and uses holy sounding religious language and terminology in order to go forth to deceive and conquer.

There is another white horse in Revelation. The rider of the white horse in Revelation 19 also goes out to conquer, but He ushers in peace and salvation. The impact of the two white horses are in stark contrast to one another. The white horse of the four horsemen in chapter 6 brings the age-old recurring story of death and mayhem, while the white horse of Jesus Christ in chapter 19 brings about a new heaven and a new earth.

The Red Horse

The second horse is the red horse of war. Whether this horse causes war solely in the name of governments or in the name of religion or in some kind of unholy combination of the secular and the supposedly sacred, the result is the same: hatred, violence, and bloodshed. What do we call them? Holy wars! The Inquisitions, the Crusades, Christians versus Moslems, Christians versus the infidels, Christians versus the pagans, Christians versus Jews, and Christians versus Christians. The sad fact is that those who have flown the flag of Christianity have been among the most bloodthirsty of all groups, even shedding the blood of their fellows in the name of God.

Warfare is one of the natural by-products of human indifference to the Lamb of God. When we reject the Lamb who died for us, we can wind up killing each other in a vain attempt to establish our own superiority.

I believe the virus of legalism exists within all humans. We are generally more emotionally and spiritually comfortable with some authority specifying right and wrong, even if we have no intention of following that authority. Some humans, because of their culture and background, are more resistant to the virus of legalism than others. Those whose spiritual immunities are weak are the prey upon which the virus of legalism thrives. Some humans, for a variety of reasons, are better hosts to the virus of legalism than others.

Legalistic religion prospers in an atmosphere where people yearn for concrete answers and clear, decisive leadership. At such times and places it is a relatively easy task to convince humans that they must make God happy by their performance of righteous deeds. Wanting to please and appease God, humans attempt to jump through all the prescribed religious hoops, only to fail because we humans by nature are flawed and broken. We are not capable of being righteous. Apart from Christ, we aren't even capable of coming anywhere close to moral perfection! Our desire to please God, goaded on and fueled by religious demands, frustrates us because we are incapable of ever doing enough to please God.

Our frustration leads us to try harder to do better. Our answer for guilt and condemnation, apart from Jesus Christ, is the same answer that religious legalism gives us. Do more, try harder, which only leads to even more heartache and pain.

At some point in this vicious, legalistic not so merry-go-round, we humans start to look for company. Misery loves company, and when those who are enslaved by religious legalism find others who are not as miserable as they are, then they do their best to make them miserable. According to Jesus, legalists do not rest until they impose the same oppression they suffer and endure upon others (Ma 23:4). We, in the words of Revelation 6:4, begin to spiritually slay one another. The red horse and its rider are thus the very antithesis of "the peace of God, which surpasses all understanding" (Ph 4:7). The red horse brings animosity, bitterness, discord, gossip, back-stabbing, hatred, and bigotry, often in the name of God.

The Black Horse

The third horse is the black horse of famine. Its rider has a pair of scales in his hand. He offers a pitiful wage for a day's work. Perhaps this horse is a symbol of our inhumanity to each other. The black horse reminds us of our oppression of each other, the gross injustice and inequity that almost always accompanies human attempts to govern and rule, whether by an established government or by a religion or by some combination of both. The message is clear: humans will chew you up and spit you out in the name of God.

The rider of the black horse demonstrates famine by the scales he holds. What spiritual commodity is in short supply? Our world has never experienced a famine of religion based upon human performance. Our world has never lacked for religion that worships something or someone other than the Lamb of God. The warning attached to the black horse is, if you seek a relationship with God apart from Jesus Christ, you will wind up beaten and battered, much like the man in the parable of the Good Samaritan who was mugged and beaten by robbers. The spiritual famine announced by the rider of the black horse is a famine of the proclamation of God's amazing grace.

The message of the parable of the Good Samaritan (Lk 16) is not that we humans should be kind to our neighbors and help them when they are in distress. Of course we should do that; but that parable, like the entire Book of Revelation and like the entire new covenant, insists that there is but one Lord, one Christ, one Master. In Him and Him alone we have hope. In Him and Him alone will we find compassion, care, and love. He alone will stop and stoop to bind up our wounds. The priests of religious legalism will pass by on the other side; but only Jesus, and in an unlikely and un-expected manner and time at that, will serve us and care for us. He will take us to an inn; He will feed us in a time of famine and injustice. He, the Bread of Life, will give us the true Bread from heaven.

What does the Good Samaritan do for the person who was mugged, beaten, and left on the side of the road like so much roadkill? He uses oil and wine to bind up the wounds of the suffering person. The only other time in all of the New Testament where that same phrase, "oil and wine," is used is here in Revelation 6:6. Oil and wine is what the Good Samaritan uses: oil, the Holy Spirit; and wine, the blood of the Lamb of God. He anoints us and cleans us and heals us.

What can we expect from Christ-less religion? Emptiness, famine, spiritual and physical hunger. A void that yearns to be filled. Jesus and Jesus alone can fill the God-shaped hole each of us have, so that we will never again hunger or thirst. He is the river of living waters for those who live in a world where the black horse of famine rides. Spiritual fam-ine and starvation are often caused by the tyranny of religion, which promises us fulfillment and significance, but which, in the end, brings nothing but junk food for the soul.

The Pale Horse

The fourth horse is the pale horse of death. The Greek word actually implies a yellowish-green color, like that of a corpse. This pale horse is symbolic of those who are the walking dead, who seem to have life, but are spiritually and emotionally dead.[8] The rider of this horse is called Death, and Hades is following close behind him. You may remember that the first chapter of the Book of Revelation identifies Jesus, the author, the subject, and object of this book, as having the keys of death and Hades. He alone gives eternal life. He alone leads us to pass from death to life as John tells us in his Gospel (Jo 5:24).

Whenever and wherever the pale horse rides, there are always those who accept Jesus Christ as their Savior, who believe and trust in Him alone, by faith alone, by grace alone, and by Christ alone. They reject all claims of sovereignty by governments, philosophies, isms, and religions; and they accept Jesus alone as their Savior.

Those who accept Jesus Christ are immune from the spiritual destruction, bondage, and oppression of the pale horse, even though they are subject to his physical punishment. But for those who are not sealed by Jesus, death is the end result of any path they may choose, because it is not based upon and centered in the Lamb of God. Whether it be new-age religion, pop psychology, positive thinking, socialism, communism, atheism, agnosticism—or that part of Christendom that is nothing more than religion appropriating the name of Christ—nothing and no one can deliver you or me from the power of death and the grave, except Jesus Christ.

And don't fall for the line, which some proclaim, that Jesus is good and helpful; but He needs a little improvement or help, which that particular guru, priest, potion, philosophy, notion, ritual, tradition, or ceremony will give you. An improved Jesus is a lie and no Jesus at all. An improved Jesus is the pale horse of death.

The Fifth Seal—Death by Martyrdom

The fifth seal is opened, and we see the brutal reality of death by martyrdom suffered by those who believe in Jesus Christ. Persecution and martyrdom of Christians is a present reality in our world. "The shocking, untold story of our time is that more Christians have died this century simply for being Christians than in the first nineteen centuries after the birth of Christ."[9] Many of these Christian martyrs have died at the hands of religion. Sometimes it was a religion that did not call itself Christian while at other times it was a religion that appropriated the name of Jesus Christ.

Revelation is crystal clear about this theme: the real enemy for Christians is Christ-less religion. Authentic Christianity is not just another religion. Authentic Christianity teaches that we do not need religious rites, relics, and rituals; we only need Jesus Christ. Performance-based religion says that we must qualify, we must produce, we must perform, we must do more and more and more—and, in the end, it's always the same—more is never enough for the harsh and unrelenting taskmaster of religion that seeks to control through its legalisms. Authentic and biblically based Christianity sets us free from all the slavery of oppressive religion.

The Sixth Seal—Literal or Symbolic Upheaval?

And now the sixth seal is opened. It's a gigantic cosmological upheaval. The earth reels from the impact of earthquake-like disasters with the stars falling, the sun becoming black, and mountains and seas being moved out of their places.[10]

In the Old Testament, the "Bible" known to the original recipients of Revelation, earthquakes were often used to describe divine intervention. At Mount Sinai "the whole mountain shook violently" (Ex 19:18). The writer of the Epistle to the Hebrews contrasts the physical shaking of the old covenant mountain with the new covenant given us in Christ.

> You have not come to something that can be touched, a blazing fire, and darkness, and gloom, and a tempest, and the sound of a trumpet, and a voice whose words made the hearers beg that not another word be spoken to them... But you have come to Mount Zion and to the city of the living God, the heavenly Jerusalem, and to innumerable angels in festal gathering, and to the assembly of the firstborn who are enrolled in heaven, and to God the judge of all, and to the spirits of the righteous made perfect, and to Jesus, the mediator of a new covenant, and to the sprinkled blood that speaks a better word than the blood of Abel.
> *Hebrews 12:18-19, 22-24*

One of the cardinal themes of dispensationalism is the rule of interpreting Scripture literally. Long before dispensationalism received a popular following, Martin Luther, one of the great reformers, insisted that the Bible should be interpreted according to its literal sense. While there is much to be said for always attempting a literal meaning of a passage, to suggest that all Scripture only has a literal meaning and that any attempt at symbolic interpretation is suspect is to ignore the way in which God inspired the Bible. Symbolic meanings were often inspired by God, because they convey truth in a profound way that literal language cannot.

The Bible should always be interpreted literally, in the sense that we should carefully consider the history, culture, grammar, and linguistic genre that are part of the words on the pages of the Bible. That is the literal background we must consider when reading and studying the Bible. The Bible is literally true; it is not myth. But much of the language God inspired within the Bible should not be understood or interpreted literally. Poetry, with its symbolism and metaphor, is found throughout the Bible. An attempt to literalize the profound meaning that poetry and idioms convey at best diminishes and damages the intended meaning. Beyond that, it may twist and confound the intended meaning.

Of course, we should understand and interpret Revelation literally: which means we should read and study it within its literal, original, context and historical setting. We should also understand the literary genre that Jesus used in giving this message to John. Sadly, some actually believe that any symbolic interpretation of the Bible (even of symbolic and poetic passages) is watered-down, less than accurate, and "liberal."

If we insist on literalizing the symbolic language of Revelation, such as the "great earthquake" (v. 12), we must either determine which past earthquake fulfilled this description, or we must place it in the future. If we choose to do either, we may well miss the deeper meaning of this earthquake. When the church was founded, on the day of Pentecost, Peter said (Acts 2:16-21) that day was fulfilling a time spoken of by Joel when wonders would occur in the sky and the sun would become dark and the moon turn into blood (Joel 2:28-32). He was describing the earth in spiritual upheaval as God the Holy Spirit, the prophesied and promised Comforter, had now come to dwell in men and women.

Following the cross of Christ, and the resurrection of our Lord from the tomb, the beginning of the church was another sign of the end of Satan's hold on all humanity. The establishment of the church was another of God's judgments on all of the idolatry, bloodshed, hatred, lust, and evil Satan had perpetrated on the earth until that time, evil that has been consistent throughout history. But the church was established with a new covenant. It was a new beginning: the birthday of the body of Christ, the gift of the Holy Spirit, another sign of the beginning of the end for suffering and inhumanity. Suffering and inhumanity have continued, of course, perhaps at times intensified; for as chapter 12 of Revelation tells us, Satan is angry when the gospel of grace is proclaimed.

There may be a great physical future earthquake with all of the physical consequences described in verses 12-17. And, of course, there have also been great earthquakes since the time of the writing of the Book of Revelation that could also provide a literal fulfillment of this passage. We could make a list of them all, and arbitrarily decide if any of them fulfilled this verse; or we could just as arbitrarily decide that none of them were catastrophic enough to qualify. If we did make such a list, we would have to join a long line of those who have already taken this step.

But far beyond any physical earthquake is the ongoing fact: *when God's grace and human government and Christ-less religion collide,* there are always earthquakes.[11] Grace leads to inevitable earthquake-like conflicts between earth and heaven, between evil and good, between religious legalism and God's grace, between human attempts at self-justification that only lead to self-righteousness and the final, perfect, sufficient, and righteous work on the cross whereby the Lamb of God did for us what we can never do for ourselves. When the world of the kingdom of men collides with the kingdom of heaven, earthquakes and conflict always result.

CHAPTER SEVEN

The Rapture—
Religion's Fear Factor

Bombs are falling in the Middle East. CNN reports pre-emptive strikes and counter-strikes, with the death toll already in the tens of thousands. Panic and pandemonium overcome civilian populations from Nairobi to Teheran. International tensions among the mega powers of the west are approaching a meltdown. The United Nations meets, but it's powerless to intervene.

Suddenly, without warning, hundreds of thousands of people disappear. Empty coats, dresses, suits, and overalls fall to the ground as those who were wearing them vanish without a trace. Airplanes whose pilot and co-pilot seats are suddenly vacated crash into skyscrapers. Driverless trucks and cars careen off the road, slaughtering hapless pedestrians. Trains without engineers plow full-throttle through cities and into crowded stations. Confusion, mayhem, and bloodshed are rampant among those who are *left behind*. Meanwhile, those who have mysteriously vanished are enjoying the pleasures of paradise.

Does this sound like some biblical disaster? In fact, this scene is not completely grounded in the Bible, but millions of people believe it is. This is the end-time scenario of the futuristic, dispensational teaching of the Rapture, an event vividly portrayed in the enormously popular *Left Behind* series of books and movies.

Many Christians assume that the Rapture theory they have read, heard about, and believe is a sound, biblically based viewpoint and interpretation.

But like many of the ideas about prophecy and the Book of Revelation, the Rapture theory is filled with assumptions, speculations, and illogical conclusions. Peter Hiett cites the astute observation of G.K. Chesterton, "Though St. John the Evangelist saw many strange monsters in his vision, he saw no creature as wild as one of his own commentators."[1]

The Rapture, specifically the futuristic, dispensational teaching of the Rapture, is the idea that believers will be taken to heaven just as the world is on the brink of seven years of tribulation, preceding the second coming of Christ and the end of history.[2]

The Rapture theory or teaching is based on *dispensationalism*, a method of interpreting the Bible that was not popularly known or believed until the early nineteenth century. Dispensationalism is actually a subset of futurism. In the first chapter, we defined the futurist interpretation as one that sees virtually everything described after the second and third chapter of Revelation as yet-to-be-fulfilled, literal end time prophecies. Dispensationalism teaches that God has divided human history into seven dispensations, each of which God has administered in different ways. Premillennial dispensationalism favors a literal interpretation of the symbolic Book of Revelation and a belief that Christ will return to the earth and establish a one thousand year earthly reign. Hyperbole and speculation about the return of Jesus Christ have always been natural by-products of dispensationalism.

It may surprise many to learn that dispensationalism was never widely believed by Christians until fairly recently. It is true that there were those who taught that their generation was living in the "end times." In our second chapter, we mentioned Montanus, who lived in the second century, and the large following he attracted until his prophecies failed. Others speculated that history would be divided into 6,000 years followed by the second coming of Jesus Christ and a 1,000 year millennium.

But none of these dispensational elements were regarded as credible in the historic church. Neither Roman Catholics nor Eastern Orthodox taught a dispensational view of biblical prophecy (and still don't). Martin

Luther apparently never heard of dispensationalism, nor did John Calvin, nor any other reformer. Premillennial dispensationalism was not popularized, nor was it given credibility until the methodology and framework taught by John Nelson Darby came along.

Darby was a nineteenth-century British pastor of Irish parents who was, perhaps, the best known developer of dispensationalist teaching in the 1830s. He personally brought his teaching to North America in a series of visits between 1859 and 1874. Darby tried to summarize and synthesize the Bible's many prophetic passages into his own interpretative scheme. He believed that world history, past and future, was divided into distinct eras, or dispensations, and that God had a different way of dealing with humanity in each of them.

One of the most famous followers of early dispensationalism was a man named William Miller. Miller's powerful preaching and teaching led his followers to believe that Jesus Christ would return in 1844. When Jesus didn't jump through humanly devised hoops of prophetic prediction, this non-event, this failed prediction, became known as the Great Disappointment.

Great Dispensational Disappointments

Like Miller's Great Disappointment, every prediction of Jesus' return has failed to date, and premillennial dispensationalism is batting .000. Every specific prediction about the second coming and immediate events surrounding it has failed. The legacy of dispensationalism is a public relations nightmare for Christianity.

Remember the Y2K hysteria at the beginning of this century, when Christian survivalists were storing food and ammunition to protect themselves in case a worldwide computer meltdown ended the world as we know it? Y2K fears were fueled and fanned by Christian bookstores, magazines, radio programs, and many pulpits. Y2K was yet another failed prophecy, a specific event that was hyped by premillennial dispensationalists. Y2K predictions were all wrong.

The idea of the dispensational Rapture is based on a shaky biblical interpretation of 1 Thessalonians 4:13-18:

> But we do not want you to be uninformed, brothers and sisters, about those who have died, so that you may not grieve as others who have no hope. For since we believe that Jesus died and rose again, even so, through Jesus, God will bring with him those who have died. For this we declare to you by the word of the Lord, that we who are alive, who are left until the coming of the Lord, will by no means precede those who have died. For the Lord himself, with a cry of command, with the archangel's call and with the sound of God's trumpet, will descend from heaven, and the dead in Christ will rise first. Then we who are alive, who are left, will be caught up in the clouds together with them to meet the Lord in the air; and so we will be with the Lord forever. Therefore encourage one another with these words.

The dispensational Rapture (and the plot of the fictional *Left Behind* series) is based on one possible interpretation of this passage.[3] If this teaching about the Rapture is true, then Christians everywhere will be "caught up in the air" by Jesus while the unsaved are left to suffer the agonies of worldwide tribulation. Then, after seven years of tribulation (from which those who believe in the premillennial dispensational Rapture will presumably be safe with Jesus), Jesus will come again. So, if we accept the dispensational Rapture, we have to believe there will be two second comings, or to put it another way, a second coming that the Bible promises, and a third coming the Bible says nothing about.

First of all, we need to define our terms and understand that the Bible does teach "a" rapture. We will use a small, lowercase "r" to distinguish the biblical rapture (about which little information is given) from the dispensational redefinition of this word, which will be designated with an uppercase "R," as it is a specific teaching incorporating and importing special meaning into the general term. The biblical teaching about a rapture offers little detail and needs to be distinguished from the speculative and hyperbolic teaching of the uppercase "R" Rapture, about which much has been written.

What does the Bible say about the rapture? In the passage in 1 Thessalonians, Paul says that Christians will be "caught up" in the air, the origin of the word *rapture,* at the second coming of Jesus Christ. That's what the Bible teaches about the rapture, and that's it. But that paucity of information would never sell more than 60 million books in 34 languages without a little creative embellishment, would it?

Rapture Speculations

The dispensational Rapture proposes the idea that Christians will be saved from physical pain that others will suffer for seven years in the great tribulation while the horrible plagues described in the Book of Revelation ravage humanity. Then, according to the teaching of this futuristic, dispensational Rapture invented by John Nelson Darby, after seven years, Jesus will return a second time (His third coming).

To accept Rapture speculation involves building assumption upon assumption. The futuristic, dispensational Rapture paints a picture of a God who will save Christians from physical distress that others, the unsaved, will experience. But the new covenant that Christians are given by Jesus Christ is not about physical comforts or health. The gospel of Jesus Christ is all about spiritual salvation, not about physical salvation.

Word and visual pictures of the dispensational Rapture have airliners crashing, as "Rapture-ready" Christians, who are piloting them, are whisked out of the cockpits to be saved, presumably because God loves them more than some of the doomed, unsaved passengers who go down in flames since they happened to have the misfortune of having a Christian pilot.

What are some practical implications of the Rapture as popularly taught by dispensationalism? First of all, if you think the Rapture might be a biblically correct teaching, there is a better than average chance you'll be concerned that if you don't get right, you will get left (behind). Agonizing about whether one will be good enough to be Raptured is a classic example of how prediction addiction, an obsession with eschatology, can join with its cousin, legalistic religion, to distort the gospel.

If you believe in the Rapture, but have real concerns that you will be left behind because you aren't Rapture-ready, then whenever you take a commercial airline flight, you should always insist on a pilot who is not a Christian. If the Rapture occurs while you are in the air, and if the pilot is Raptured but you are not Rapture-ready and therefore you don't qualify to join him or her, you are history. Choosing a non-Christian pilot will ensure your physical safety, give you more time to do more stuff to make God happy and eventually qualify for God's kingdom of heaven, even if it means having to experience the great tribulation. I know this is not the official Rapture teaching, but I am proposing, tongue firmly tucked in cheek, that these are logical and practical implications of any sincere belief in the dispensational Rapture.

A further pragmatic consideration of the Rapture would involve Christian airline pilots (among other professionals). Our society does not think twice before restricting or prohibiting those who have physical limitations, or who may be chemically impaired, from operating vehicles of transportation. For these people not only place their own lives in peril but the lives of others. We have laws that prohibit airline pilots from flying if they are impaired in some way. What about "Rapture-ready" Christian pilots?

The enormously popular *Left Behind* series illustrates the horrific consequences when airline pilots, bus drivers, and drivers of privately owned automobiles are Raptured, preventing the drivers from performing their vital tasks and thus placing the lives of passengers and innocent bystanders in harm's way.

If the Rapture teaching of dispensationalism is true beyond a doubt, and if it is ethical for it to be used to "scare people out of hell," then those who actually believe in the Rapture teaching should voluntarily refuse to engage in any vocation or activity that could place the lives of others in jeopardy in the event such Christians are Raptured. Careers that would therefore be out of bounds for "Rapture-ready" Christians would surely include police and fire jobs, military pursuits, doctors, health care professionals, bus and truck drivers, and airline pilots, among others. Avoiding such professions would seem to be mandatory for any Christian who believes in the Rapture, for Christians exemplify Jesus' love (Jo 13:34-35).

The dispensational Rapture teaches that Christians around the world, regardless of how important or precarious an activity they are involved in, may suddenly be, without warning, "called home"—all at exactly the same time. Some who believe in the Rapture have actually posted a notice on the dashboards of their cars: "If I'm Raptured, take the wheel." But why would God sponsor an event in which vehicles of all sizes and shapes suddenly careen out of control, killing and maiming those who are "left behind"? What about the patient on the operating table whose surgeon suddenly vanishes? Is this a true and accurate picture of the God of the Bible? Fear religion, speculations, and outlandish predictions about the future sell books and videos. But at what cost?

What about the views of other Christians, many, if not the majority, of whom believe in *a* rapture but not *the* Rapture?[4] And what about all those Christians who lived and died up until the early nineteenth century who knew nothing of the dispensational Rapture? What about the faith of those who pin all their hopes on such ideas, victims of "prediction addiction," who have their hopes dashed? What about those who find such hype and promotion nothing more than a traveling carnival show and therefore dismiss all of Christianity as irrational and silly, and as a result, find it difficult even to believe in God?

Jesus Christ told us He would return to this earth. He did not say He would return twice—once to save the necks of those who believe in the dispensational Rapture—and then again, seven years later, after seven years of hell has been unleashed on this earth. Jesus told us in no uncertain terms that we would not be able to accurately predict His second coming (Ma 24:36, 42, 44, 50; 25:13). Considering the track record of past speculations and predictions we would do well to take Christ at His word, trusting Him as to whenever and however His return might be.

There is no doubt that the Bible should be interpreted literally. But reading and studying the Bible's literal intent means to literally understand the manner in which God inspired it. Huge portions of the Bible were written as poetry; they were never intended to be understood in a woodenly literal sense. But the literal meaning of such passages is understood when they are read symbolically. Most literature, including the Bible, uses devices such as metaphor and idiom. Non-literal (not to be confused with untruthful) meanings are common.[5] For example, poetry is used to convey a depth of meaning that a literal interpretation cannot.

There are several ways to interpret biblical prophecy, and the speculative events of the Rapture have never been, and are not now, favored by a large percentage of Christians.

Determine the *Original* Readers' and Listeners' Application and Context

If we accept the dispensational Rapture, a basic principle of understanding the Bible must be thrown to the wind. A fundamental rule of understanding the Bible is to read a passage in its context. What was the message in its original context to its original readers and listeners? As students of the Bible, our first task is to discover the original application of the message for its original audience. Then, and only then, are we free to make an interpretation for our lives.

Contemporary applications of Scripture must always be based upon the original meaning. Bypassing the boring historical details in order to arrive at a sensational application makes for captivating and interesting reading; but if that is our primary goal, we should stick with racy, supermarket tabloids. This cardinal rule of Bible study—understanding the original context, audience and application—must be ignored if we accept the dispensational Rapture. Richard Jeske notes that many authors have used the Book of Revelation as a foil for their own personal agenda and in the process ignore obvious principles of understanding the Bible.[6]

Earlier, we looked at 1 Thessalonians 4:13-18. Paul's original intent in writing this passage was not even close to the Rapture theory that was forced on this text almost 1,800 years later.

The text simply explains that at the second coming of Jesus Christ those who are dead in Christ as well as those who are alive will rise to meet Him in the air. They will thus be raptured—but this is not the Rapture of dispensationalism.

The Rapture teaching of dispensationalism also violates one of the very "rules" of those who teach it. Dispensationalism and its followers have long favored the practice of proof-texting: "proving" a particular teaching by quoting multiple passages that happen to include a particular word or phrase.

Overwhelming a topic with the sheer number of passages intended to prove a point, regardless of the context and genre of literature used by each passage, is, of course, a serious abuse of the Bible. Some call it "spoof texting." Others call it "Scrip-torture." Think of proof-texting as loading up a dump truck with biblical passages that mention a specific word or phrase and then dumping that load on the head of the as-yet-unconvinced individual.

But in the case of the Rapture, even this commonly used dispensational device is ultimately abandoned, since only a few passages can even remotely be "used" to prove such an event. Those who believe and teach the Rapture can't even agree among themselves; and no wonder, for they lack firm biblical foundation for this fictional teaching.

Some believe that the Rapture will be secret and quiet; that is, only Christians will see Jesus Christ, and the rest of the world will have no idea that anything has happened. Others believe the Rapture will be audible and noisy; so that those who are not Christians will see and hear the spectacle of Christians being whisked away to safety while they are left behind, having to suffer the emotional agony of knowing that safety has been denied them and that excruciating suffering awaits.

But the Bible tells us that God does not motivate us with fear, and we should not attempt to persuade others that He does so. Roman 8:15 tells us, "For you did not receive a spirit of slavery to fall back into fear, but you received a spirit of adoption." Paul adds, in 2 Timothy 1:7, "For God did not give us a spirit of cowardice, but rather a spirit of power and of love and of self-discipline." God loves all His children, whether we happen to believe we will be Raptured or not.

Further, the Bible teaches that there is only one second coming. For the Bible there is no such thing as a second, second coming—or, if you prefer, a third coming.

What's the Problem With Believing in a Dispensational Rapture?

Well, you may ask, "What difference does it make if you believe the end is just around the corner? Doesn't it help to motivate us to be good, assuming that only those who are ready will be Raptured? Why not be ready for the Rapture just in case? How can that hurt anyone?"

Jesus tells us to "Beware of false prophets" (Ma 7:15); that they will be known "by their fruits" (Ma 7:20), and that not everyone who says or does something in His name will enter the kingdom of heaven (Ma 7:21). He even calls some who will teach in His name "evildoers" (Ma 7:23).

What is the fruit of this unwarranted emphasis on the dispensational Rapture? Is teaching the Rapture harmless?

The Dispensational Rapture:

- Detracts from the central message of the gospel: Jesus gave His life to save the world.
- Is based on and encourages further unsound and speculative interpretation of the Bible.
- Focuses on human authorities who must constantly reinterpret prophecy

in light of world events and then announce the latest recalculation or resetting of dates to their followers.

- Appeals to the human desire to avoid pain and suffering. While the Bible tells us that God loves us and protects us, nowhere does the Bible promise that Christians will not suffer along with non-Christians or that we will be saved from physical suffering in some special way. The primary concern of the Book of Revelation, indeed of the new covenant given to us in Christ's blood, is our spiritual salvation, not our physical salvation. The dispensational Rapture appeals to the flesh, motivates using the fear factor, rather than by God's grace.[7]

- Encourages legalism, because it emphasizes what you can *do* to escape the tribulation. The idea of a second coming combined with a third coming encourages the idea that you can qualify to be good enough to be saved by the second coming, so that you need not suffer the great tribulation.

- Distorts the gospel, interpreting Revelation in terms of escape from earthly violence rather than in terms of the victorious new life Jesus gives us. The Rapture teaching follows the dispensational agenda, stressing that a specific generation's time is probably the end time, artificially inducing Christians into behaviors on the basis of fear.

- Discourages responsible stewardship of our lives, our responsibilities in our world, and its environment: "The world will end soon, so why bother?"

- Produces an unstable faith, focused on changing world events, rather than upon our firm foundation on the Rock, Jesus Christ.

- Burns Christians out. After failed predictions, many lose faith and give up on Christianity, some before they even begin to walk with God, because they assume all Christians to be Rapture-happy.

Some dispensational advocates will contend that I am taking the "big stick" out of their hands if I insist that special rewards won't be given to Rapture-believing believers. But it seems to me that such a concern is a concern of performance-based religion, not a concern of authentic, Christ-centered Christianity. God never gave the "big stick" of the Rapture to Christianity in the first place. Authentic Christianity does not offer a carrot that promises escape from physical suffering. Christian concerns within the body of Christ do not include control, intimidation, and manipulation. Surely Christians do not believe that the end justifies the means, do we?

The Rapture teaching is tailor-made for religious legalism. Oppressive and controlling religion is always looking for big sticks to control people. Religion under the guise of Christianity often seeks to control and manipulate in order to encourage people to behave as Christians. No Christian has any biblical authority to mislead people, even if we believe that the end justifies our questionable methodologies.

Religious baggage must be *left behind* as we enter the Word of God, so that we might be taught from God, rather than from narrow, sectarian interpretations. Futurism can be a valid perspective; and indeed, many passages in Revelation are hard to understand without seeing a future fulfillment. But the extreme views of dispensationalism and the Rapture run counter to the grace-based message of the Revelation of Jesus Christ.

Are you or is someone you know concerned and anxious about the end times? Do you worry about whether you will have done enough or performed enough righteous deeds so that you will qualify to be caught away with the saints from the horrible events of the great tribulation? Are you concerned that you might not be counted worthy to experience the dispensational Rapture? Do you worry about your friends and loved ones having to endure the terror of the tribulation and the reign of Antichrist?

If so, you've been listening to, reading, and allowing yourself to be enslaved by unbiblical teaching. You need to discover the Prince of Peace, the Lamb of God, the Alpha and the Omega, who gave you the Book of Revelation, the unveiling of the wonderful truth that Jesus has conquered all religious pretenders; and that we are free in Him from unbiblical notions of fear and worry.

CHAPTER EIGHT

Eternally Sealed From the Religious Jungle

It's a jungle out there! The very religion Revelation warns us about, that the cross of Christ frees us from, and that Jesus encourages each of the seven churches to conquer, has done its best to recast the theme of the Book of Revelation. The same religious legalisms from which the Lamb of God seals us warp and distort the message of Revelation so that many open the pages of this book looking for sensational and lurid predictions of the immediate future. It seems that performance-based religion has successfully removed itself as the villain of Revelation by providing a salacious theological interpretation of these words of life. Do many miss the point of Revelation because they are addicted to prediction?

Some justify "prophecy preaching" and "a little speculation and prediction" as victimless theological crimes. After all, preachers will be preachers, and they are prone to making wild predictions. Thus the havoc left in the wake of spurious claims about the meaning of Revelation is often dismissed as harmless.

When I was a young boy, I loved sports (and still do). Sports fascinated me, I wanted to make either participation in or reporting about athletic endeavors my life. My mother, though she and my stepfather were often hard-pressed to pay all their bills, recognized my desire and purchased a subscription to *Sports Illustrated (SI)* for me. Almost 50 years ago *SI* was a magazine that a parent could provide for a ten-year old boy like me who aspired to some kind of career in athletics and sports.

Over the years *SI* apparently determined to grow its circulation and demographic appeal by catering to a wider audience than simply sports fans who wish to read unembellished accounts of athletic endeavors. In a thinly veiled (pun intended) attempt to increase circulation, *SI* added an annual swimsuit issue. After all, *SI* could reason, women's swimsuits are at least ostensibly produced for swimming, and swimming is a sport. Such reasoning does not change the fact that many parents today would not consider a subscription to a magazine that included the *SI* swimsuit issue for their ten-year-old son.

What does the *Sports Illustrated* annual swimsuit issue have to do with the Book of Revelation? Dispensationalism has added a new sensational spin on Revelation, seducing the curious with peek-show like promises of insights about the future. Religious oppressors and profiteers have turned this sacred book into a prophetic strip show, luring the unsuspecting into its twisted and perverted interpretations while emptying their pockets. This twist on the Book of Revelation was not at all the message intended by the Messenger.

If those who have made wild and irresponsible claims and predictions about the book were car mechanics, they would be out of a job. If their efforts to fix and repair cars had failed over and over again, as evidenced by vehicle after vehicle being returned to their repair shop, they would either be out of business or at the very least in trade school learning to be mechanics. But visit your Christian bookstore, and you will see material that is based upon ideas and methods and interpretations that have failed over and over again; and this stuff continues to sell like hotcakes. It's repackaged to have a fresh appeal, updated for a new generation, but it's the same old stuff.[1]

It is a religious jungle out there, and those who believe in the Lamb of God need to be rescued, saved, and protected. The Book of Revelation describes this protection as being "sealed."

God's Servants Sealed and Healed

[1] After this I saw four angels standing at the four corners of the earth, holding back the four winds of the earth so that no wind could blow on earth or sea or against any tree. [2] I saw another angel ascending from the rising of the sun, having the seal of the living God, and he called with a loud voice to the four angels who had been given power to damage earth and sea, [3] saying, "Do not damage the earth or the sea or the trees, until we have marked the servants of our God with a seal on their foreheads."

[4] And I heard the number of those who were sealed, one hundred and forty-four thousand, sealed out of every tribe of the people of Israel:

[5] From the tribe of Judah twelve thousand sealed,
from the tribe of Reuben twelve thousand,
from the tribe of Gad twelve thousand,
[6] from the tribe of Asher twelve thousand,
from the tribe of Naphtali twelve thousand,
from the tribe of Manasseh twelve thousand,
[7] from the tribe of Simeon twelve thousand,
from the tribe of Levi twelve thousand,
from the tribe of Issachar twelve thousand,
[8] from the tribe of Zebulun twelve thousand,
from the tribe of Joseph twelve thousand,
from the tribe of Benjamin twelve thousand sealed.

[9] After this I looked, and there was a great multitude that no one could count, from every nation, from all tribes

and peoples and languages, standing before the throne and before the Lamb, robed in white, with palm branches in their hands. [10]They cried out in a loud voice, saying,

"Salvation belongs to our God who is seated on the throne, and to the Lamb!"

[11] And all the angels stood around the throne and around the elders and the four living creatures, and they fell on their faces before the throne and worshiped God, [12] singing,

"Amen! Blessing and glory and wisdom
and thanksgiving and honor
and power and might
be to our God forever and ever! Amen."

[13] Then one of the elders addressed me, saying, "Who are these, robed in white, and where have they come from?" [14] I said to him, "Sir, you are the one that knows." Then he said to me, "These are they who have come out of the great ordeal; they have washed their robes and made them white in the blood of the Lamb.

[15] For this reason they are before the throne of God,
and worship him day and night within his temple,
and the one who is seated on the throne will shelter them.

[16]They will hunger no more, and thirst no more;
the sun will not strike them,
nor any scorching heat;

[17] for the Lamb at the center of the throne will be their shepherd, and he will guide them to springs of the water of life, and God will wipe away every tear from their eyes."

Revelation 7:1-17

Suddenly, in chapter seven everything is put on hold until an extremely important piece of business is taken care of. The servants of God must be "sealed" and protected. Upon an initial reading of this passage (especially if that initial reading is informed by a purely futuristic and perhaps premillenial dispensationalist perspective) chapter seven seems to be a picture of future judgment.

However, to the degree that futuristic, dispensational baggage can be set aside, and to the degree that we insist on seeing our interpretation through first-century eyes and ears, then a different picture emerges.

One hundred forty-four thousand are sealed, 12,000 from each of the tribes of Israel, a symbolic number depicting the great number of God's faithful who bear His seal and are under His spiritual protection. These tribes, by the way, are not the same as those listed in the Old Testament, so this list cannot literally represent Israel as a nation. These tribes symbolically represent spiritual Israel, the universal church.[2] The great multitude that no one could count represents another view of God's faithful who come out of great tribulation and wear clean robes of righteousness made white in the blood of the Lamb.

The emphasis in the New Testament is on the spiritual people of God, the universal body of Christ. The church is diverse in gender, ethnicity, and socioeconomic standing (Ga 3:28). Those who believe in Christ are the New Testament people of God who replace the racially defined people of God of the old covenant (Ro 2:29; Ph 3:3). The New Testament church is God's holy, spiritual nation, His new chosen people (1 Pe 2:9).

The specific number of 144,000 might be used because the new Jerusalem (mentioned in chapter 21) is built upon the 12 names of the 12 apostles of the Lamb of God, as well as the 12 names of the 12 tribes of Israel headed by the Lion of Judah. The walls of the new Jerusalem are 144 "cubits" thick. They are 12,000 stadia long, wide, and high. All of these numbers are multiples of 12, having something to do with 144,000.

What is the significance of this precise number of 144,000? If you're looking for some dogmatic insight or some spellbinding and mesmerizing speculation, you're reading the wrong book. Years ago I accepted arbitrary, esoteric, mystical, and superstitious interpretations for the numbers and symbols of Revelation. No more. Those kinds of ideas are without merit, integrity, or validity. They mock God's word and turn it into a sleazy carnival.

What's the significance of the 144,000? Paul insisted that Jesus is the chief cornerstone (Ep 2:20), the foundation and ground zero of our faith. He told the Corinthians:

> For the message about the cross is foolishness to those who are perishing, but to us who are being saved it is the power of God…. For Jews demand signs and Greeks desire wisdom, but we proclaim Christ crucified, a stumbling block to Jews and foolishness to Gentiles, but to those who are the called, both Jews and Greeks, Christ the power of God and the wisdom of God. For God's foolishness is wiser than human wisdom, and God's weakness is stronger than human strength.
> *1 Corinthians 1:18, 22-25).*

The exact and precise identity of the 144,000, who and what they are and represent, is the wrong question. Multiple trips around the block of religious dogmatism and speculation have taught me several lessons, among them this: if we ask the wrong question, we will probably get the wrong answer. The primary question that this passage is answering is posed by the last verse of the chapter that precedes it, "for the great day of their wrath has come, and who is able to stand?" (6:17). The last verses of chapter six explain that many of the rich, mighty, powerful, and famous will seek shelter from the wrath of the Lamb (6:15-16). Chapter seven answers the question of who will stand before God and on what basis they will do so.

Those who stand before God do so because of the Lamb, and they do so in and through His name. They stand before God by God's grace, not because of their own human abilities, morality, character, talent, or spiritual prowess. They stand because their robes have been washed in the blood of the Lamb (v. 14).

The meaning and significance of the 144,000 to us today remains exactly the same as it was to the original readers of Revelation. One hundred forty-four thousand is a symbolic number, signifying an imprecise but large group of people who by God's grace inhabit the new Jerusalem. One hundred forty-four thousand is a deliberately mysterious number representing those who, by God's grace, inhabit eternity.[3] They are sealed and receive eternal spiritual healing, sealed and healed by the blood of the Lamb.

One hundred forty-four thousand is a mysterious number, but it is not arbitrary. One hundred forty-four thousand is an exact number derived from multiples of 12, with many biblical precedents, including the twelve tribes and the twelve apostles.

The 144,000 are sealed by God's grace. This sealing demonstrates that no one can separate them from the love of God in Christ Jesus. Nothing can separate them, "neither death, nor life, nor angels, nor rulers, nor things present, nor things to come, nor powers, nor height, nor depth, nor anything else in all creation" (Ro 8:38-39).

What does it mean to be sealed by God? It means that if you have accepted Jesus Christ, no one can separate you from Him. Not your church, not your pastor, not the most powerful religious leader on earth. No one. No rule, no regulation, no ritual or restriction. No potion or priest. No ceremony, no secret knowledge, no password, no better revelation, no amount of character that you have failed to build, no bad habit that you just can't completely conquer. Nothing can separate you from God. You are sealed. That's the message of the 144,000. Don't get sidetracked by some juicy speculation about the exact demographic, racial, and chronological identification of the 144,000.

What does it mean to be spiritually sealed and healed? It means that Jesus lives His resurrected life in you (Ga 2:20). It means that while we will experience life in this body of flesh, enduring diseases and suffering accidents, the ultimate victory over death and the grave is shared with us by the risen Lord (1 Co 15:57).[4] No political, military, or religious beast power can remove the eternal healing given to us by the Great Physician.

A second group in chapter seven is called a great multitude. Like the 144,000, this group is a big group. A great multitude is not just a little handful of separated, holy living, "better than everyone else," one-true-church commune way back in the hills, far from the closest sin and city. The 144,000 and, even more so, the great multitude are larger and more inclusive than religion would allow if it had the final say.

The great multitude is an even bigger number than the 144,000, and it seems that they have survived, by God's help, slightly differing challenges of persecution and tribulation. Once again, some are quick to pinpoint exact time lines and chronologies that distinguish these two groups; but neither calendrical, chronological precision, nor mathematical exactness is suggested or hinted at in this chapter. *When* and precisely *how many* is what we don't know from chapter seven.

But what can we know from chapter seven? What is crystal clear is that God will make a way. Even in spite of overwhelming tribulation and persecution, even though the pressure may seem so severe that we may wonder whether we or anyone could be saved by God because of the horrible circumstances we encounter and endure (or perhaps even at times bring upon ourselves), the message is that God not only saves a somewhat specific group like the 144,000, but He also saves a huge group like the great multitude. The message that the Messenger is giving us in chapter seven is that He is saving more people than we might imagine; and we humans, along with created angelic beings, are overwhelmed when we realize that He has, is, and will do such a thing (v. 9-11).

Jacques Ellul implies that the two groups of people in this chapter may simply represent two facets, two visions, which, taken together, form a complete picture of the "entire people of God."[5]

That's another reason why the gospel is such good news. *There will be more people in God's kingdom of heaven than we humans would invite or allow.* God is more generous (the word the Bible often uses for spiritual generosity is grace) than anyone of us. The Lamb of God is more generous than religion. When the rubber hits the road, the truth is that it is in the best interests of legalistic religion for its followers to live in fear, never being sure if they will make it into the new Jerusalem. Religious legalism wants to dangle your feet over the fires of hell to get you to shape up and start obeying its rules and regulations. Oppressive religion uses a big stick to keep you in line. Performance-based religion wants its heaven to be exclusive, given the general assumption that the more unique and esoteric a club is the more energies and resources humans will willingly expend to join.

But the Lamb of God, the Good Shepherd, the Good Samaritan, is not a captive of religious tradition, methodology, ideology, exclusivism, or dogmatism. The Lamb of God gently guides and leads us, using a shepherd's crook to nudge us in the direction we need to go, protecting us as we journey through the valley of the shadow of death.

This sealing and healing is spiritual, with no promise that Christians won't be exposed to the physical dangers of the Four Horsemen, the deceptive seductions of the white horse, the violence of the red horse, the suffering and misery of the black horse, or the death and Hades of the pale horse.

The fifth seal, in fact, tells us that many will be martyred because of their faith in Christ. They are sealed spiritually in Christ, but they will be killed and martyred.

Jesus Christ promises, "You will be betrayed even by parents and brothers, by relatives and friends; and they will put some of you to death. You will be hated because of my name. But not a hair of your head will perish. By your endurance you will gain your souls" (Lk 21:16). Christians are spiritually sealed with God's protection through Christ. We are spiritually healed by the stripes voluntarily endured on our behalf by the Lamb of God (1 Pe 2:24-25). We can be sure of our salvation. Nothing can touch us. We are protected from God's anger and wrath that is directed toward the inhumanities of war and oppression of all kinds, including religious oppression and abuse. Our eternal life is guaranteed, in God's presence, in the new Jerusalem, before His throne forever.

The Seven Trumpets

[1] When the Lamb opened the seventh seal, there was silence in heaven for about half an hour. [2] And I saw the seven angels who stand before God, and seven trumpets were given to them.

[3] Another angel with a golden censer came and stood at the altar; he was given a great quantity of incense to offer with the prayers of all the saints on the golden altar that is before the throne. [4] And the smoke of the incense, with the prayers of the saints, rose before God from the hand of the angel. [5] Then the angel took the censer and filled it with fire from the altar and threw it on the earth; and there were peals of thunder, rumblings, flashes of lightning, and an earthquake.

[6] Now the seven angels who had the seven trumpets made ready to blow them.

[7] The first angel blew his trumpet, and there came hail and fire, mixed with blood, and they were hurled to the earth; and a third of the earth was burned up, and a third of the trees were burned up, and all green grass was burned up.

[8] The second angel blew his trumpet, and something like a great mountain, burning with fire, was thrown into

the sea. [9] A third of the sea became blood, a third of the living creatures in the sea died, and a third of the ships were destroyed.

[10] The third angel blew his trumpet, and a great star fell from heaven, blazing like a torch, and it fell on a third of the rivers and on the springs of water. [11] The name of the star is Wormwood. A third of the waters became wormwood, and many died from the water, because it was made bitter.

[12] The fourth angel blew his trumpet, and a third of the sun was struck, and a third of the moon, and a third of the stars, so that a third of their light was darkened; a third of the day was kept from shining, and likewise the night.

[13] Then I looked, and I heard an eagle crying with a loud voice as it flew in mid-heaven, "Woe, woe, woe to the inhabitants of the earth, at the blasts of the other trumpets that the three angels are about to blow!"

Revelation 8:1-13

For a short time after the opening of the seventh seal nothing happens while the prayers of the saints ascend to God. Is this a "time" that happens only once in human history, or in "God's time" is this a recurring interval of what we experience as time? Time and prayer are here linked as factors that lead to the seventh seal being opened, and there is a time when nothing happens while prayers ascend to God. This, of course, is all metaphorical language.

If we avoid twisting and contorting this language into some literal application, then a fascinating window into how prayer "works" in God's time opens. We humans are often confused by Jesus' absolute promise to answer prayer (Ma 7:7-11) followed by what we can only interpret as a failure on God's part to answer. Prayers here symbolically ascend to God, but they are not answered for "half an hour" (v. 1).

Of course, we would be delighted if it only took 30 minutes for God to answer our prayers, but our experience is that we may have prayed about something for years without receiving an answer, or at least the answer we asked for. Perhaps God does not calculate His time in the same way we humans measure and experience time (2 Pe 3:8)? Translating timeless, eternal truth into our corrupted world of time and space is risky since we are so prone to "strain out a gnat but swallow a camel" (Ma 23:24). This passage once again teaches us that it is futile to literally calculate statements filled with symbolism and metaphor. We are so busy determining an exact date when Jesus will return and a precise time when the Rapture will happen that we miss His message!

The angel takes the collected prayers of the saints and hurls them to the earth (v. 5) as the dramatic symbol of God's answer, resulting in divine judgment against all the wickedness that the enemies of God and of His Lamb have perpetrated on His people. Jesus Christ, the slain Lamb, has opened the scroll, and the judgment of God has begun.

A series of seven trumpets, sounded by seven angels, now begins. Each trumpet signals a different disaster sent to drive an unrepentant humanity to its knees. These plagues are described in symbolic terms: hail and fire mixed with blood, a third of the ocean turning to blood, a falling star that poisons a third of all fresh water, and darkening of the sun, moon, and stars.

When do these plagues happen? How can we identify them when they do? Once again, many have been trying to answer the wrong questions. Some have constructed elaborate computations in order to determine what these plagues are and how to identify them as specific events, conditions, or objects. But all attempts have fallen like a theological house of cards or, to use a biblical reference, as a house built upon sand (Ma 7:26-27).

The description of these plagues is part of the complex and somewhat mysterious symbolic language of the apocalyptic style in which Revelation was both inspired and written. The original audience, the seven churches to whom the Book of Revelation was addressed in the first century, undoubtedly understood some of this symbolism better than we do—while many extensive efforts to transfer and interpret Revelation into a specific generational experience of time and space have merely obscured it.

The last three trumpets are accompanied by "woes." Especially severe plagues and disasters intended to bring the people of earth to repentance.

A Prophecy of Tanks and Helicopters?

[1] And the fifth angel blew his trumpet, and I saw a star that had fallen from heaven to earth, and he was given the key to the shaft of the bottomless pit; [2] he opened the shaft of the bottomless pit, and from the shaft rose smoke like the smoke of a great furnace, and the sun and the air were darkened with the smoke from the shaft. [3] Then from the smoke came locusts on the earth, and they were given authority like the authority of scorpions of the earth. [4] They were told not to damage the grass of the earth or any green growth or any tree, but only those people who do not have the seal of God on their foreheads. [5] They were allowed to torture them for five months, but not to kill them, and their torture was like the torture of a scorpion when it stings someone. [6] And in those days people will seek death but will not find it; they will long to die, but death will flee from them.

[7] In appearance the locusts were like horses equipped for battle. On their heads were what looked like crowns of gold; their faces were like human faces, [8] their hair like women's hair, and their teeth like lions' teeth; [9] they had scales like iron breastplates, and the noise of their wings was like the noise of many chariots with horses rushing

into battle. [10] They have tails like scorpions, with stingers, and in their tails is their power to harm people for five months. [11] They have as king over them the angel of the bottomless pit; his name in Hebrew is Abaddon, and in Greek he is called Apollyon.

[12] The first woe has passed. There are still two woes to come.

[13] Then the sixth angel blew his trumpet, and I heard a voice from the four horns of the golden altar before God, [14] saying to the sixth angel who had the trumpet, "Release the four angels who are bound at the great river Euphrates." [15] So the four angels were released, who had been held ready for the hour, the day, the month, and the year, to kill a third of humankind. [16] The number of the troops of cavalry was two hundred million; I heard their number. [17] And this was how I saw the horses in my vision: the riders wore breastplates the color of fire and of sapphire and of sulfur; the heads of the horses were like lions' heads, and fire and smoke and sulfur came out of their mouths. [18] By these three plagues a third of humankind was killed, by the fire and smoke and sulfur coming out of their mouths. [19] For the power of the horses is in their mouths and in their tails; their tails are like serpents, having heads; and with them they inflict harm.

[20] The rest of humankind, who were not killed by these plagues, did not repent of the works of their hands or give up worshipping demons and idols of gold and silver and bronze and stone and wood, which cannot see or hear or walk.

Revelation 9:1-20

The fifth trumpet, and the first "woe," brings stinging locusts from a bottomless pit, to torment the earth's inhabitants. The sixth trumpet, the second "woe," unleashes an army of two hundred million demonic horsemen, who kill a third of the world's population.

Commentators, pastors, and teachers have perched on precarious limbs and branches, outdoing themselves trying to identify these images with literal objects and events. In the past few decades some have speculated that the stinging locusts from the abyss might resemble helicopters dispensing biological toxins. That interpretation gives supposed credibility to the idea that no one could fully understand the Book of Revelation until the helicopter was invented and built. Wow, what an unbelievable idea! But not so unbelievable if you once believed it, as I did.

Some suggest that the horsemen might resemble a future army of tanks with flame throwers. Once again, no tanks or flame throwers existed until the twentieth century. So if you accept this kind of "never-before-possible" interpretation, you accept a provocative idea that caters to human vanity: the idea that those of us who live in the twenty-first century understand what the vast majority of Christians never did. What an intoxicating message! How seductive! One has to admit that such preposterous claims sell books, but we are left to grapple with how much truth is dispensed via promotional hype and sensationalism.

The idea that we in the twenty-first century understand the message of Revelation better than anyone ever has is not only fatally flawed, but it is also simply another example of the mindless narcissistic drivel that caters to our me-first world. Such an interpretation teaches that no one could understand the Book of Revelation until the modern weapons of warfare were manufactured. Like any book of the Bible, authentic Christianity demands that the Book of Revelation be interpreted in a Christ-centered way, and that means *our generation, when we live, what we do, and where we live is not the primary focus of the Book of Revelation.*

Even if we are the generation who will be alive when Jesus returns (and, of course, eventually there will be one), the idea that Revelation is written primarily to us remains a teaching at odds with the gospel. If we attempt to impose our place in history upon Revelation—when we live and where we live and who we are and what we do—we are in danger of becoming more fodder for the gristmill of oppressive and opportunistic religion.

This is not to say that the Book of Revelation is irrelevant or without any significance for the twenty-first century. It's not a case of either Revelation being only about our lives, our times and our world, or not about us at all. Of course, Revelation has significance for us. But, please, don't let anyone tell you that Revelation is finally being understood "in these end times." Revelation had an original meaning to its original readers, and it has continued for almost 2,000 years to proclaim a timeless, meaningful message for Christians.

Picture this. You, along with other twentieth and twenty-first century Christians, are receiving an orientation to God's kingdom of heaven. You have "arrived" in eternity. Jesus clears His throat, "About all these ideas some of you had about prophecy and the Book of Revelation. Remember when you were told that your generation had a better understanding of Revelation than any other generation of Christians who had ever lived?" Jesus pauses and then, with a smile, continues, "Actually, the truth is the exact opposite of what you were told. Let me explain." I have to tell you that I find such a scene far more plausible than the Rapture.

Those who struggle to force a literal interpretation into the symbolic images of Revelation risk missing its real message: Christ has and will triumph over all such evil power, whether it be religious, military, or political. The battle belongs to the Lord.

Jesus' revelation tells us that regardless of when the "woes," judgments, and plagues God sends come, and, in spite of their consequences, there are those who refuse to acknowledge Him as Lord. John tells us, "The rest of mankind, who were not killed by these plagues, did not repent of the work of their hands or give up worshiping demons and idols of gold and silver and bronze and stone and wood, which cannot see or hear or walk. And they did not repent of their murders or their sorcery or their fornication or their thefts" (v. 20).

We human beings are stubborn. Even in the midst of severe trials, we will assert our independence rather than surrendering to our Creator, who is the source of true freedom. In the face of extreme adversity some continue to assert that religious legalism and tradition is the answer. Many of us trust in our own moral strength rather than God's grace. Some congregations, in defiance of the gospel, will effectively blackmail their pastor, insisting that if too much Jesus is preached and if God's unconditional gift of grace is proclaimed without equivocation, people will use it as an excuse for sin. They are worried that the gospel of Jesus Christ will encourage people to try to get away with something! Does that sound like the Jesus of your Bible, or does that sound like judgmental, opinionated, hyper-critical religion that enslaves and controls?

In the apocalyptic imagery of the Book of Revelation, people are either with Christ or against Him. There is no large group of well-meaning people who are searching for a spiritual direction, looking at crystals, sitting inside a miniature pyramid to get good vibrations or chanting some mantra. You are either with Christ or against Him. There is no middle ground and no ambiguity. After all, those who are suffering persecution, such as the original readers of this book, do not need ambiguity. They need black and white reassurance, and that's the way Revelation is written.

Jesus is With, In, and Among us Now

> [1] And I saw another mighty angel coming down from heaven, wrapped in a cloud, with a rainbow over his head; his face was like the sun, and his legs like pillars of fire. [2] He held a little scroll open in his hand. Setting his right foot on the sea and his left foot on the land, [3] he gave a great shout, like a lion roaring. And when he shouted, the seven thunders sounded. [4] And when the seven thunders had sounded, I was about to write,

but I heard a voice from heaven saying, "Seal up what the seven thunders have said, and do not write it down." [5] Then the angel whom I saw standing on the sea and the land raised his right hand to heaven

[6] and swore by him who lives forever and ever, who created heaven and what is in it, the earth and what is in it, and the sea and what is in it: "There will be no more delay, [7] but in the days when the seventh angel is to blow his trumpet, the mystery of God will be fulfilled, as he announced to his servants the prophets."

[8] Then the voice that I had heard from heaven spoke to me again, saying, "Go, take the scroll that is open in the hand of the angel who is standing on the sea and on the land." [9] So I went to the angel and told him to give me the little scroll; and he said to me, "Take it, and eat; it will be bitter to your stomach, but sweet as honey in your mouth." [10] So I took the little scroll from the hand of the angel and ate it; it was sweet as honey in my mouth, but when I had eaten it, my stomach was made bitter.

[11] Then they said to me, "You must prophesy again about many peoples and nations and languages and kings."

Revelation 10:1-11

The interlude between the sixth and seventh trumpets is marked by teaching about God's faithfulness to His people. Before the seventh and final trumpet and the third "woe," John is given another vision. An angel, descending from heaven, plants his right foot on the sea and his left foot on the land, depicting the power of God over all things (v. 2). His arrival is accompanied by seven thunder-like messages, but John is instructed not to publish these messages (v. 4). This divine instruction reminds us that some aspects of God's work are simply not revealed to us. We must be content with an incomplete understanding, and that would include exact, literal meanings for every symbol and metaphor in the Book of Revelation.

The angel raises his right hand to heaven and swears, "There will be no more delay!" (v. 6). What did this mean to original readers of Revelation? Perhaps they thought about another apocalyptic book they were familiar with, the Book of Daniel. Toward the end of the Book of Daniel, an Old Testament apocalyptic writing filled with symbols and images, Daniel saw two men. One man asked the other, "How long shall it be until the end of these wonders?" (Da 12:6). The other man responded that "it would be for a time, two times, and half a time, and that when the shattering of the power of the holy people comes to an end, all these things would be accomplished" (Da 12:7).

The original recipients of the Book of Revelation remembered that the temple in Jerusalem, Herod's Temple, had been utterly destroyed in A.D. 69-70. Not one stone was left standing on top of another (Ma 24:2). Organized Christianity did not officially break the yoke of the religion of Judaism until the temple and all of its ceremonies were utterly destroyed almost four decades after the cross of Christ and His resurrection. For Christians reading the Revelation given to John by the Lamb of God, there was no more delay.

The power of oppressive religion was officially ended at the moment of Jesus' atoning death on the cross: "At that moment the curtain of the temple was torn in two, from top to bottom" (Ma 27:51). No more separation between man and God. No more human priesthood as intermediaries. No more ceremonies, sacrifices, or rituals required as a condition of reconciliation with God. The power of the holy people of the old covenant came to an end (Da 12:6). A new day was born. The Lamb of God did what no one could ever do; He opened the way for humans to have a personal relationship with God. The kingdom of our Lord and Savior was launched, with His birth, life, death, and resurrection showing the way.

Religion, at that time primarily Judaism, did not react kindly to Christianity. This new "way" was seen as a threat to religion's livelihood. Religion resisted Jesus then, and has continued to resist and revolt against Him and revise His message ever since. The destruction of the Jewish temple, almost 40 years after the cross and the resurrection, closed another door whereby religion could assert itself and claim relevance and importance and so compete with the gospel of Jesus Christ.

In contrast to the message given to Daniel, a message that clearly pointed to the ministry and work of Jesus as the fulfillment of all its prophecies, the angel in Revelation announces that there is no delay. The kingdom is here. The kingdom is now. The kingdom is *already*, in the person of the risen Christ who lives His life within those who accept Him; and it is *not yet*, because, until Jesus' second coming, legalistic religion will continue to compete with the pure, unadulterated, grace-filled message of the Messenger.

We need not allow the message of Revelation to be buried under mountains of speculation about history and past events. Neither must looking for future fulfillments of Revelation sidetrack us. The kingdom is now. The kingdom is here. In the person of the risen Lord, we experience the kingdom now; we are now seated with Him in heavenly places (Ep 2:6). We need not consult prophecy charts, newspapers, or prophecy teachers and gurus. A greater than all of these is here now, with us, in us, and among us. There is no delay!

The angel gives John a small scroll (in contrast to the large scroll in Re 5:1) and directs him to eat it. This action of ingestion symbolized the vision that John is commissioned to internalize and later write to God's people. The little scroll is pleasant tasting in John's mouth but unpleasant in his stomach. The job of a faithful prophet, pastor, and teacher pastor may initially appear attractive; but it often involves more sacrifice and suffering than most humans are able to tolerate on the basis of human strength and resources alone.

The Two Witnesses and the Last Trumpet

> [1] Then I was given a measuring rod like a staff, and I was told, "Come and measure the temple of God and the altar and those who worship there, [2] but do not measure the court outside the temple; leave that out, for it is given over to the

nations, and they will trample over the holy city for forty-two months. [3] And I will grant my two witnesses authority to prophesy for one thousand two hundred and sixty days, wearing sackcloth."

[4] These are the two olive trees and the two lamp stands that stand before the Lord of the earth. [5] And if anyone wants to harm them, fire pours from their mouth and consumes their foes; anyone who wants to harm them must be killed in this manner. [6] They have authority to shut the sky, so that no rain may fall during the days of their prophesying, and they have authority over the waters to turn them into blood, and to strike the earth with every kind of plague, as often as they desire.

[7] When they have finished their testimony, the beast that comes up from the bottomless pit will make war on them and conquer them and kill them, [8] and their dead bodies will lie in the street of the great city that is prophetically called Sodom and Egypt, where also their Lord was crucified. [9] For three and a half days members of the peoples and tribes and languages and nations will gaze at their dead bodies and re-fuse to let them be placed in a tomb; [10] and the inhabitants of the earth will gloat over them and celebrate and exchange presents, because these two prophets had been a torment to the inhabitants of the earth.

[11] But after the three and a half days, the breath of life from God entered them, and they stood on their feet, and those who saw them were terrified. [12] Then they heard a loud voice from heaven saying to them, "Come up here!" And they went up to heaven in a cloud while their enemies watched them. [13] At that moment there was a great earth-quake, and a tenth of the city fell; seven thousand people

were killed in the earthquake, and the rest were terrified and gave glory to the God of heaven.

¹⁴ The second woe has passed. The third woe is coming very soon.

¹⁵ Then the seventh angel blew his trumpet, and there were loud voices in heaven, saying,

"The kingdom of the world has become the kingdom of our Lord

and of his Messiah,

and he will reign forever and ever."

¹⁶ Then the twenty-four elders who sit on their thrones before God fell on their faces and worshiped God, ¹⁷ singing,

"We give you thanks, Lord God Almighty,

who are and who were,

for you have taken your great power

and begun to reign.

¹⁸ The nations raged,

but your wrath has come,

and the time for judging the dead,

for rewarding your servants, the prophets

and saints and all who fear your name,

both small and great,

and for destroying those who destroy the earth."

¹⁹ Then God's temple in heaven was opened, and the ark of his covenant was seen within his temple; and there were flashes of lightning, rumblings, peals of thunder, an earthquake, and heavy hail.

Revelation 11:1-19

The "two witnesses" have been the subject of speculation for centuries. Some see them as literal individuals in the future. Some believed, and still do, that they were Luther and Calvin. Many scholars interpret them as being symbolic of Moses and Elijah, two great prophets of the Old Testament.

They have authority to "shut the sky" (v. 6) which would have reminded the original reader of Elijah's prayer that caused a drought in ancient Israel (1 Ki 17). The New Testament book of James illustrates the power of prayer with Elijah's prayer and notes that the drought caused by his prayer lasted three and one-half years (Ja 5:17), which is the same length of "time" of the ministry of the two witnesses. "I will grant my two witnesses authority to prophesy for one thousand two hundred sixty days" (v. 3).

Jacques Ellul comments on the "many interpretations" of the time periods of forty-two months (11:2) or 1,260 days (11:3 and 12:6) or three and one-half years (11:9, 11). His Christ-centered perspective finds the primary significance as being the "duration of the ministry of Jesus on earth."[6] Thus we once again are reminded of the divine *who* of Revelation, even though specific language seems to insist on human days, months, and years.

John then says, "When they have finished their testimony, the beast that comes up from the bottomless pit will make war on them and conquer them and kill them" (v. 7). This beast is a picture of Antichrist, the personification of the evil, religiously driven power obsessed with the total destruction of Christ and His church. The power behind Antichrist, of course, is Satan. In the Book of Revelation, Antichrist is associated with the ancient city of Babylon. The original readers of the Book of Revelation would have recognized the figurative reference to Sodom and Egypt (v. 8) as one and the same as Babylon, itself symbolic of the Roman Empire that oppressed them. At the time an emperor intent on eradicating Christianity from his domain headed Rome.

After lying dead for three and a half days, the two witnesses are called up to heaven. Their death and resurrection mirror the death and resurrection of Jesus. They remind us that accepting suffering in the name of Christ may conquer evil.

Finally in verse 15, the seventh trumpet sounds. This final trumpet marks the triumph of Christ over human kingdoms and governments that have long resisted and persecuted God's people. The 24 elders who sit before God in His throne room, falling on their faces before God, give a perfect summary of the impact of the properly understood message of Revelation.

"We give you thanks, Lord God Almighty, who are and who were, for you have taken your great power and begun to reign. The nations raged, but your wrath has come, and the time for judging the dead, for rewarding your servants, the prophets and saints and all who fear your name, both small and great, and for destroying those who destroy the earth" (vv. 17-18).

Verse 19 speaks of the temple of God being opened *in heaven*, and the ark of His covenant being seen. "Then God's temple in heaven was opened, and the ark of his covenant was seen within his temple; and there were flashes of lightning, rumblings, peals of thunder, an earthquake and heavy hail." For decades, rumors have circulated and people have debated and pondered when, or if, a new temple might be built in Jerusalem. This speculation has been fueled by rumors that the ark of the covenant is buried in a complex of tunnels beneath the Temple Mount, or that it resides in a shrine in Ethiopia, or some other location. Intense interest has centered on "news" reports of quarries where stones are being prepared for this literal edifice or where red heifers are being raised for temple sacrifice (Nu 19:2).

The Book of Hebrews tells us that the temple and its furnishings were only physical representations of heavenly things, "a sanctuary that is a sketch and shadow of the heavenly one" (He 8:5). The old temple and ark of the old covenant were only a shadow that pointed toward the new reality. The Book of Revelation explains the spiritual reality, the genuine articles, the real and true temple and the ark of the covenant in heaven. Isn't it somewhat ironic then that some, who claim to take the

Book of Revelation "literally," do not take this passage literally but are intensely interested in finding the physical remains of the ark of the old covenant or the evidence of the building of a new, physical temple in Jerusalem on earth?

This forced interpretation is a result of a literal understanding of the Book of Revelation that insists upon a series of events that eventuate in the rebuilding of a literal temple in Jerusalem with a literal future Antichrist playing a key role. But the emphasis of the Book of Revelation points us to Jesus, the new covenant and the new Jerusalem above, not upon deciphering and reporting about the latest attempt to rebuild a temple in Jerusalem.

The seventh trumpet has sounded. The kingdoms of the world are now the kingdom of God. But the battle is not yet over. And what about the third woe? In our next chapter we will encounter the third woe and we will witness the losing battle of Satan against the people of God.

Do you feel as though a sword is hanging over your head, as though the world is about to be plunged into indescribable chaos and that your loved ones and family who are not "Rapture ready" will have to face the horrors described in the Book of Revelation? That's not the message God is sending you. He wants you to be keenly aware of His wrath and judgment, to be sure. But His wrath is directed against an evil system that threatens to enslave you and your loved ones.

There are imposters and con artists who live in the religious jungle. They are ready to mug you, in the name of God, and take your freedom in Christ and exchange it for a lie. The lesson of the Book of Revelation is that, no matter how dark conditions may seem, you can be sealed, safe, and secure in Christ.

CHAPTER NINE

The Beast of the Month

Chances are, even if you are not a student of the Bible, you have heard of some of the names, images, and specific numbers found in Revelation. You have heard of the beast of Revelation. If you have been around the theological block a few times, or up and down the aisles of a Christian bookstore for that matter, you have read or heard a speaker, author, or pastor give a precise and specific identification to the beast of Revelation. I have heard of so many potential beasts that I once thought of starting a "beast-of-the-month" club. Potential members of my beast-of-the-month club include all religious and political leaders who have been predicted to lead the Antichrist revolt at the time of the second coming of Jesus Christ.

I haven't started my club yet, so please don't write me and ask for next year's calendar. Seriously, I don't think I will ever start my club, but if I ever do, I would have no problem selecting poster persons. Actually, many of them no longer qualify as candidates to lead an "end-time" revolt against Jesus because they are dead and buried. In fact, speaking of the dead, *all* of those who predicted these dead and buried beast-of-the-month poster persons were dead wrong.

This morbid curiosity and search to specifically identify the evil described in the Book of Revelation, exemplified by a burning desire to identify the beast of Revelation, not to mention the manipulative merchandising of this macabre inquisitiveness, overshadows and can overwhelm the good news Revelation proclaims. Jesus Christ is the revelator, the Messenger, and the subject of the revelation. He brings good news about *who* he is, and part of that good news is that no beast we will ever encounter has any spiritual power over those who are sealed by the Lamb of God.

God is Active and Involved

[1] A great portent appeared in heaven: a woman clothed with the sun, with the moon under her feet, and on her head a crown of twelve stars. [2] She was pregnant and was crying out in birth pangs, in the agony of giving birth. [3] Then another portent appeared in heaven: a great red dragon, with seven heads and ten horns, and seven diadems on his heads. [4] His tail swept down a third of the stars of heaven and threw them to the earth. Then the dragon stood before the woman who was about to bear a child, so that he might devour her child as soon as it was born. [5] And she gave birth to a son, a male child, who is to rule all the nations with a rod of iron. But her child was snatched away and taken to God and to his throne; [6] and the woman fled into the wilderness, where she has a place prepared by God, so that there she can be nourished for one thousand two hundred and sixty days.

[7] And war broke out in heaven; Michael and his angels fought against the dragon. The dragon and his angels fought back, [8] but they were defeated, and there was no longer any place for them in heaven. [9] The great dragon was thrown down, that ancient serpent, who is called the Devil and Satan, the deceiver of the whole world—he was thrown down to the earth, and his angels were thrown down with him.

[10] Then I heard a loud voice in heaven, proclaiming,
"Now have come the salvation and the power
and the kingdom of our God

and the authority of his Messiah,

for the accuser of our comrades has been thrown down,

who accuses them day and night before our God.

[11] But they have conquered him by the blood of the Lamb

and by the word of their testimony,

for they did not cling to life even in the face of death.

[12] Rejoice then, you heavens and those who dwell in them!

But woe to the earth and the sea,

for the devil has come down to you with great wrath,

because he knows that his time is short!"

[13] So when the dragon saw that he had been thrown down to the earth, he pursued the woman who had given birth to the male child. [14] But the woman was given the two wings of the great eagle, so that she could fly from the serpent into the wilderness, to her place where she is nourished for a time, and times, and half a time. [15] Then from his mouth the serpent poured water like a river after the woman, to sweep her away with the flood. [16] But the earth came to the help of the woman; it opened its mouth and swallowed the river that the dragon had poured from his mouth. [17] Then the dragon was angry with the woman, and went off to make war on the rest of her children, those who keep the commandments of God and hold the testimony of Jesus.

Revelation 12:1-17

For almost 200 years the fruit of futuristic dispensationalism has included a preoccupation with the beast of Revelation, with people wondering and speculating about who or what it might be. In the last 50 to 60 years the dizzying daze of dispensationalism has identified the beast with governments in Europe, Russia, China, North Korea, and Iraq, among others. North American prophecy teachers, viewing the Book of Revelation through a provincial national lens of our culture and time, have predicted that a potent economic and political confederacy of nations and religious power would eventually rival and then surpass the United States in military and industrial might, paving the way for the beast and the Antichrist. It just hasn't happened as the prophecy pundits have predicted.

Since specific predictions about nations and world leaders have been wrong, does that mean that the Book of Revelation is flawed? Perhaps we have been missing the forest for the trees! Perhaps our tunnel vision has caused us to obsess on the lineup of potential beasts, while all around us, beginning with the original audience to whom this book was written, the real beast of Revelation has been deceiving, abusing, and enslaving (v. 9).

In the first eleven chapters of Revelation, we have learned *who* is in control of the great themes underlying human history. The outcome of the monumental, ongoing battle between the forces of evil and the forces of God is not in question. The battle belongs to the Lord. The major events, trends, and movements of history are never out of the supervision of Jesus Christ. The disasters that seem to blindside us, confuse us, and disorient us, and leave us asking "why?" never come as a surprise to God.

We have learned that, while there are times when it seems that God is not acting, He is still on His throne and is deeply involved in human events and lives. He is active and He is involved according to His own eternal timetable, not ours. That insight is a lesson learned for those who are able, by God's grace, to see through the haze generated by the dizzying daze of dispensationalism. The destiny of God's people is never in question.

We have seen that Revelation insists there are two ways of life: one being an acceptance of Jesus Christ, who alone can save and rescue us apart from any righteous activity that we might attempt to generate or produce. Faith alone, grace alone, Christ alone. On the other hand, Revelation vividly depicts another way of life—using symbols, metaphors, and illustrations of unknown and apocalyptic beasts as well as powerful animals known to us in our world—explaining that our culture is filled with the spirit of Antichrist. The spirit of Antichrist is present in materialism, relativism, pluralism, consumerism, socialism, and humanism. Antichrist is alive and well in our politically correct, tolerance-is-god, multicultural, postmodern, value-neutral, and value-free western culture.

But Antichrist is not restricted to the secular world according to the Book of Revelation. Revelation depicts Antichrist as thriving in religion, including religion that masquerades as Christianity.

In the first century, Christians who were under pressure and persecution for their faith needed reassurance that Jesus Christ is Lord of lords and King of kings, the Alpha and Omega, "who is and who was and who is to come" (1:4, 8). That message is needed today just as much as it was then.

A War For the Ages

As we begin chapter twelve of the Book of Revelation, the seventh trumpet has sounded. Chapter 11:15 tells us, "The kingdom of the world has become the kingdom of our Lord and of his Messiah." These powerful words are a spiritual call to arms for Christians; they are our hope and our quest. You may best remember this passage in another form as a refrain in Handel's Messiah, a traditional and perennial favorite often performed during the month of December, as we are reminded of both the first and second comings of Jesus.

This seventh and last trumpet introduces the third woe, as God prepares to deliver more judgment on a world that defies the Lamb of God. God's judgments come to 1) a religious world that counterfeits the Lamb and 2) to a secular world that disregards the call to come to Christ and instead seeks to conquer through lust, pride, envy, and vanity.

In Revelation 12:1-5, we read:

> A great portent appeared in heaven: a woman clothed with the sun, with the moon under her feet, and on her head a crown of twelve stars. She was pregnant and was crying out in birth pangs, in the agony of giving birth. Then another portent appeared in heaven: a great red dragon, with seven heads and ten horns, and seven diadems on his heads. His tail swept down a third of the stars of heaven and threw them to the earth. Then the dragon stood before the woman who was about to bear a child, so that he might devour her child as soon as it was born. And she gave birth to a son, a male child, who is to rule all the nations with a rod of iron. But her child was snatched away and taken to God and his throne.

This portent is a historical overview. It doesn't necessarily happen at any one specific point in time; rather, it is a portrait that Jesus is painting for us, a summary of world history of the time between His first and second comings. Chapter twelve sets the theme for the chapters that follow—the recurring theme of history for the last 2,000 years and Satan's efforts to destroy the Messiah and the church.

Conflict is the theme of this chapter, as well as of chapter thirteen. In chapter twelve we read of the conflict between the woman and the dragon, then of the conflict between Michael, an angel of God, and the dragon, and then finally of the conflict between the woman's children and the dragon. In chapter thirteen, Jesus reveals visions of the conflict between the woman's children and two beasts, one that comes out of the sea and the other that comes out of the earth.

Who is the woman of chapter twelve? The woman is the eternal home and dwelling place of Jesus Christ.[1] The woman is eternity, the eternity of God's heaven that gives birth to a male child, who in turn will rule all nations. The Book of Galatians uses similar language when speaking of Jerusalem above, contrasting it with the literal city of Jerusalem. Jerusalem above, according to Galatians 4:26, is our mother.

The breathtaking new Jerusalem is painstakingly and majestically illustrated in Revelation chapter twenty-one. The Book of Revelation itself contrasts the new Jerusalem, the origin and the goal of all true believers, with the earthly city of Babylon, which is another woman. The woman of Babylon, according to chapter 17:5 is "the mother of whores" and, according to chapter 17:18, "is the great city that rules over the kings of the earth."

Jesus is revealing another comparison between good and evil, a familiar literary device throughout the Bible and throughout this Book of Revelation. The woman here in chapter twelve is not any physical woman, not the virgin Mary, not Eve, and not the nation of Israel. This woman stands for eternity, for heaven, holiness, and perfection. Jesus came out of eternity to become one of us. He is the male child spoken of in verse five. Jesus was born of a physical woman, the virgin Mary, but as God in the flesh His eternal divine home was and is heaven.

The enormous red dragon mentioned in verse three is clearly identified as "that ancient serpent, who is called the Devil and Satan, the deceiver of the whole world" (v. 9).

The dragon persecutes the woman, who not only symbolizes heaven but also is a symbol of heaven on earth, in the sense that the body of Christ is composed of earthbound Christians who accept, believe in, and trust in Jesus Christ. The woman can also stand for individual Christians within the universal body of Christ; for Jesus lives His risen life within us, giving us eternal life. Even though Christians live physical lives in which we suffer pain and tribulation, the spiritual reality is that we are saved. We are sealed and healed. We are assured of eternal salvation. The spiritual reality is that we Christians already inhabit eternity even while we live in this body of flesh. As Paul says in Ephesians 2:4-6, "But God, who is rich in mercy, out of the great love with which he loved us even when we were dead through our trespasses, made us alive together with Christ—by grace you have been saved—and raised us up with him and seated us with him in the heavenly places in Christ Jesus."

The woman, in this case representing Christians who are alive in Christ even though they still live in bodies of flesh in an imperfect world, flees to the desert after the male child is snatched up to God and His throne. After His atoning work on the cross, the Lamb of God bodily ascends to heaven, and the woman is then in conflict with the dragon and all who represent him. The woman is taken care of by God for 1,260 days, probably not a literal period of time either of years, months, or days that some attempt to fit into the past or the future, but a term which is used to convey the idea that there is a limited period of human history that the body of Christ on earth will be subject to the dragon's anger.

When the woman escapes from the dragon, the dragon takes his angels and wages a war in heaven against the angel Michael. The dragon is, of course, defeated and thrown back to earth. Jesus is assuring us that the woman, authentic Christians in the body of Christ, always spiritually escapes from the dragon, even though the dragon may take the physical lives of individual Christians. Jesus tells us in Matthew 10:28, "Do not fear those who kill the body but cannot kill the soul." Neither the dragon nor any of his earthly representatives can take our souls.

An angel announces, "Now have come the salvation and the power and the kingdom of our God and the authority of his Messiah, for the accuser of our comrades has been thrown down, who accuses them day and night before our God. But they have conquered him by the blood of the Lamb and by the word of their testimony, for they did not cling to life even in the face of death" (vv. 10-11).

G.B. Caird concludes that a literal, concrete interpretation of the war in heaven in which Michael and his angels are victorious over the dragon and his angels overlooks a Christ-centered interpretation that finds cosmic significance in the cross.[2]

The dragon, the serpent in the Garden in the beginning, is deceptive and seductive. He accuses the brethren, who are part of the woman, the body of Christ. He accuses Christians by trying to convince them that God is mad at them, God is not pleased with them, and Jesus is not enough to secure their salvation. The dragon accuses Christians and attempts to enslave them with superstition, fear, and ritual. The dragon attempts to turn humans away from God's grace by turning them into judgmental clones of himself—and he often does this in God's name, within four walls where God is ostensibly worshiped.

The dragon attempts to turn the grace of God into performance-based religion, which will turn humans away from the one who enables them to conquer manipulative religious devices. The dragon uses false prophets who come in Jesus' name, in sheep's clothing, to manipulate, mislead, and deceive. Jesus tells us about these false prophets who are inwardly "ferocious wolves" (Ma 7:15). Satan is the master deceiver who is able to enslave people, even in the name of God. In verse 11 Jesus tells us that those who are not persuaded by the dragon overcome the dragon "by the blood of the Lamb."

The dragon is the ongoing adversary of the people of God; and, while we are given victory over him, we would be wise to remember that, as Peter tells us in 1 Peter 5:8, "Like a roaring lion your adversary the devil prowls around, looking for someone to devour." James tells us to submit to God, and resist the devil (Ja 4:7).

Peter Hiett quotes J.R.R. Tolkien, perhaps best known as the author of the book trilogy *Lord of the Rings*, who often wrote with Christian metaphor, symbolism, and significance in mind. In his book *The Hobbit,* he speaks of dragons and advises, "It does not do to leave a live dragon out of your calculations, if you live near him."[3] Satan is very much a presence in our lives; he is not only active in our neighborhood, but also sometimes he sneaks into in our homes, schools, courts and, yes, even some churches.

The good news of the gospel of Jesus Christ, the good news proclaimed by the Book of Revelation, is that, although Satan—the dragon, the serpent—is still active on earth, he is already defeated. Though many heretical philosophical ideas and human religious notions and traditions are being taught because of Satan's influence, the Lamb of God has already defeated all ideas that are Antichrist.

Names and Claims—The Beasts That Emerge From the Sea and Earth

[1] And I saw a beast rising out of the sea, having ten horns and seven heads; and on its horns were ten diadems, and on its heads were blasphemous names. [2] And the beast that I saw was like a leopard, its feet were like a bear's, and its mouth was like a lion's mouth. And the dragon gave it his power and his throne and great authority. [3] One of its heads seemed to have received a death-blow, but its mortal wound had been healed. In amazement the whole earth followed the beast. [4] They worshiped the dragon, for he had given his authority to the beast, and they worshiped the beast, saying, "Who is like the beast, and who can fight against it?"

[5] The beast was given a mouth uttering haughty and blasphemous words, and it was allowed to exercise authority for forty-two months. [6] It opened its mouth to utter blasphemies against God, blaspheming his name and his dwelling, that is, those who dwell in heaven. [7] Also, it was allowed to make war on the saints and to conquer them. It was given authority over every tribe and people and language and nation, [8] and all the inhabitants of the earth will worship it, everyone whose name has

not been written from the foundation of the world in the book of life of the Lamb that was slaughtered.

⁹ Let anyone who has an ear listen:

¹⁰ If you are to be taken captive,

into captivity you go;

if you kill with the sword,

with the sword you must be killed.

Here is a call for the endurance and faith of the saints.

¹¹ Then I saw another beast that rose out of the earth; it had two horns like a lamb and it spoke like a dragon. ¹² It exercises all the authority of the first beast on its behalf, and it makes the earth and its inhabitants worship the first beast, whose mortal wound had been healed. ¹³ It performs great signs, even making fire come down from heaven to earth in the sight of all; ¹⁴ and by the signs that it is allowed to perform on behalf of the beast, it deceives the inhabitants of earth, telling them to make an image for the beast that had been wounded by the sword and yet lived; ¹⁵ and it was allowed to give breath to the image of the beast, so that the image of the beast could even speak and cause those who would not worship the image of the beast to be killed. ¹⁶ Also it causes all, both small and great, both rich and poor, both free and slave, to be marked on the right hand or the forehead, ¹⁷ so that no one can buy or sell who does not have the mark, that is, the name of the beast or the number of its name. ¹⁸ This calls for wisdom: let anyone with understanding calculate the number of the beast, for it is the number of a person. Its number is six hundred sixty-six.

Revelation 13:1-18

The conflict continues between the dragon and the children of the woman. The beast that comes out of the sea represents political authorities, religious powers, and civil governments that have opposed authentic Christianity through the ages.[4] Multiple heads and crowns represent not just one government, but many over time. The blasphemous names on each crown represent government and religion that presumptuously claim to directly speak for God, to be His representative, and to bear His authority. Protestants often quickly point to Catholics as the prime example of this.

But lest anyone settle into smug Protestant self-righteousness, there are profane religious titles in the Protestant world: titles and names that ascribe divine authority to religious leaders. Some speak of themselves as being "anointed," while others outrageously assert that they receive direct revelation from God far beyond what He has given lesser mortals like you and me in Holy Scripture.

The monster of Revelation is not confined to any one legal entity, religious incorporation, or religious-political alliance. The original readers of Revelation almost certainly did not view the beast of Revelation as some future power. They either interpreted such a passage as speaking specifically of the power of Rome at that time or of the scourge of religious oppression that would continue throughout history.

To Christians living in the first century, pretentious and pompous religious titles were spiritually obscene: signs of the power of the Roman Empire that explained how Satan used political and religious authority to oppose the church.

As with other symbols in the Book of Revelation, this beast had meaning for the original audience and readership of Revelation.[5] To early Christians, the seven heads and ten horns of the monster from the sea may well have symbolized the emperors of Rome after Augustus, seven significant emperors but ten in all. Roman emperors demanded worship as gods. The fatal wound that had been healed may have been understood to be the death of Nero in A.D. 68, which was almost three decades before this book was written. Nero's death was followed by the restoration of order to the empire under Vespasian.

This beast is "uttering haughty and blasphemous words" against God (vv. 5-6). He is worshiped by "all inhabitants of the earth" (v. 8). Human beings respond to heroes, larger than life fellow humans who promise the masses the proverbial pot of gold at the end of the rainbow in return for their worship. "Support me" goes the cry, "and I will give you more, and life will be better for you than it was before."

Revelation reveals that the real power behind the throne of the emperor worship of Rome and, for that matter all other false religious systems, is the devil himself (Re 12:8-9). The sea monster, the beast from the sea, has seven heads and ten horns (v.1), just like the dragon of Revelation 12:3, who deceives the entire world.

But not all inhabitants of the earth fall for the blasphemy and lying words of the beast, only those whose names are not written in the book of life. This book belongs to the Lamb that was slain from the "foundation of the world" (v. 8). This book of life contains the names of those who accept the Lamb as their Savior, their Lord, and their Master, in spite of the religious Antichrist heroes that entice and attempt to seduce them.

The Second Beast From the Earth—666!

In verse 11, a second beast arises, who forces the world's inhabitants to worship the first beast. This beast comes from the earth. This beast has two horns like a lamb, an obvious reference to counterfeits of authentic Christianity that are based upon the one and only unique Lamb of God (v. 8). Again, as we seek to identify one or both of these beasts, we recall that they may not appear as evil and sinister at all. In the Sermon on the Mount Jesus said, "Beware of false prophets who come to you in sheep's clothing" (Ma 7:15).

These two beasts, one from the sea and one from the land, work as a team to do the work of the dragon on this earth. The first beast may be symbolic of great military-political-economic powers, with the second

beast representing religious leadership, providing rituals and religious ide-
ologies that deceive the inhabitants of the world.[6] This co-mingling of the
powers of religious influence with civil authority is one of Revelation's
themes, explaining how the dragon deceives the entire world (12:9).

For the past few decades in the United States, a growing number of
Christians have been flexing their political muscles. They often complain
that national laws are conspiring against all Christians, and they cite the
constitutional guarantee that religion will be protected from the state.
There is no doubt that civil governments can become a beast, much like
that described here in chapter thirteen. But we American Christians should
also realize and appreciate that the United States constitution also protects
the state from religion. Religion itself can become a monster; it can camou-
flage itself in Christian attire and divert attention from its oppressive
abuses by redirecting our attention to political beasts.

Speculation from some in Christendom has been focused on beasts
who are outside of their own religious traditions and national origins.
Limiting potential beasts to "outsiders" leaves an obvious blind spot. What
about the subversive beast within?

In verse 17 we come to the mysterious mark of the beast. This mark is
described as the name of the beast or the number of his name, calculated
as 666. Some interpret 666 as the numerical value of the letters of the Greek
or Hebrew alphabet that spell the name of a literal person who is the beast.
Some scholars believe 666 represented Nero, who had become an enemy
of Christians, and therefore stood for the persecuting Roman government.
However, like much of the imagery in Revelation, translating Jesus' words
literally is a fool's errand, an exercise that attempts to force wooden literalism into symbolic language.

Throughout the past 2,000 years the number 666 has given rise to religious fanaticism and phobias that fuel efforts to decipher and decode it.
Many of these attempts have been subjective and arbitrary concoctions
using any methodology possible to twist 666 into becoming the enemy of

that particular brand of religion. Spurred on by the prospect of coming up with an incredible "find," many spend years using elaborate codes applied to a variety of languages in an attempt to come up with some human being, past, present, or future, whose name equates to 666.

Not long ago, U.S. Highway 666 was renamed because some citizens felt that the number itself was unlucky, a bad omen, or perhaps even satanic. Fascination with 666 and other symbolic language in the Book of Revelation provides a ready market for those who willingly tap into macabre interest in apocalyptic disasters.

In order to understand any number, color, or symbol in Revelation we must remember that Revelation is written in an apocalyptic style, a style that relies heavily on symbolism. Attempts to assign specific meaning or identity to the number 666 fail primarily because they do not interpret it within the linguistic style God inspired. Revelation is simply saying that 666 is the number of the beast's name.

The number six is often used, throughout the Bible, to describe human sin and imperfection compared to the holiness and perfection of God. Six Hundred Sixty-Six is triple imperfection and sin, a reference to the complete moral failure and bankruptcy of humans to solve their own problems via their governments and religions. While Nero epitomized evil when Jesus originally gave the message to John, even that specific identification is not the primary meaning of this number.[7]

From our vantage point in the twenty-first century we can see many monsters from the sea and the earth exhibited in past religious systems and governments. We can see that some religious and political beasts oppose Christianity even now, such as those in Muslim and communist countries where Christians are imprisoned and tortured. Christians represent a threat to despotic power because our primary citizenship is in heaven (Ph 3:20). There is no doubt that fascism, Islam and communism have been three major beasts of the twentieth and now twenty-first centuries that have opposed all that Christians hold sacred. Beast-driven persecution also arises in our secular western societies, where Christian values and beliefs stand in sharp opposition to immoral laws and policies and the prevailing relativistic and materialistic culture.

Unfortunately, the dispensational methodology of many prophecy teachers drives them to place these beasts at a specific place and time, usually somewhere in the not-too-distant future from the vantage point of the preacher, teacher, or author. Those who are cautious play safe by assigning a date after their own lifetimes to the specific identities of their predicted beasts. Such narrow interpretations miss one of Revelation's themes: even though Satan has and will continue to oppose the people of God through whatever means he has at his disposal, he has already failed, and Jesus has already triumphed.

The mark of the beast (vv. 16-17) is the religious alternative of being sealed by the Lamb of God. Identifying a literal mark of the beast (vv. 16-17) is another endless source of bizarre predictions. Literal interpretations include a tattoo or brand of some kind, perhaps using a national identification number, such as Social Security in the United States. Some predictions are blatantly self-serving, teaching that the mark of the beast is a practice to which members of that particular group do not subscribe.

The mark of the beast simply means to be in accord and agreement with the cultural, political, and religious systems that are the enemies of God. Religious pride is certainly part of the religious mark of the beast when we mark others as being spiritually defective or inferior because they fail to adhere to, or measure up to, our religious beliefs and performance standards.

The End Result of *Bad News Religion*

[1] Then I looked, and there was the Lamb, standing on Mount Zion! And with him were one hundred forty-four thousand who had his name and his Father's name written on their foreheads. [2] And I heard a voice from heaven like the sound of many waters and like the sound of loud thunder; the voice I

heard was like the sound of harpists playing on their harps, [3] and they sing a new song before the throne and before the four living creatures and before the elders. No one could learn that song except the one hundred forty-four thousand who have been redeemed from the earth. [4] It is these who have not defiled themselves with women, for they are virgins; these follow the Lamb wherever he goes. They have been redeemed from humankind as first fruits for God and the Lamb, [5] and in their mouth no lie was found; they are blameless.

[6] Then I saw another angel flying in mid-heaven, with an eternal gospel to proclaim to those who live on the earth—to every nation and tribe and language and people. [7] He said in a loud voice, "Fear God and give him glory, for the hour of his judgment has come; and worship him who made heaven and earth, the sea and the springs of water." [8] Then another angel, a second, followed, saying, "Fallen, fallen is Babylon the great! She has made all nations drink of the wine of the wrath of her fornication."

[9] Then another angel, a third, followed them, crying with a loud voice, "Those who worship the beast and its image, and receive a mark on their foreheads or on their hands, [10] they will also drink the wine of God's wrath, poured unmixed into the cup of his anger, and they will be tormented with fire and sulfur in the presence of the holy angels and in the presence of the Lamb. [11] And the smoke of their torment goes up forever and ever. There is no rest day or night for those who worship the beast and its image and for anyone who receives the mark of its name."

[12] Here is a call for the endurance of the saints, those who keep the commandments of God and hold fast to the faith of Jesus.

[13] And I heard a voice from heaven saying, "Write this: Blessed are the dead who from now on die in the Lord." "Yes,"

says the Spirit, "they will rest from their labors, for their deeds follow them."

[14] Then I looked, and there was a white cloud, and seated on the cloud was one like the Son of Man, with a golden crown on his head, and a sharp sickle in his hand! [15] Another angel came out of the temple, calling with a loud voice to the one who sat on the cloud, "Use your sickle and reap, for the hour to reap has come, because the harvest of the earth is fully ripe." [16] So the one who sat on the cloud swung his sickle over the earth, and the earth was reaped.

[17] Then another angel came out of the temple in heaven, and he too had a sharp sickle. [28] Then another angel came out from the altar, the angel who has authority over fire, and he called with a loud voice to him who had the sharp sickle, "Use your sharp sickle and gather the clusters of the vine of the earth, for its grapes are ripe." [19] So the angel swung his sickle over the earth and gathered the vintage of the earth, and he threw it into the great wine press of the wrath of God. [20] And the wine press was trodden outside the city, and blood flowed from the wine press, as high as a horse's bridle, for a distance of about two hundred miles.

Revelation 14:1-20

Chapter fourteen answers two questions: 1) what happens to those who die for refusing to receive the mark of the beast?, and 2) what happens to the beast and his followers?

In the first verse, we see the 144,000 who were sealed in chapter seven, standing victoriously on Mount Zion. This is not the geographical Mount Zion in Jerusalem, but the spiritual Zion, the same Mount Zion mentioned in Hebrews 12:22: "the city of the living God, the heavenly Jerusalem" and "the Jerusalem above" mentioned in Galatians 4:26.

These 144,000 are those "who have not defiled themselves with women, for they are virgins" (v.4) meaning that they are redeemed men and women who are not corrupted by the spiritual adulteries of Babylon the Great. Here is an obvious example where forcing a literal interpretation on symbolic language would be silly; implications of such a view would lead to the conclusion that only males who never had sexual relations with a woman may stand with the Lamb on Mount Zion! This group of 144,000 represents the universal body of believers: Christians who are visible and known to us, as well as those who are invisible, unknown to us but known by God.[8] They have the name of the Lamb and of God the Father written on their foreheads, in contrast to those who have the mark of the beast written on them.[9] In the first century, such a brand or mark was a brand of ownership, indicating a person or entity to whom a slave belonged. In the Book of Revelation, all people are either servants of Satan or servants of Christ. There are no "free agents." You are on one team or the other.

In verses six and seven, an angel issues a final warning, a final offer of the gospel to all of the earth. This is the only place in Revelation where the word *gospel* is used, and it is employed in the middle of a desperate time of conflict and battle. The angel proclaims the fear of God, which, in the context of this passage and of the entire Book of Revelation is to fear the consequences of rejecting God's grace, which alone can save us.

In verse eight, a second angel proclaims that Babylon, the world's anti-God and Antichrist system of materialism and idolatry, has fallen. And in verse nine, a third angel warns that those who receive the mark of the beast will receive the punishment of the beast as well. Those who have the mark of the beast are bewitched by oppressive religion and, under its spell, believe that those who accomplish, achieve, and produce according to a religious meritocracy will earn their entrance into God's kingdom of heaven. Such people are captives of the beast, branded by the beast with its mark.

Jesus then reveals God's judgment upon all who counterfeit authentic Christianity—all who enslave others through political or religious ideology, all who lead people away from the one true God. Here is God's judgment upon evil, as depicted by three metaphors: first, in verse 10, wine in the cup of God's wrath; second, in verses 14-16, the earth being harvested as grain; and third, in verses 17-20, the earth being harvested like a vineyard (see Is 63:1-6). Verse 20 offers the gruesome image of a 200-mile-long river of the spilled blood of the enemies of God.

For first-century Christians and all Christians who have shared in the sufferings of Jesus, the message is clear: God is absolutely and dogmatically against those who deceive, seduce, and twist the truth into a lie. Those who blaspheme God's name will eventually face the consequences. This judgment is given explicitly without reservation or qualification. God's judgment is not couched as fear religion, not as a threat, nor as a motivation for Christians to ensure they walk the straight and narrow, nor as a reason for Christians to be assured that the bad guys will get theirs. Judgment belongs to God, and He will reward those who traffic in human misery and heartache, both physically and spiritually. God's judgment is certain.

Preparing to Pour the Plagues

¹Then I saw another portent in heaven, great and amazing: seven angels with seven plagues, which are the last, for with them the wrath of God is ended.

²And I saw what appeared to be a sea of glass mixed with fire, and those who had conquered the beast and its image and the number of its name, standing beside the sea of glass with harps of God in their hands. ³And they sing the song of Moses, the servant of God, and the song of the Lamb:

"Great and amazing are your deeds,

Lord God the Almighty!

Just and true are your ways,

King of the nations!

⁴Lord, who will not fear

and glorify your name?

For you alone are holy.

All nations will come

and worship before you,

for your judgments have been revealed."

⁵ After this I looked, and the temple of the tent of witness in heaven was opened, ⁶ and out of the temple came the seven angels with the seven plagues, robed in pure bright linen, with golden sashes across their chests. ⁷ Then one of the four living creatures gave the seven angels seven golden bowls full of the wrath of God, who lives forever and ever; ⁸ and the temple was filled with smoke from the glory of God and from his power, and no one could enter the temple until the seven plagues of the seven angels were ended.

Revelation 15:1-8

The scene again returns to the victorious saints in heaven, who watch as seven angels receive seven golden bowls filled with the wrath of God ready to be poured on the earth. Some scholars believe these plagues are the "third woe" announced in Revelation 11:14. Meanwhile, the saints sing the Song of Moses from Exodus 15, which celebrates the victory of God over the Egyptians at the Red Sea. Some of these plagues are reminiscent of the plagues of Egypt, when the people of God of the Old Testament were enslaved by the military power of Egypt.

This chapter draws a parallel between the continuing crisis that faces the body of Christ and the historical crisis that faced the people of God in Egypt. Deliverance from Egypt, a nation controlled by pagan polytheism, given over to worship of the created rather than the creator (Ro 1:21-25), was a hallmark of the history of the people of God in the Old Testament. Their salvation history was rooted in the story of divine rescue from the slavery and bondage of Egypt, symbolic of all who opposed the one true

God. The song of Moses is sung along with the song of the Lamb, the Savior who redeems under the new covenant in His blood.

These seven angels with seven plagues contained in seven bowls are ready to pour out God's wrath upon the earth, and we will take a closer look at these seven plagues in seven bowls in our next chapter.

We are again reminded of the central subject, object, and divine person of the Revelation. This book is all about Jesus Christ. Revelation is an indictment of religious tyranny and all perversions of the grace of God that lead people away from the Lamb of God and His cross. The beast of Revelation is not limited to one month, one generation, or one lifetime. The beast of Revelation is "the Devil and Satan, the deceiver of the whole world" (12:9). The good news is that the battle belongs to the Lord, not the beast of the month. May God fill you with the riches of His grace as we continue to consider this great message and the even greater Messenger and Messiah.

CHAPTER TEN

Babylon and Its Religions Go to Hell

When you begin reading a book, you don't pick it up and start reading page 78, do you? You know that there is no way you will be able to make sense of the plot, the story thread, the theme, or the main characters if you just plunge into the story without understanding the background. If you go to a movie, you try to arrive before it starts. You don't want to miss anything you will need to understand as the story unfolds.

We all like to see movies from the very beginning, and we all know that it's hopeless trying to read a 600-page book in about 15 or 20 minutes by starting to read on page 575.

But when it comes to the Bible, the story seems different for us. Many seem to have no problem whatsoever opening the Bible to some portion of a book, in this case the Book of Revelation, reading a portion of one verse, and then coming to some over arching, all encompassing theological conclusion.

Obviously, there is a problem with reading the Bible in this manner. Your comprehension and understanding of exactly what is going on is going to suffer, and the possibility that you will fall for some bogus interpretation of what the Bible is saying will increase dramatically if you just flip to a passage and read it or allow someone else to flip to a passage and tell you what you should believe about it. With the Book of Revelation, it is extremely important to initially gain and then maintain a contextual understanding of the theme of the book, the background, the linguistic style in which it was inspired and written; and the original audience must be taken into account and, finally, the immediate context of the passage you are reading must be considered.

We have emphasized that Revelation is written in an apocalyptic style or genre. We must read it within those boundaries. Consider your daily newspaper. When you read the front page, you assume that you are reading hard news, reporting of actual events. Hard, factual news on the front page is radically different from opinion pieces about the same events printed on the editorial page. And it goes without saying, as you read the news on the front page, you realize that you are not reading the comics, the obituaries, or the classified ads.

When you read each portion of the newspaper you, of course, hope you are reading true and factual information; but you realize truth can be communicated in a variety of literary styles and contexts. In order to understand the intent of different styles of writing within the same newspaper, without thinking, you automatically switch literary gears. The athletic prowess and achievements of the sports page, the biting analysis of the editorial page, and the cryptic abbreviations of the classified ads all have their place, and are rightly understood within their context and their style of writing. If you're anything like me, sometimes you find the real truth about the news in the comics and through the cartoons on the editorial pages.

We must do the same switching of gears as we read the Bible; for Genesis is not Matthew, Proverbs is not Ezekiel, and Deuteronomy is not Galatians. And Revelation is none of these. As we continue our survey of this blockbuster epic of Revelation, let's stop to get our bearings, and repeat some of the themes we have discussed in previous chapters.

The Good Guys and the Bad Guys

Who is the human author of this book? The apostle John. But he didn't write the book as much as he reported about the visions and insights he was given by the divine Author. Who is the divine Author? Jesus Christ. What is the theme of the book? Jesus Christ. Who is the main character of the book? The Lamb of God, King of kings, Lord of lords, our Savior, Jesus Christ. This book is the revelation of Jesus Christ about Jesus Christ.

How about the bad guys, the villains? Who are they? The dragon (Satan), the beast, Babylon, the fallen woman, and the harlot. What was the original occasion of this book and the original audience? Christians for whom this book was originally intended were under intense persecution; some were being tortured and martyred because of their faith in Christ. They were being persecuted by the Roman Empire—a beast power that combined the overwhelming strength of religious ritual and regulation, governmental laws, and the brute force of the military.

The original audience provides an initial touchstone for the many centuries of Christians who have turned to this book for hope and encouragement, for focus and faith, for a Christ-centered understanding of their lives, even in the middle of pain and difficulties.

Sadly, there have been and are many who misrepresent and distort this message so filled with symbolism and poetry. Many over-literalize the numbers, colors, dimensions, symbols, and metaphors and, unfortunately, in some cases twist and distort the message, in the process maybe even missing the Messenger who revealed it. The twisting and manipulation, not to mention sensationalizing of the Book of Revelation, has served the goals of religion. Revelation itself tells us that counterfeit Christianity is religious identity theft on a grand scale, perpetuated by the spiritual personification of evil, "the Devil and Satan, the deceiver of the whole world (12:9).

With that thought in mind, we turn our attention to chapter sixteen, but as we do so, let's also recall a summary of chapter fifteen. The scene is a victory celebration in heaven, with the celebrants being those who yield their lives to the Lamb of God through whose earthly lives Jesus Christ continuously conquers the beast and his image. They sing praises to God, singing a variation of the song of Moses, who also gave thanks to God for delivering him and his people from religious and political oppression and slavery.

During the celebration, seven angels with seven plagues, contained in seven bowls, prepare to pour out these plagues, plagues that are not unlike the plagues which God gave the Pharaoh of Egypt and his people, because they refused to "let my people go." Behind every oppressive pharaoh was an abusive and controlling legalistic religion, and behind those who counterfeit Christianity is the master manipulator, the "deceiver of the whole world" (12:9).

The Location of a Future Mega-Battle and Earthquake?

[1] Then I heard a loud voice from the temple telling the seven angels, "Go and pour out on the earth the seven bowls of the wrath of God."

[2] So the first angel went and poured his bowl on the earth, and a foul and painful sore came on those who had the mark of the beast and who worshiped its image.

[3] The second angel poured his bowl into the sea, and it became like the blood of a corpse, and every living thing in the sea died.

[4] The third angel poured his bowl into the rivers and the springs of water, and they became blood. [5] And I heard the angel of the waters say,

"You are just, O Holy One, who are and were,
for you have judged these things;
[6] because they shed the blood of saints and prophets,
you have given them blood to drink.
It is what they deserve!"
[7] And I heard the altar respond,
"Yes, O Lord God, the Almighty,

your judgments are true and just!"

⁸The fourth angel poured his bowl on the sun, and it was allowed to scorch people with fire; ⁹ they were scorched by the fierce heat, but they cursed the name of God, who had authority over these plagues, and they did not repent and give him glory.

¹⁰The fifth angel poured his bowl on the throne of the beast, and its kingdom was plunged into darkness; people gnawed their tongues in agony, ¹¹ and cursed the God of heaven because of their pains and sores, and they did not repent of their deeds.

¹² The sixth angel poured his bowl on the great river Euphrates, and its water was dried up in order to prepare the way for the kings from the east. ¹³ And I saw three foul spirits like frogs coming from the mouth of the dragon, from the mouth of the beast, and from the mouth of the false prophet. ¹⁴ These are demonic spirits, performing signs, who go abroad to the kings of the whole world, to assemble them for battle on the great day of God the Almighty. ¹⁵ ("See, I am coming like a thief! Blessed is the one who stays awake and is clothed, not going about naked and exposed to shame.") ¹⁶And they assembled them at the place that in Hebrew is called Harmagedon.

¹⁷The seventh angel poured his bowl into the air, and a loud voice came out of the temple, from the throne, saying, "It is done!" ¹⁸ And there came flashes of lightning, rumblings, peals of thunder, and a violent earthquake, such as had not occurred since people were upon the earth, so violent was that earthquake. ¹⁹The great city was split into three parts, and the cities of the nations fell. God remembered great Babylon and gave her the wine-cup of

the fury of his wrath. [20] And every island fled away, and no mountains were to be found; [21] and huge hailstones, each weighing about a hundred pounds, dropped from heaven on people, until they cursed God for the plague of the hail, so fearful was that plague.

Revelation 16:1-21

The angels pour out their bowls on the earth. In rapid succession those who follow the beast are stricken with boils, the sea turns to blood, the rivers and springs turn to blood, the sun becomes intensely hot, and darkness covers the kingdom of the beast. The Euphrates river is dried up, preparing the way for the evil kings of the east to come and battle the army of God at Armageddon (Harmagedon in the NRSV translation).

While these judgments are almost certainly not a blueprint-like description of coming judgments but rather graphic, metaphorical illustrations of the sure judgment of God, many dispensationalists offer incredibly minute, yet-to-come details of literal fulfillments.

Today the actual site of Megiddo (Harmagedon; see v. 16) in Israel is an obligatory stop for busloads of North American Christian tourists, with many who visit this site believing it to be the actual spot where this final climactic battle of Armageddon will take place. But is Jesus Christ revealing the exact physical location of some future physical battle, or is He using "Megiddo" as a symbol of the battle between the Dragon, Satan, and the Lamb of God?

The Old Testament records many battles fought on a plain close to the mountain and city of Megiddo. It's possible this reference to Harmagedon is a symbol for a decisive conflict, either a specific one or any battle in which the Lamb of God emerges victorious. Perhaps a titanic, final spiritual battle will include a physical gathering of armies of nations, but we should be careful not to limit the message and revelation of Jesus to only one such event.

Almost 150 years before the Book of Revelation was written, Julius Caesar was the Roman governor of Gaul, supported by a large and seasoned army. No Roman commander was allowed to take soldiers outside of his province without the permission of the Roman Senate. Julius Caesar decided to march south to occupy Rome.

The Rubicon River separated Gaul from ancient Italy. When Julius Caesar marched his armies across the Rubicon, he was declaring war on Rome, and there was no turning back. Caesar's act was irreversible, resulting in a bloody civil war that left Julius Caesar as the ruler of the Roman world. "Crossing the Rubicon" has come to mean the act of making an irrevocable decision. The term has far more meaning than the act of crossing a literal river at a specific point in time.

The site of Megiddo is better known as Armageddon and is also translated as Harmagedon. As a result of dispensational futurism and its interpretation of Revelation, many see Armageddon as a specific battle that will be fought in a specific place in the future. But the term Armageddon is more accurately employed to speak of any decisive confrontation, much the way "Crossing the Rubicon" is used.

Finally, when the seventh angel pours out his bowl, frightening thunder and lightening accompanies an earthquake described in verse 18 as "a violent earthquake, such as had not occurred since people were on the earth."

Is this passage predicting a future, literal earthquake that will dwarf all previous earthquakes? If so, has that earthquake already happened? And if it has, could another one happen in the future? If this is a future earthquake, one that has not yet happened, then where will it be? Revelation says this earthquake will split the city of Babylon into three parts. Are the earthquake and the city intended to be understood literally? Or is only the earthquake literal, but not the specific location of the city?

The literal city of Babylon is in Iraq, and by no means fits the descriptions of the political, religious, and commercial center given in the Book of Revelation. While Iraq has indeed been one of many countries suffering from religious oppression, Babylon today is not even a primary commercial center in Iraq.

Babylon was once a mighty city-empire, but that was well over 2,500 years ago, centuries before the Book of Revelation was written. So does that mean, as some propose, the earthquake mentioned in Revelation 16 is literal but the name of the city is symbolic of a literal, modern city of another name that our generation must select because it fits the description given here? And by what authority or methodology would we pick and choose, from the same text and the same description, an event to be understood literally while not interpreting its geographical reference point in the same manner? And how do we understand the other earthquakes mentioned in Revelation (6:12; 8:5; and 11:13)?

Perhaps the actual city of Babylon in Iraq will eventually become exactly what the Book of Revelation describes, and perhaps its rise from oblivion will be a sign that a future generation is finally living in the end times. If that is the case, it will almost certainly take a few decades, at the very least, for the current Babylon to become what Revelation describes.

Here's the point. The conclusion that many people arrive at—this is a literal earthquake upon a literal city of Babylon—is not usually based upon careful study of the Book of Revelation.[1] Such a conclusion is arrived at and accepted (about this passage as well as many others in the Bible for that matter) because some person they believe to be a good Bible teacher, or whom they regard as a prophet or bishop, or someone they have accepted as specially "anointed" tells them what to believe. Many of us allow and trust someone to tell us what the Bible says because we believe they have been given extra insight by God, as some people say, "in these end times."

We can, of course, allow a religious authority to dictate our beliefs to us. But we must be careful about placing our trust in any human interpretation, no matter how much we may trust a pastor or religious authority (1 Jo 4:1). What about the someone who revealed the Revelation, who alone is worthy of our trust? What does He say?

If you blindly accept what someone tells you the Bible means, you are in danger of allowing someone to turn God's grace into a mindless religious exercise. Shallow, empty, bogus, and just plain wrong interpretations of the Bible and of this Book of Revelation place us in danger of joining forces with the wrong side. Giving unquestioned allegiance to legalistic religion may cause us to unwittingly become a part of the religious Babylon that opposes the Lamb of God.

Authentic Christianity does not oppose reason, logic, and thought. Counterfeit Christianity, in order to protect itself, encourages its followers to check their brains at the door of the church. Surrendering our God-given ability and gift to listen to the message of Revelation to some religious authority may lead us to the pits and swamps of Babylon the Great.

A Christ-centered understanding of Revelation will lead us to the big picture, and if some of the revelation has been, is being, or will be literally fulfilled, that would be God's decision. If we focus primarily on the physical and literal "fulfillments," experience and history shows it is possible to become enraptured by physical details, lost in predictive tunnel vision, and, in time, we can lose sight of the Lamb of God.[2]

So, again, we need to remember that Jesus is revealing this message using symbols and apocalyptic language.[3] If the earthquake is literal, one day we will know that. The focus of Revelation is not physical details but on the ongoing cosmic struggle of Satan and his religions against the grace of the Lamb of God.

Revelation says, when the seventh plague is poured out, Babylon is split into three parts, and collapses, along with the cities of all the nations. Here is the fall of the great false religious system that has opposed the Lamb of God since His human birth in Bethlehem. When Jesus was born, Herod the king, a secular authority, attempted to kill Him. The religious leaders saw the adult Jesus as a threat to the status quo and were ultimately instrumental in persuading the Roman military power to crucify Him. This power of religion and all of its legalisms continues to this day, by different names, with slightly different methods; but Revelation warns that a day of reckoning is coming for any system that opposes the Lamb of God.

Revelation says that the universal downfall of the system of Babylon is punctuated by a colossal earthquake and hailstorm. This is a description of the devastating punch God delivers to religion that controls humans with its edicts and dictates. We know that God will conquer religion; and that when bogus belief systems fall, the world is turned upside down. If a physical earthquake accompanies the earthquake-like demolition of religious Babylon, so be it. But we know that God does not need to use a physical earthquake to destroy spiritual Babylon. In spite of the destruction of Babylon, Revelation tells us that the inhabitants of earth who have refused to acknowledge the Lamb of God still remain unrepentant.

A Summary of the Messenger's Message

[1] Then one of the seven angels who had the seven bowls came and said to me, "Come, I will show you the judgment of the great whore who is seated on many waters, [2] with whom the kings of the earth have committed fornication, and with the wine of whose fornication the inhabitants of the earth have become drunk." [3] So he carried me away in the spirit into a wilderness, and I saw a woman sitting on a scarlet beast that was full of blasphemous names, and it had seven heads and ten horns. [4] The woman was clothed in purple and scarlet, and adorned with gold and jewels and pearls, holding in her hand a golden cup full of abominations and the impurities of her fornication; [5] and on her forehead was written a name, a mystery: "Babylon the great, mother of whores and of earth's abominations." [6] And I saw that the woman was drunk with the blood of the saints and the blood of the witnesses to Jesus.

When I saw her, I was greatly amazed. [7] But the angel said to me, "Why are you so amazed? I will tell you the mystery of the woman, and of the beast with seven heads and ten horns that carries her. [8] The beast that you saw was, and is not, and is about to ascend from the bottomless pit and go to destruction. And the inhabitants of the earth, whose names have not been written in the book of life from the foundation of the world, will be amazed when they see the beast, because it was and is not and is to come.

[9] "This calls for a mind that has wisdom: the seven heads are seven mountains on which the woman is seated; also, they are seven kings, [10] of whom five have fallen, one is living, and the other has not yet come; and when he comes, he must remain for only a little while. [11] As for the beast that was and is not, it is an eighth but it belongs to the seven, and it goes to destruction. [12] And the ten horns that you saw are ten kings who have not yet received a kingdom, but they are to receive authority as kings for one hour, together with the beast. [13] These are united in yielding their power and authority to the beast; [14] they will make war on the Lamb, and the Lamb will conquer them, for he is Lord of lords and King of kings, and those with him are called and chosen and faithful."

[15] And he said to me, "The waters that you saw, where the whore is seated, are peoples and multitudes and nations and languages. [16] And the ten horns that you saw, they and the beast will hate the whore; they will make her desolate and naked; they will devour her flesh and burn her up with fire. [17] For God has put it into their hearts to

carry out his purpose by agreeing to give their kingdom
to the beast, until the words of God will be fulfilled. [18]The
woman you saw is the great city that rules over the kings
of the earth."

Revelation 17:1-18

Chapters seventeen and eighteen are one unit, which viewed together, provide a devastating portrait of God's earthquake-like devastation on the religious-political system of Babylon. Our interpretation of chapter seventeen may actually control and govern our interpretation of the entire Book of Revelation because of the way in which it brings so many symbols and characters into sharp focus in one place, one chapter, and one setting.

In this chapter, God minces no words, comparing the enticements, temporary pleasures, and ultimate emptiness of legalistic religion to a whore. Protestants have historically found immense satisfaction and comfort in interpretations of this metaphor that brand the Roman Catholic Church as one and the same as the whore of Revelation.

I will always remember a good friend telling me about a class he took at Candler School of Theology at Emory University in Atlanta (a Protestant seminary). The class, *Introduction to the New Testament*, was taught by the Catholic scholar, Luke Timothy Johnson. One day Dr. Johnson began his lecture by saying, "Class, it is now time to discuss the Book of Revelation. That's right; we will be talking about such things as the Great Whore, which some Protestants believe to be a symbol for my church. We will also be talking about the Great False Prophet, who some Protestants believe to be symbolic of the man I call His Holiness. Clearly, among Christians there exists more than one way of interpreting the symbols of the Book of Revelation."

The whore of Revelation certainly seems to include many of the practices and teachings of the Roman Catholic Church. But to limit the whore of Revelation to only one incorporated church is a textbook example of human denial, folly, and vanity. To limit the whore of Revelation to only one religious institution is to seriously underestimate the book's scope and power. All churches and denominations have the capability of prostituting themselves by allowing the seductive powers of religious legalism to have their way with them. Babylon is a symbol of all opposition and resistance to God, regardless of the brand name, size, shape, or description. Babylon represents any and all political and religious power that wars against the Lamb of God, oppressing, seducing, deceiving, and enslaving its followers.

Ellul observes that this whoredom is not a sexual prostitution. This "sacred" religious prostitution is a sign of infidelity; and it includes power and money, key elements of prostitution.[4]

Many who profess the name of Christ can fall for the temptation of selling themselves for the price of self-sufficiency, pride, and vanity. We are not immune, corporately or individually, from being bewitched and ensnared by the great whore of Revelation, by the enticing promises of legalism that promise us eternity while enslaving us in spiritually degrading servitude. Hundreds of millions of Christians have been seduced by the great whore and smooth-talking pimps of religion and have lived lives of misery in spiritual gutters and ghettos. God calls legalistic religion what it is, a great whore. May we not find artificial comfort in deluding ourselves into thinking that one denomination or incorporated religious entity is the only group that has bewitched others. Such a view is pompous and arrogant.

Chapter seventeen begins by describing a whore riding the beast with seven heads and ten horns, first introduced in chapter thirteen. The fallen woman is "drunk with the blood of the saints" (v. 6).

As John is astonished and confused over what he is seeing, an angel comes to explain the vision to him. The angel explains that the seven heads of the beast represent seven hills or mountains and seven kings. The ten horns are ten lesser kings who rule with the beast. The ocean or water upon which the prostitute sits represents the nations of the world. The beast revolts against the whore, who represents a religious system that rules the whole world.

For Christians in the first century this city would have represented Rome. The beast would have represented the political power of Rome; its seven heads would have corresponded to the seven hills of Rome as well as to the succession of emperors during the first century. The ten horns may represent lesser kings ruling within the empire.

But is this initial interpretation and immediate application to the original audience all that God intended by using this graphic and alluring imagery? Or does some future similar system and alliance of church and state represent the primary meaning the Messenger of Revelation is revealing? There is no way to interpret all of the details in this chapter as historic fulfillments, at least with our present knowledge of history.

The best interpretative lens, therefore, by which we might view this critical chapter, would include historical fulfillment that we know about and future fulfillments we might imagine. But let us not stop there; for the whore and the beast are the archetypes of every evil system opposed to God throughout the ages, including specific applications of which we are unaware. The sin, deception, and abuse of whore and beast go far beyond human comprehension. Revelation is all about the Lamb of God; therefore our primary interpretation should be to view the whore and the beast as any and all efforts to diminish, devalue, and destroy Jesus Christ.[5]

The whore is the great religious system that has controlled the history of the world. She is the economy and the culture, and the rulers of the world hate her because she controls them; but they are in bed with her because they want what she provides.

Thus we see a bigger picture of the enemies of God, as religion and governments and military powers. Yes, but more than that, here is a religious kingdom and empire that exhibits incomparable economic power; religion exerting power over political kingdoms as a seductive woman can bewitch a more physically powerful man.[6] This human kingdom of religion sets itself against the kingdom of God. This is a description of the kingdom of human ingenuity, invention, prowess, skill, and effort versus the kingdom of God powered by His grace.

Written at the end of the first century, this is an overview of the next 2,000 years of human history and perhaps more (notwithstanding the predictions of the "end times" to come in our generation). It's also a summary of religious oppression before the birth of Christ, including the great pagan religions of Egypt and Babylon. Read your history books, and you will discover the intercourse in which politicians and religious leaders have engaged. History documents the intoxicating power that ideas and philosophies and isms have exercised over the church. Also, religious vision and philosophy have often conquered or controlled the secular power.

Verse 18 tells us that religious authority and power "rules over the kings of the earth." It may be communism, materialism, atheism, Islam, or Buddhism. It may even be a system that incorporates Christian terminology and symbols and counterfeits Christianity. Whatever its specific name may be, it is a legalistic religion that controls, enslaves, and conquers.

And once again we are assured and comforted about our ultimate victory; the battle belongs to the Lord. Verse 14 speaks of this powerful beast with ten horns that the woman rides making war with Jesus Christ, but as verse 14 says, "The Lamb will conquer them, for he is Lord of lords and King of kings, and those with him are called and chosen and faithful."

A Blow by Blow Description

[1] After this I saw another angel coming down from heaven, having great authority; and the earth was made bright with his splendor. [2] He called out with a

mighty voice,

"Fallen, fallen is Babylon the great!

It has become a dwelling place of demons,

a haunt of every foul spirit,

a haunt of every foul bird,

a haunt of every foul and hateful beast.

[3] For all the nations have drunk

of the wine of the wrath of her fornication,

and the kings of the earth have committed forni-

cation with her,

and the merchants of the earth have grown rich

from the power of her luxury."

[4] Then I heard another voice from heaven saying,

"Come out of her, my people,

so that you do not take part in her sins,

and so that you do not share in her plagues;

[5] for her sins are heaped high as heaven,

and God has remembered her iniquities.

[6] Render to her as she herself has rendered,

and repay her double for her deeds;

mix a double draught for her in the cup she mixed.

[7] As she glorified herself and lived luxuriously,

so give her a like measure of torment and grief.

Since in her heart she says,

'I rule as a queen;

I am no widow,

and I will never see grief,'

[8] therefore her plagues will come in a single day—

pestilence and mourning and famine—

and she will be burned with fire;

for mighty is the Lord God who judges her."

[9] And the kings of the earth, who committed fornication and lived in luxury with her, will weep and wail over her when they see the smoke of her burning; [10] they will stand far off, in fear of her torment, and say,

"Alas, alas, the great city,
Babylon, the mighty city!
For in one hour your judgment has come."

[11] And the merchants of the earth weep and mourn for her, since no one buys their cargo anymore, [12] cargo of gold, silver, jewels and pearls, fine linen, purple, silk and scarlet, all kinds of scented wood, all articles of ivory, all articles of costly wood, bronze, iron, and marble, [13] cinnamon, spice, incense, myrrh, frankincense, wine, olive oil, choice flour and wheat, cattle and sheep, horses and chariots, slaves—and human lives.

[14] "The fruit for which your soul longed
has gone from you,
and all your dainties and your splendor
are lost to you,
never to be found again!"

[15] The merchants of these wares, who gained wealth from her, will stand far off, in fear of her torment, weeping and mourning aloud,

[16] "Alas, alas, the great city,
clothed in fine linen, in purple and scarlet,
adorned with gold, with jewels, and with pearls!

[17] For in one hour all this wealth has been laid waste!"

And all shipmasters and seafarers, sailors and all

whose trade is on the sea, stood far off [18] and cried out
as they saw the smoke of her burning,

"What city was like the great city?"

[19] And they threw dust on their heads, as they wept
and mourned,

crying out,

"Alas, alas, the great city,

where all who had ships at sea

grew rich by her wealth!

For in one hour she has been laid waste."

[20] Rejoice over her, O heaven, you saints and
apostles and prophets!

For God has given judgment for you against her.

[21] Then a mighty angel took up a stone like a great
millstone and threw it into the sea, saying,

"With such violence Babylon the great city

will be thrown down,

and will be found no more;

[22] and the sound of harpists and minstrels and

of flautists and trumpeters

will be heard in you no more;

and an artisan of any trade

will be found in you no more;

and the sound of the millstone

will be heard in you no more;

[23] and the light of a lamp

will shine in you no more;

and the voice of bridegroom and bride

will be heard in you no more;

for your merchants were the magnates of the
earth,

and all nations were deceived by your sorcery.
[24] And in you was found the blood of prophets
and of saints,
and of all who have been slaughtered on earth."
Revelation 18:1-24

Chapter eighteen gives us a detailed description of God's judgment on the great satanic system of Babylon that has plagued humankind throughout history. This chapter is a funeral dirge for the system of Babylon, harkening back to the dirges sung by the Old Testament prophets over the ancient cities of Babylon and Tyre.

In verse four, a voice from heaven, echoing the words of the prophet Jeremiah (Je 50:39; 51:6, 9, 45), commands, "Come out of her, my people, so that you do not take part in her sins, and so that you do not share in her plagues." Jeremiah wrote of the fall of physical Babylon; but the Book of Revelation is telling us of a greater victory, not over just a city, but over the entire system of human achievement and accomplishment that exalts itself rather than worship the Lamb of God, who alone is worthy to be praised.

Revelation 18:4 is not a literal call to God's people to physically remove themselves from a city or a nation or a culture; rather it is a call to shun the ensnarement of the world's evils. Some completely misunderstand the force of this passage, and simply explain that it means we should not listen to modern music (whatever "modern" music means), go to movies, that women should not wear cosmetics, that we must not use birth control, and similar restrictive regulations of religion. There are obvious problems with that kind of simplistic, overly literal misuse of this passage.

First of all, such a view of verse four misses the big picture given by the context of the chapter and the book. It misses the message of the Messenger that identifies the foe as religious legalism, and thus this interpretation of verse four winds up being quoted in favor of enforcing more legalism! Religious tyranny tries to interpret Revelation in such a way as to miss the forest of the gospel by nitpicking us with the trees of legalistic rules and regulations, offering us tantalizing predictions along the way. Curiosity not only kills cats, it also leads many deep into the swamps of legalism.

The second problem is that this kind of interpretation itself leads us into oppression and bondage; it leads us into the middle of the Babylon that we think we're leaving as a result of observing all of our do's and don'ts. Religious Babylon leads us to self-righteousness. Performance-based religion leads us to focus on what we can do ourselves. Legalistic religion tells us that holiness and sanctification and perfection is up to us. That's one reason why the dragon is so deceptive; he uses a form of religion to ensnare us, even when we think we are running away from it and toward God. Abduction and the enslavement of others is a crime; and make no mistake, the dragon is a criminal. Legalistic religion is a co-conspirator, aiding and abetting him.

Given the immediate context of the Book of Revelation, and the larger context of the cross of Christ and God's amazing grace, verses four and five of chapter eighteen might be paraphrased something like this: *My people, come out of oppressive religion that seeks to control and enslave you, so that you won't share in its sins. The sins of performance-based religion and all of its legalisms are piled up to heaven, and God remembers her crimes.*

In the Book of Galatians, Paul uses a phrase, "the elemental spirits of the world" (Ga 4:3)—referring to the way human beings operate, the way our spiritual economy works. Chapters seventeen and eighteen of the Book of Revelation talk about the linkage of the spiritual and physical economies of this all encompassing false system that enslaves and controls. It's the way Babylon works.

You do something for me, and I have to pay you or do something in return. That's the way we humans operate; that's the system we understand. "The elemental spirits of the world" results in an economic, emotional, psychological, and religious barter system. The religions of Babylon tell us that if we expect its gods to do things for us, we are going to have to do things for him/her/them. Such religion lies to us, telling us that the one true God is displeased with us because we are sinners; and, of course, religion doesn't have to prove to us that we are imperfect. Legalistic religion then works on us, using shame and guilt, to ensure that we will fall into obedience to its dogmas, conventions, and ceremonies. Religion uses the "elemental spirits of the world" to control us.

In Revelation chapters seventeen and eighteen we read that Babylon glorifies what humans can accomplish.[7] The spiritual economy of Babylon is not driven by faith in the one true God, it is driven by faith in human abilities, human wisdom, innovation, and hard work. There is no room for God's amazing grace in Babylon, because the pride and vanity of Babylon occupies all the available space. There is no need for God's righteousness given because of the cross of Christ, because religion has convinced the citizens of Babylon that their self-righteousness and fruit of their human effort will somehow be enough to gain them salvation, however that salvation may be defined.

But the truth of the gospel is the diametric opposite. The gospel is driven by another spiritual economy.[8] The Lamb of God works, but He doesn't work the way we work. God's grace is not given to us because of our good works and deeds. God's grace is given to us in spite of who we are, not because of who we are. God's grace is given not because we are good but because God is good.

Christians do not produce the fruit of God's righteousness; the Holy Spirit produces that fruit in us. Our good deeds are *God's produce*. The Bible tells us to rest in Christ. Religion tells us that we must work hard, every day of our lives, and tells us that our deeds and accomplishments are never good enough. The mark of the beast is upon those who are enslaved because they are convinced that their salvation is up to them. Those who are sealed by the Lamb of God rest in Him and enter His rest.

In authentic Christianity, there is no possibility of the spiritual economy of Babylon, because all authentic Christians accept the fact that they are powerless to save themselves. The spiritual currency of Babylon is worthless in the kingdom of heaven. Authentic Christians recognize they are powerless to build huge churches and fill their parking lots with thousands of cars on Sunday mornings. God may fill those parking lots —while they may be filled through other methods as well!—but if the huge crowds that gather for worship are from God, Christ will always be the center of faith and belief. For Christians grace is everything, and what we can accomplish in our lives apart from God is nothing. What we do is not the issue with God, what Christ has done, is doing, and will do is the issue—the only issue.

We, as Paul says, count all of what we have accomplished and achieved as loss. Actually, he gets a little more graphic in Philippians 3:8. He says he counts all that he can do on his own, apart from God, as rubbish. Here's one verse where I like the plain, clear language of the Authorized King James Version. The King James doesn't sanitize this word by calling our accomplishments rubbish, garbage, or trash. Paul is not talking about old newspapers, milk cartons, eggshells, and empty cans. The King James says that Paul compared the legalistic religious economy, the "elemental spirits of the world," (Ga 4:3) to dung.

Rubbish is tossed into trashcans inside the house. We grind up garbage in disposers. Rubbish and garbage are not strong enough word pictures for how useless our works and deeds are in terms of our salvation. All of our performance and all of the rituals and ceremonies of legalistic religion are compared to human waste we flush down the toilet or to animal excrement we bury, use for fertilizer, or throw directly into trash cans we keep outside of our homes.

If we take Fido for a walk in our neighborhood, we courteously pick up anything he "deposits" on city or private property and take the dung home to be disposed of. Not so in spiritual Babylon! Citizens who have been seduced by the religious legalisms of Babylon actually take pride in the religious waste that litters the streets of their spiritual city. The stench reaches to high heaven.

Babylon tells us that our spiritual well-being and security depends on our behavior; it's all about us. Authentic Christianity, the gospel of Jesus Christ, and this powerful Revelation of Jesus Christ tells us that our salvation is all about Jesus. It's all about the Lamb of God.

Wherever there is self-glorification, wherever there is pride and arrogance, wherever there is self-sufficiency, wherever there is spiritual arrogance and self-righteousness, wherever there is hypocrisy and double standards, wherever there is abuse and authoritarianism, wherever there is tyranny and oppression, wherever there is reliance on human power and strength, there is Babylon. Jesus empowers Christians to separate themselves spiritually and ideologically from that evil system wherever it manifests itself. By God's grace we are beckoned and empowered to come out of the religions of Babylon.

In verse nine we read that the "kings of the earth" mourn the demise of Babylon because they are in the grip of this evil system. They "committed fornication with her" (vv. 3, 9). In the first century, kings of the nations who cooperated with and gave their allegiance to Rome were richly rewarded. As part of the Roman Empire, they enjoyed the protection of Roman legions, who quickly put down any revolts and protected these kings from foreign aggression. Their countries reaped the economic benefits of Rome: free trade within the Roman Empire. They were also obliged to open their countries to the Roman religious system, which involved honoring the emperor as a God.

In the apocalyptic imagery of the Book of Revelation none of the "kings of the earth" are joyful at the fall of Babylon. None of them welcome Christ's coming, whether that coming is past, present, or future. All human governments are portrayed as being willingly enslaved by the "beast" system to some degree. They once celebrated their captivity; now they mourn the fall of the very system that held them in bondage.

In verse 11, the merchants and business people join the dirge, later to be joined by the world's mariners and sea captains. The economic system of Babylon and that of Rome was built on commerce, filling the demand for luxury goods and slaves. Verse 13 mentions trade in "human lives." Roman civilization was built on slavery, which enabled its wealthy citizens to live in the greatest opulence and luxury the world had ever seen. The physical economy of religion and religious legalism is often based upon a spiritual slave trade that impoverishes while making religious entities and empires rich.

Ultimately the Babylon of Revelation represents all the great political, religious, and economic systems that have opposed God. Babylon continues to dominate the world, with rampant greed and commercialism, with oppression and exploitation of the poor and

disadvantaged, with immorality and violence, and with religious fanaticism, paganism, and godless materialism. Babylon rewards its
own: those who cheat, steal, deceive and manipulate, with power
and opulence. The inspiring message of Revelation is that all this will
one day come to an end. As verse 21 assures us, Babylon "will be
thrown down, and will be found no more."

Where do your loyalties lie? Whose name or mark is on your forehead? Is it the great religious system of Babylon, or is it the Lamb of
God? There is no middle ground.

CHAPTER ELEVEN

The Music and the Millennium of Revelation

The Book of Revelation is filled with music reflecting the sweet, harmonious sounds of heaven. Included in the Book of Revelation's greatest hits is the song in Revelation chapter five, "Worthy is the Lamb." In chapter fourteen, the 144,000 sing on Mt. Zion with the Lamb of God. A new song, the song of the Lamb, based upon the song of Moses, is given to us in Revelation chapter fifteen. What is the music of Revelation telling us? What message is God giving us with "Revelation's Greatest Hits?"

Chances are music is an important part of your life. With some people music is almost a second language; they listen to its sounds, tunes, and lyrics everywhere they go. They are plugged in and turned on by the message of music.

There are times when the older generation, out of its frustration to comprehend a new musical form, the strange new musical language of the younger generation, condemns music, or at least all music that was written and composed after their generation passed the ages of 40 or 50. But when that happens, the older generation has lost its short-term memory of how its own music was often viewed as scandalous and even immoral by the older generation that preceded it. Our acceptance or connection with a specific musical form or genre does not validate or dismiss its ability to communicate. The music of Revelation is similar—we may reject it altogether, or we may attempt to force it into an entirely different context than was originally intended—but its music still contains a message, whether we hear it or accept it.

Music is an important element in the Book of Revelation, just as music is critically important to any movie. Next time you watch TV, a video, or a DVD turn down the volume, and you'll see what I mean. Hit the mute button on your remote; and even if you have a feature on your television that provides written text of the spoken words, even though you will see the actors and scenery and read the written script, the important dimension of music will be missing. Without the music you may not know when or how much to cry, when to be excited, or when to be afraid. Music speaks to our hearts. Music alerts us, giving us a cue that something bad is about to happen, and it lifts our emotions when we view an inspiring moment.

In a similar way music is important to our worship of God, ask any church that has been through its own version of "worship wars." The great old classic hymns face off against the new, upbeat contemporary Christian music. Many people come to church only for the music, and when that music is changed, they leave their home church of many years. Music can be a source of unity in worship as well as a source of division. A joke, which has made the rounds of the evangelical church, acknowledges the power that church musicians either have or feel they have: "What's the difference between a terrorist and a worship leader?" Answer: "You can negotiate with a terrorist."

The message of music may be good or bad, but it is critically important because it is persuasive. Whether it's classical, hip-hop, country, blues, rap, or that old-time rock and roll, music is a powerful and effective mode of communication. What is the music saying? What is the music encouraging us to do? What is the message of the music of Revelation, the message of the greatest hits of Revelation?

In the last chapter we discussed Babylon, the great city Revelation speaks of as a metaphor for the political and religious system that dominates the world. Its final defeat is at the hands of the Lamb of God, Jesus Christ. The mood music was that of a triumphant victory song, for God conquered a great and powerful system.

We begin looking at Revelation chapter nineteen and discover that much of the chapter is one big "Hallelujah Chorus."

A Song of Doom for Babylon

[1] After this I heard what seemed to be the loud voice
of a great multitude in heaven, saying,
"Hallelujah!
Salvation and glory and power to our God,
[2] for his judgments are true and just;
he has judged the great whore
who corrupted the earth with her fornication,
and he has avenged on her the blood of his servants."
[3] Once more they said,
"Hallelujah!
The smoke goes up from her forever and ever."
[4] And the twenty-four elders and the four living creatures fell down and
worshiped God who is seated on the throne, saying,
"Amen. Hallelujah!"
[5] And from the throne came a voice saying,
"Praise our God,
all you his servants,
and all who fear him,
small and great."
[6] Then I heard what seemed to be the voice of a great
multitude, like the sound of many waters and like the

sound of mighty thunder-peals, crying out,

"Hallelujah!

For the Lord our God

the Almighty reigns.

[7] Let us rejoice and exult

and give him the glory,

for the marriage of the Lamb has come,

and his bride has made herself ready;

[8] to her it has been granted to be clothed

with fine linen, bright and pure"—

for the fine linen is the righteous deeds of the saints.

[9] And the angel said to me, "Write this: Blessed are those who are invited to the marriage supper of the Lamb." And he said to me, "These are true words of God." [10] Then I fell down at his feet to worship him, but he said to me, "You must not do that! I am a fellow-servant with you and your comrades who hold the testimony of Jesus. Worship God! For the testimony of Jesus is the spirit of prophecy."

[11] Then I saw heaven opened, and there was a white horse! Its rider is called Faithful and True, and in righteousness he judges and makes war. [12] His eyes are like a flame of fire, and on his head are many diadems; and he has a name inscribed that no one knows but himself. [13] He is clothed in a robe dipped in blood, and his name is called The Word of God. [14] And the armies of heaven, wearing fine linen, white and pure, were following him on white horses. [15] From his mouth comes a sharp sword with which to strike down the nations, and he will rule them with a rod of iron; he will tread the wine press of the fury of the wrath of God the Almighty. [16] On his robe and on his thigh he has a name inscribed, "King of kings and Lord of lords."

¹⁷Then I saw an angel standing in the sun, and with a loud voice he called to all the birds that fly in midheaven, "Come, gather for the great supper of God, ¹⁸ to eat the flesh of kings, the flesh of captains, the flesh of the mighty, the flesh of horses and their riders—flesh of all, both free and slave, both small and great." ¹⁹ Then I saw the beast and the kings of the earth with their armies gathered to make war against the rider on the horse and against his army. ²⁰ And the beast was captured, and with it the false prophet who had performed in its presence the signs by which he deceived those who had received the mark of the beast and those who worshiped its image. These two were thrown alive into the lake of fire that burns with sulfur. ²¹ And the rest were killed by the sword of the rider on the horse, the sword that came from his mouth; and all the birds were gorged with their flesh.

Revelation 19:1-21

The Best of Times and The Worst of Times

Chapter nineteen begins with a great celebration in heaven. In verse seven the heavenly multitude shouts: "Hallelujah! For our Lord God the Almighty reigns. Let us rejoice and exult and give him glory, for the marriage of the Lamb has come, and his bride has made herself ready."

The chapters leading up to chapter nineteen have described the complete and final destruction of the whore, the woman who sits on the beast, the spiritual, theological, and religious power that enslaves the whole world. The power is spoken of metaphorically as Babylon.

Some 60 years before this Revelation was given to John, Jesus Christ arrived at the city of Jerusalem at the end of His earthly life. Passion week, the events of the last week of His life, was spent in Jerusalem, a city whose citizens were held captive by religious traditions. Jesus came to this citadel of religion to put an end to religion. He died on the cross and rose victoriously from a tomb that could not hold Him, overcoming all powers, taking captive all religions, conquering death and the grave and all who use death as a religious threat and bargaining chip with which to control us in this life.

Now in chapter nineteen Jesus is the rider on a white horse. He has destroyed Babylon and all counterfeit religion that enslaves men, women, and children. He is called Faithful and True. His name is the Word of God. He is King of kings and Lord of lords; He prepares a great supper of God, inviting all the fowls of the air. And the entrée is the flesh of all those who opposed God's grace, and his Lamb, slain from the foundation of the world. An incredible study in contrasts!

Chapter nineteen contrasts the whore and her lovers from Babylon with the Lamb of God and His bride. The bride is the heavenly city, new Jerusalem, the church, the people of God down through time. Christ's bride wears white clothing in contrast to the purple and red clothing of the great prostitute. The bride is *given* her garments, which symbolize righteousness, reminding us that our righteousness is *given* to us because of Jesus Christ, by God's grace. We have done nothing to earn it. By contrast, any clothing that you wear as a slave of religion is earned by your works.

The whore of Babylon *earns* her purple and red clothing by her profession, which degrades, brutalizes, and abuses her. The bride of Christ wears clothing that is purchased by the blood of the Lamb. The bride does not earn her position or purchase her wedding garments. She accepts the love of the Lamb, who died and gave Himself for her. A wedding supper is *given* for her. The other supper mentioned in this chapter consists of the flesh of those who oppose the Lamb "to eat the flesh of kings, the flesh of captains, the flesh of the mighty, the flesh of horses and their riders—flesh of all, both free and slave, both small and great" (v. 18). Birds eat this flesh.

The victorious Christ sits on a white horse and heads a column of the armies of heaven. He is "Faithful and True, and in righteousness he judges and makes war" (v. 11) in contrast to the powers of the religious Antichrist who deceives, lies, intimidates, abuses, and manipulates. Jesus is the good guy on the white horse. He marries the bride who is chaste, dressed in the white garments she has been given. This is the best of times for those who worship the Lamb.

The powers that have always opposed the Lamb of God, be they political or religious, or a combination of both, gather their armies against Him as they always have. They are cowards and crooks and deceivers. They are themselves deceived by the great Dragon, Satan, and together they form an army of snakes. They enslave billions, using and abusing them, insisting that they jump through the hoops of religious legalism. But this great battle in Revelation chapter nineteen is not primarily a military conflict. It is the King of kings and Lord of Lords executing justice on tyrants and dictators whose hands are filled with the blood of innocents. This is the worst of times for all who align themselves against God.

In verse 17, an angel issues a call to all scavenger birds to come and feast on the enemies of God who are about to die. These are the armies who started to assemble at the sixth plague to battle Christ under the leadership of the kings of the earth.

The Battle That Is No Contest—The UNbattle

This conflict between the forces of Christ and the kings of the earth is the legendary Battle of Armageddon—called Harmagedon in the New Revised Standard Version—an event most people vaguely identify with the "end of the world." Many recent interpreters place this battle at a specific site, Megiddo, an ancient town in the Valley of Jezereel, north of Jerusalem (see pages 174–175 commenting on Re 16:16). But it's doubtful that John's readers in Asia Minor would have known about this specific place. The word has several other possible generic meanings, including simply, "a gathering of troops."

It is likely that John's first-century readers understood this as an account of the defeat of their Roman oppressors by Christ. But history tells us that the Roman Empire did not end this way.

John describes the action in verse 20: "And the beast was captured, and with it the false prophet who had performed in its presence the signs by which he deceived those who had received the mark of the beast and those who worshiped his image. The two were thrown alive into the lake of fire that burns with sulfur. And the rest were killed with the sword of the rider on the horse, the sword that came from his mouth; and all the birds were gorged with their flesh."

If this is a battle, it is certainly one-sided. In fact, there is *no* battle. Christ summarily and effortlessly destroys His enemies. Neither is this the end of the world. Rather, it is symbolic of the overthrow of the religious forces of evil that have oppressed and enslaved the world for so long. And it is the beginning of the freedom that Christ brings.

Whether or not Harmagedon (Armageddon) is to be considered a literal event in a literal place, the message here is clear: there is never any contest with Christ. His enemies were and are already defeated—at the cross. In this battle Jesus dispatches His enemies and finishes the job once and for all. The battle belongs to the Lord.

Some today have a great preoccupation with "spiritual warfare," where practitioners struggle to drive out real or imagined forces of evil and ruling spirits. They believe that it is necessary, in God's name, to carefully follow formulas and procedures, invoking and commanding demonic spirits by name, arguing, disputing, and negotiating with them until the spirits reluctantly comply. Ideas and activities such as generational curses, mapping, and binding and loosing Satan may resemble voodoo or witchcraft more than they do authentic Christianity. Much of what is popularly known as spiritual warfare and deliverance ministry seems to be just another permutation and variation of religion that fascinates, intrigues, and then seduces us. Once we are in the web of deception, religious legalism springs its trap.

Spiritual warfare is of course described in the Bible. Simply because religious extremists have co-opted and hijacked the term does not diminish the validity and truth behind its practice. In the sixth chapter of Ephesians, Paul notes that the enemies of Christians are often beyond what we can observe with our human faculties (Ep 6:12). Dark spiritual forces energize and motivate earthly manifestations of power and prestige. But Paul does not direct us, as Christians, to match specific geographic locations under a supposed particular curse with the specific demonic power that rules this territory. As Christians we are assured that the one who is in us is greater than the one who is in the world (1 Jo 4:4).

We do resist Satan and his demons; but there is no need for the kind of spiritual warfare some practice today. That is, there is no need for someone to name specific demons of geographic areas or zip codes by name so that they can be conquered. Our Lord and Savior has already done that kind of "conquering." God does not direct us or need us to delve into the spirit world to do warfare with already vanquished demons. Some, in the name of God, may tell you it's necessary, but the authentic gospel of Jesus Christ says otherwise.

The forces of evil are never a match for the power of the Lamb of God. He may allow them to continue for a while in this world, but they are already defeated by the awesome and infinite power of Christ and those who place their trust in Him.

In verse 20 and 21, the result of this battle is recorded, with the beast and the false prophet thrown into a lake of fire; and the rest of the army, which gathered against the King of kings and Lord of lords, is killed, the birds of the air gorging themselves on flesh in a great supper of God to which all the fowls of the air are invited.

This is a picture of the judgment against legalistic religion, when oppressive, authoritarian religion and all that opposes Jesus Christ finally and completely goes to hell. It's a time of great celebration: two suppers, one a festive wedding supper, and one featuring the bloated bodies of those who oppose the Lamb of God being eaten by vultures! In perfect justice, scavengers eat the world of corrupt and perverted religion. The great supper of God with religious oppressors as the entrée provides a striking contrast with the marriage supper of the Lamb.

Just What Does Revelation Mean—The Millennium?

[1] Then I saw an angel coming down from heaven, holding in his hand the key to the bottomless pit and a great chain. [2] He seized the dragon, that ancient serpent, who is the Devil and Satan, and bound him for a thousand years, [3] and threw him into the pit, and locked and sealed it over him, so that he would deceive the nations no more, until the thousand years were ended. After that he must be let out for a little while.

[4] Then I saw thrones, and those seated on them were given authority to judge. I also saw the souls of those who had been beheaded for their testimony to Jesus and for the word of God. They had not worshiped the beast or its image and had not received its mark on their foreheads or their hands. They came to life and reigned with Christ for a thousand years. [5] (The rest of the dead did not come to life until the thousand years were ended.) This is the first resurrection. [6] Blessed and holy are those who share in the first resurrection. Over these the second death has no power, but they will be priests of God and of Christ, and they will reign with him for a thousand years.

[7] When the thousand years are ended, Satan will be released from his prison [8] and will come out to deceive the nations at the four corners of the earth, Gog and Magog, in order to gather them for battle; they are as numerous as the sands of the sea. [9] They marched up over the breadth of the earth and surrounded the camp of the

saints and the beloved city. And fire came down from heaven and consumed them. [10] And the devil who had deceived them was thrown into the lake of fire and sulfur, where the beast and the false prophet were, and they will be tormented day and night forever and ever.

[11] Then I saw a great white throne and the one who sat on it; the earth and the heaven fled from his presence, and no place was found for them. [12] And I saw the dead, great and small, standing before the throne, and books were opened. Also another book was opened, the book of life. And the dead were judged according to their works, as recorded in the books. [13] And the sea gave up the dead that were in it, Death and Hades gave up the dead that were in them, and all were judged according to what they had done. [14] Then Death and Hades were thrown into the lake of fire. This is the second death, the lake of fire; [15] and anyone whose name was not found written in the book of life was thrown into the lake of fire.

Revelation 20:1-15

Chapter twenty introduces another layer of complexity into our study of Revelation as we are introduced to the thousand-year reign of the saints. The phrase "thousand years" has in turn been popularly interpreted and referred to by many Christians as the millennium, so much so that many Christians are surprised when they fail to find the precise term *millennium* in the Bible.

Steve Gregg notes that the final three chapters of Revelation, beginning with chapter twenty, comprise "what is arguably the chief controversy in eschatological studies, if not in all evangelical theology."[1]

The thousand years, or as popularly known, the millennium, is yet another of the many symbolic and metaphorical terms that comprise the apocalyptic genre of biblical literature. This term has engendered enormous speculation as many have turned themselves into eschatological pretzels attempting to turn this symbol into a literal, specific, blueprint-like precise number of years. And it isn't difficult to arrive at a specific one thousand year period of time as we measure it, if we ignore the literary genre in which the Lamb of God revealed this message, and if we ignore the consistent context of the entire book!

As we begin this chapter, we begin our study and reading under a warning flag—a caution to remember the symbolism of this book, the language and linguistic forms chosen by Jesus, the Revelator, to describe the Message, which is, again, all about Him. If we place these words under the methodology of some humanly devised interpretive microscope, we may miss much of the message. This chapter, more than any other chapter of the Book of Revelation, has been the happy hunting ground for wild, silly, illogical, and irresponsible interpretations.

The "thousand years" is the time period commonly referred to as the millennium. Many believe this is to be understood literally as a thousand-year time period, yet it is the only passage in the Bible that mentions a thousand years for Christ's reign with the saints. But in a book that is loaded with symbolism, where numbers are employed figuratively and symbolically—numbers like 3½, 7, 12, 144,000, 666—do we have any reason to categorically determine that this mention of one thousand years is literal, based upon earth-based chronology? I think not!

Passages elsewhere in the Bible give no limitation for the reign of the Messiah, yet the fact that this one reference in one chapter of Revelation is the only place for a reference to a time period of one thousand years has not stopped tens of millions from using it to construct and believe in a precise dispensational chronology of God's plan and schedule for humans. Once again, are we primarily looking for Christology, the divine *who*, or chronology, the *when*, as we read Revelation?

Interpretations that impose a mechanistic and myopic literalism on the grand, panoramic sweep of Revelation's literary style are not new. One of the early church fathers, Gregory of Nyssa (336-395) lamented such short-sighted devaluations of the Christ-centered message of Revelation:

> Now if we loudly preach all this, and testify to all this, namely that Christ is the power of God and the wisdom of God, always changeless, always imperishable, though He comes in the changeable and the perishable; never stained himself, but making clean that which is stained; what is the crime we commit, and wherefore are we hated?... Do we announce another Jesus? Do we hint at another? Do we produce other scriptures?... Do we romance about three Resurrections? Do we promise the gluttony of the Millennium? Do we declare that the Jewish animal-sacrifices shall be restored? Do we lower men's hopes again to the Jerusalem below, imagining its rebuilding with stones of a more brilliant material?[2]

In the Book of Psalms, the psalmist tells us that God owns the cattle on a "thousand hills" (Ps 50:10). Is this mention of the one thousand years somewhat like the poetic cattle on a "thousand hills"? Is the one thousand years of Revelation symbolic of a length of time that is a long, long period, longer than any human being will experience in their lifetime, or is it a specific, precise, literal period of time? Further, even if we conclude that this one symbolic term in the Book of Revelation is literal and precise, then on what authority do we further assume that the one thousand years should be measured by time as we know it?

A Christo-centric focus on the Book of Revelation and on its original audience also leads us to consider that the thousand years may have been a way to help counter the Jewish idea that the kingdom of God would center around one cultural/racial group of people. Revelation insists that the universal body of Christ receives God's grace; and therefore salvation is by grace, not race. This chapter may have originally been inspired by the Lamb of God to help cement the gospel's teaching that salvation is available to all, and the gates of God's kingdom are open regardless of nationality.

Throughout the history of the Christian faith, there have been three prevalent ideas about this one thousand years:

Postmillenialism was the prevailing Protestant idea until about 150 years ago. In postmillennialism, Jesus' second coming occurs *after* the thousand year millennium. Postmillennialism looks for a thousand-year period of peace on earth to be brought about by the evangelistic work of Christianity, after which Jesus would return to defeat Satan and rule forever. The assumption of this view is that the work of Christianity brings worldwide conversions, either by preaching and teaching or by the imposition of Christian-sponsored political and military power. Obviously, this kind of millennium has not yet started. Peace does not reign supreme on this earth. So, unless we assume that the thousand years of worldwide evangelism has not yet started, this view seems to lack credibility.

Premillennialism (popular among many evangelical Christians) teaches that Christ will return, followed by an exact one thousand year reign, followed by the removal of Satan. In premillennialism the second coming occurs *before* the thousand-year millennium. There are two distinct groups of premillennialists: dispensational premillennialists and historic premillennialists. Dispensationalists, as discussed in chapter six, believe that Christians will be taken in the Rapture seven years before the millennium, thus, in effect, requiring two second comings of Jesus. Historic premillennialists see the rapture, the catching up of Christians to meet Christ in the clouds, occurring at the same time as the second coming and the beginning of the literal one thousand years.

Amillennialism is based upon a belief that the thousand years is a symbolic and imprecise period of time of the "Church age," the time between Christ's resurrection and His return. In amillennialism the second coming occurs *after* the thousand-year millennium, with the proviso that there is no way of knowing exactly how long and when the thousand years may be. Amillennialists believe we may now be in this symbolic and imprecise one thousand year period of time. This view sees the mention of the term "thousand years" as a term that means a "long, long" time—longer than any human could live or imagine within his or her generations. They believe it is an imprecise term that describes the exact period of time between the first and second comings of Jesus Christ. Thus, the amillennial view understands the "thousand years" as simply a long period of time between Christ's return and the final judgment.

Perhaps no one of these three views represents a well-rounded or Christ-centered view of the full and complete message of Revelation.

What are the first ten verses of chapter twenty telling us about the "thousand years"? This passage contains some seemingly conflicting and even confusing information about "the thousand years," especially if we attempt to force a time-bound, wooden, literal interpretation on it. Here's what we cannot know for sure about this passage:

- This passage presents many questions—and provides few dogmatic answers—except for those doctrinaire pontifications and interpretations from sources you would probably want to second guess. For example, why, after beginning His eternal reign, would Christ bring Satan back? Why wouldn't Satan have been thrown into the Lake of Fire with the beast and false prophet back in chapter nineteen? Some believe that God wants to show that Satan can never be rehabilitated, no matter how long he is in prison. Others say that God will allow Satan to go free to prove that Satan is nothing but a loser, always has been and always will be. Some scholars point to this as evidence of divine inspiration of the Book of Revelation. No human would conceive of this convoluted plot. If a human writer were making this story up, Christ would simply return, and we would all live happily ever after.

- But God thinks differently than we do (thank God!). It takes Satan only "a short time" (v. 3) to deceive nations that have lived free from his in-fluence. Perhaps the shortcomings we realize when we try to shoehorn human time into this passage reveal the real message of this passage: it's not a chronological timetable of end time events but a theological description of the pervasive and insidious nature of human evil. The source of death and mayhem, according to this passage, is not culture or society, not evil influences around us or even the devil. The real cul-prit is the human heart. The passage explains that even when Jesus is on earth bodily (and, of course, He already has been once), and even when or if Satan is banished from deceiving our world (he hasn't been yet, as far as we know), evil still happens.

- The rebellious armies are identified as Gog and Magog, a symbolic name drawn from Ezekiel 38 and 39 for all the enemies of Christ. What is this all about? We don't know for sure; no one does. Based on their track record, and their seeming disregard for the apocalyptic literary genre of the Book of Revelation, those who pronounce with great authority that they have specific details for everything that is mentioned in chapter twenty would probably be the last sources for you to listen to.[3]

- Let's take a closer look at verse four. Let's assume that the millennium is a literal time period of one thousand years when Jesus is ruling on this earth. Many who offer such an interpretation depict the saints, those who are dead in Christ as well as those who are alive at His sec-ond coming, as ruling over this world for this one thousand year millennium. But verse four does not allow for such a teaching. If the one thousand years is a literal millennium, then only those who were dead in Christ who died as a result of being beheaded "came to life and reigned with Christ a thousand years" (v. 4).

What can we know from this passage?

- During this time (and we must understand that Jesus is probably not talking about a time measured by 24-hour days), Christ and the saints reign, and Satan is bound and sealed in the abyss. During the first phase of this time, earth is a "Satan-free" zone followed by another period of time when he is released, deceives, and is again soundly defeated by fire from heaven.

- The main point of the chapter, indeed, the entire Book of Revelation, is that even under the best of circumstances the human heart is deceitful. We easily fall prey to false religious leaders, accepting religious deception and manipulation, hook, line, and sinker. Why, once again, would Satan be brought back into a near perfect environment of this millennial utopia? Perhaps Satan will be allowed back to prove that, even when we are exposed to perfection, we are still capable of being deceived. That lesson is not just for some future time, that lesson is for Christians of all times. Satan doesn't need a horrible environment and wretched conditions to turn our hearts from the one true God.

- This final challenge from Satan to Christ's kingdom ends with fire falling from heaven and destroying the rebels. Satan is cast into the Lake of Fire where the beast and false prophet await him. Finally, we come back to the heart and core of the gospel. We are saved by grace, not by chronology or prophecy charts. Salvation is not based, nor does it depend, on having the "correct" interpretation of the thousand years. It does depend upon Jesus Christ. Once again, the theme of Revelation is *who*, with *when* usually being simply an object of conjecture and speculation. Our understanding of Revelation needs to be based on *Christology*, not *chronology*.

The Judgment

The next scene (vv. 11-15) depicts the Judgment, the dreaded event depicted in countless works of art and described vividly and horrifically in innumerable sermons.

The books are opened along with the "book of life." In verses 12-13, we read "the dead were judged according to their works, as recorded in the

211

books. And the sea gave up the dead that were in it, Death and Hades gave up the dead that were in them, and all were judged according to what they had done."

At least two books are opened. One of them includes names of those who will be judged, as verse 12 says, "according to their works." Verse 13 says "all were judged according to what they had done." This first book is contrasted with the "book of life" as verse 12 relates, "another book was opened, the book of life." In Revelation13:8 we read that this book belongs to the Lamb of God, and everyone whose name is not written in the book of life will worship the beast. The names of those who worship the beast are written in the first book "according to what they had done." We might call this *The Book of Human Merits and Works*.

What have you *done*? Are your deeds and works in the book that records things "according to what you have *done*?" Is that how you want to be judged—by what you have *done*? That's what works-based religion wants to convince you of: that you will be judged by what you have *done*. If this is your choice, consider what is recorded under your name in the book of works, whether it is literal or a metaphor for the infinite memory of God. Sure, you can remember a number of things you are proud of: accomplishments, good behaviors, times when you avoided doing bad things, and good things you did to help other people. But then there are the other things: sins you committed deliberately and publicly, as well as the sins that only you know about, and the many others you can't even remember: things you did that were selfish or greedy or that resulted in harm to others; things you hope you have successfully covered up; the times when you did things that looked good, but you did them either begrudgingly or with the most selfish of motivations. These could be written in the books.

At this point, what would you say? Many will say, "Sure, I did some bad things, but aren't those outweighed by my good deeds?" It seems that the popular conception of Judgment Day is that God will weigh your good deeds against your bad deeds, and if the good deeds outweigh the bad, you are allowed into the kingdom of heaven.

But the Bible tells us in James 2:10: "Whoever keeps the whole law and yet stumbles at just one point is guilty of breaking all of it." This is not good news for any of us, since, "All have sinned" (Ro 3:23). No one will come out of the Last Judgment looking good based on his or her deeds.

There are two ways to be judged. You may choose to be judged by your deeds and works, which is what legalistic religion always urges you to do. You can choose to be in the "book of works," or you may choose to enter the book of life, which is the book that contains the names of those who accept the futility of trying to enter into life by their own performance and throw themselves on the mercy of the Lamb of God and ask for God's grace.[4]

The good news is "anyone whose name was not found written in the book of life was thrown into the lake of fire" (v. 15). You are saved eternal damnation, not based on your deeds, but based upon whether your name is found written in the Book of Life.[5] Those whose names are in the book of life confess, with the apostle Paul in 1 Timothy 1:16, "I received mercy, so that in me, as the foremost, Jesus Christ might display the utmost patience, making me an example for those who would come to believe in him for eternal life."

CHAPTER TWELVE

Everything Is Born Again— The End of Religion

Here at the end of the Book of Revelation Jesus continues to challenge our human notions and perceptions of religion. As the divine Author, the Messenger to the human author, the apostle John, and as the message, Jesus focuses our attention on the conflict between God's amazing grace and human attempts to be religious. Here, at the end of His Revelation, Jesus wants to impress on us that—at the end of the day, all of what we do, all of what we accomplish, not just what we individually do, not just what we do as a congregation or a church, or even a generation—all human accomplishment, including all religious achievement, will be destroyed. All of our deeds, apart from Christ, will be destroyed because they are imperfect (see Ps 16:2). At the end of this grand epic of Revelation, Jesus presents a new, divine world as our heritage, rather than the world that we have lived in and, to some degree, cherished.

Sometimes we have the idea that the call to follow Christ, to give up what we want to do and how we want to live and to instead follow our Lord and Savior, is a one-time event. After we have done it, said it, memorized a creed, been baptized, received a membership certificate, been confirmed, and had our picture taken—well, it's over, isn't it? No, it's not over; it's just beginning. We're going to talk about the new beginning that awaits us all on the other side of eternity as we look at the last two chapters of Revelation.

Birth and rebirth are wonderful and fascinating themes of the Bible, and what is contained in Revelation is no exception. God is in the business of making new things. He is in the business of resurrecting and giving life. God takes something or someone that is used, abused, and worn out; and God breathes the breath of life into that thing or that person.

Even though it's uplifting and inspirational to talk about new things, about new starts, and about new lives, deep down within all of us, to one degree or another, when the rubber hits the road, we need to be transformed from who and what we are into what God wants us to be. Yet we resist. We humans usually favor the old. We like what we call the tried, the tested, and the true. One of the cries within Christendom is "give me that old time religion."

That's an interesting request. If we are calling for the essential core doctrines of historic Christianity, then that's a beautiful call for the purity and truth of the gospel of Jesus Christ. But most of the time when people cry out for "the old time religion," they are saying that they want things to remain the way they have been. We want what we have done in the past to be validated. We want to think of our spiritual investments as profitable. We want our old traditions to continue, the music and hymns we remember, we want what we have done and the contributions we have given to be inscribed and etched on monuments and pews in our church. That's not what God has in mind.

All Things Become New

[1] Then I saw a new heaven and a new earth;
for the first heaven and the first earth had passed

216

away, and the sea was no more. ² And I saw the holy city, the new Jerusalem, coming down out of heaven from God, prepared as a bride adorned for her husband. ³ And I heard a loud voice from the throne saying,

"See, the home of God is among mortals.

He will dwell with them;

they will be his peoples,

and God himself will be with them;

⁴ he will wipe every tear from their eyes.

Death will be no more;

mourning and crying and pain will be no more,

for the first things have passed away."

⁵ And the one who was seated on the throne said, "See, I am making all things new." Also he said, "Write this, for these words are trustworthy and true." ⁶ Then he said to me, "It is done! I am the Alpha and the Omega, the beginning and the end. To the thirsty I will give water as a gift from the spring of the water of life. ⁷ Those who conquer will inherit these things, and I will be their God and they will be my children. ⁸ But as for the cowardly, the faithless, the polluted, the murderers, the forni- cators, the sorcerers, the idolaters, and all liars, their place will be in the lake that burns with fire and sulfur, which is the second death."

⁹ Then one of the seven angels who had the seven bowls full of the seven last plagues came and said to me, "Come, I will show you the bride, the wife of the Lamb." ¹⁰ And in the spirit he car- ried me away to a great, high mountain and

showed me the holy city Jerusalem coming down out of heaven from God. [11] It has the glory of God and a radiance like a very rare jewel, like jasper, clear as crystal. [12] It has a great, high wall with twelve gates, and at the gates twelve angels, and on the gates are inscribed the names of the twelve tribes of the Israelites; [13] on the east three gates, on the north three gates, on the south three gates, and on the west three gates. [14] And the wall of the city has twelve foundations, and on them are the twelve names of the twelve apostles of the Lamb.

[15] The angel who talked to me had a measuring rod of gold to measure the city and its gates and walls. [16] The city lies foursquare, its length the same as its width; and he measured the city with his rod, fifteen hundred miles; its length and width and height are equal. [17] He also measured its wall, one hundred and forty-four cubits by human measurement, which the angel was using. [18] The wall is built of jasper, while the city is pure gold, clear as glass. [19] The foundations of the wall of the city are adorned with every jewel; the first was jasper, the second sapphire, the third agate, the fourth emerald, [20] the fifth onyx, the sixth cornelian, the seventh chrysolite, the eighth beryl, the ninth topaz, the tenth chrysoprase, the eleventh jacinth, the twelfth amethyst. [21] And the twelve gates are twelve pearls, each of the gates is a single pearl, and the street of the city is pure gold, transparent as glass.

[22] I saw no temple in the city, for its temple is

the Lord God the Almighty and the Lamb. ²³ And the city has no need of sun or moon to shine on it, for the glory of God is its light, and its lamp is the Lamb. ²⁴ The nations will walk by its light, and the kings of the earth will bring their glory into it. ²⁵ Its gates will never be shut by day—and there will be no night there. ²⁶ People will bring into it the glory and the honor of the nations. ²⁷ But nothing unclean will enter it, nor anyone who practices abomination or falsehood, but only those who are written in the Lamb's book of life.

Revelation 21:1-27

At the end of the Book of Revelation Jesus says that *all* things will become new. The former things, all of them, will pass away. As we prepare to understand how vast and sweeping this change will be, and why it needs to happen, let's recall several themes Jesus has given us throughout this book:

- Jesus Christ is the Author of this book. Of course, this book is more than a book; it is the gospel. Jesus is the beginning and end of everything. He is the Alpha and the Omega, the A to Z. He is the Lamb of God, slain from the foundation of the world (13:8), who takes away the sin of the world. As God in the flesh, He entered into our world, in His Incarnation. He inhabited our time, but we cannot presume to impose our human limitations of time and space upon His eternity. The eternal Son of God is described as "who is and who was and who is to come" (1:4, 8). This book is far more concerned about the divine *who* than it is about our physical *when* of time and space.
- Revelation is written to encourage and inspire Christians that

the battle belongs to the Lord. Regardless of how bleak things may seem, through the slain and risen Lamb of God, King of kings and Lord of lords, we have the victory.

- Revelation is written in a symbolic, apocalyptic style. That's the literary genre Jesus used in giving the message of Revelation to John. John was given a vision, and the revelation was portrayed to him in majestic, poetic metaphors, with known and unknown beasts, with symbolic colors and numbers. We should be careful not to diminish (and perhaps even lose sight of) the message and the Messenger by insisting upon literalisms when profound truth is being revealed through symbolic language and writing.[1]

- Revelation pulls no punches. There is good and there is evil in this world. In some respects, Revelation is one grand morality play. There is no middle ground in Revelation. There is right and wrong, good and evil. There are the forces of the Lamb of God, and then there are the forces of the great dragon who has deceived the whole world, the beast, Babylon and the fallen woman. The whore is a counterfeit of the true church; Babylon is a cheap substitute for the new Jerusalem, the beast is the religious replacement for the Lamb of God. There is authentic Christianity, and there is counterfeit religion. There is no accommodation or compromise; it is God's way or the way of Babylon. God's grace or the deeds and works of human performance.

- The messages to the seven churches of chapters two and three help us to remember that Revelation is a timeless message, relevant to every generation and to every Christian. And these churches remind us that legalistic religion is a toxic virus that exists in all churches, waiting to unleash its dogmatic demands that war against God's grace.

- War is ever present in Revelation—an inevitable and familiar conclusion to the sordid intercourse that government and commerce have with religion—the end result of spiritual lust, pride, and arrogance. Apart from Christ, hatred, oppression, slavery, war, and death are the products of religion. Eternal life is the gift of God through the work of the Lamb of God.

Many of the word pictures painted by the divine Author of Revelation conclude with a vivid depiction of victory and celebration. We have seen this theme much like a point and counterpoint throughout this book, beginning with chapters two and three and the messages to the seven churches. Many times this victory celebration is much like a cheer. The Bible says that angels cry out their praise and worship because of the triumph of the Lamb of God. At other times the victory is conveyed through magnificent choruses, in swelling anthems of praise. As we saw in chapter five, "Worthy is the Lamb." We have noted that music is an often overlooked part of Revelation as music plays a critical role in conveying joy and thanksgiving. There are many illustrations, such as Revelation 7:9-7; 11:15-19; 15:1-4; 19:1-10.

And now we come to yet another emotionally compelling scene as we build to the sweeping big picture of God's plan of His victory, peace, and joy.

> Then I saw a new heaven and a new earth; for the first heaven and the first earth had passed away, and the sea was no more. And I saw the holy city, the new Jerusalem, coming down out of heaven from God, prepared as a bride adorned for her husband. And I heard a loud voice from the throne saying, "See, the home of God is with mortals. He will dwell with them as their God; they will be his peoples, and God

himself will be with them; he will wipe every tear from their eyes."

Revelation 21:1-4

Heaven Comes to Earth

John echoes the prophet Isaiah as he describes the reality of a new heaven and new earth. The Greek word translated *new* means new and fresh in quality. As sin and death have been destroyed forever, God, who alone is holy, brings His kingdom of heaven and takes up residence on a purified earth with redeemed and glorified humans. In terms of the new heaven and new earth, William LaSor warns, "We must not press for literal or photographic details, for human eyes have not seen, no ears heard, that which lies beyond our earthly experience." [2]

In this image, there is no more sea. In ancient times, the ocean was viewed as a realm of mythical monsters, a mysterious and frightening force that regularly took human lives. In apocalyptic imagery, the sea is the source of the satanic beast. The absence of the sea is therefore symbolic of the absence of evil from the earth.

As we read symbolic literature, we are always tempted to try to reduce it to our world of reality, to take abstract, profound truth that is so overwhelming we cannot possibly embrace all that it means and whittle it down to our size. Thus, we see people speculating about how much more land there will be on this earth when there are no oceans. Others prepare elaborate charts and diagrams, using the dimensions given for the new Jerusalem later in this chapter, and placing the present city of Jerusalem at the center of the new Jerusalem, then superimposing the specifications given in Revelation on a map of the Middle East, North Africa, Turkey, and the Mediterranean. If you are tempted to interpret Revelation in such a way, you will miss the message. Step back. Take a look at the picture God is painting.

Earlier in the book, I mentioned the phrase Paul uses in Galatians, "the elemental spirits of the world." It's shorthand for our spiritual economic system based upon bartering: you give me something; I give you something back. You do something; you deserve to be paid. That system of barter and trade, deeply engrained within humans, is the host of the virus of legalism—the basic principle of this world, the way the world works. Jesus gives us these wonderful words of freedom, "The first things have passed away" (v. 4).

The new heaven and new earth are just that: new, the old has passed away. No more spiritual barter and trade. There will be no more "old time religion." No more denominations. No more "I'm better than you because..." or "my church is better than your church because...." No more "God is happy with me now; look at everything I have done." The old order of things has passed away. This is the end of religion. Thank God!

Revelation tells us that this new heaven will come to earth. Many Christians have adopted the platonic idea that everything about the physical is bad and that ultimate good dwells either within us or far apart from us—the popular Hollywood vision of heaven. Hollywood heaven usually includes bright white lights, clouds, and lots of harp music. Revelation, on the other hand, tells us another story. Just as God in the person of Jesus came down to this earth to save us, so heaven will eventually come down to this earth. The new heaven and new earth will not rise and ascend from the works, deeds, products, and accomplishments of humans, spiritually or physically. The new heaven and new earth will descend as a manifestation of God's love, a product of grace. The new heaven and new earth *come down* from God, from eternal perfection, descending into our imperfect world, transforming it from old to new, from mortal to immortal.

Everything will be new, but it will also be *here*. Heaven on earth. God will obliterate the works of human hands without revising human history. As in the Incarnation, He again comes into our world, this time perfecting all of it, including the earth itself.

This old earth has been the scene of much bloodshed, many crimes, and many sins. It will also be the place of redemption. We won't leave the earth behind; rather it will be redeemed and recycled. It was good at the beginning (Ge 1:31), and it will be good once again. The good earth started in an idyllic, lush garden created by God, and God will once again turn it into a garden paradise.

You and I have only known an earth of suffering, sin, pain, heartache, warfare, inhumanity, lust, and greed. This passage tells us that a new world is indeed coming; it's a new earth without:

- War
- Terrorists
- Bombs, tanks, or submachine guns
- Hatred or bigotry
- Torture
- Abused children
- Pedophiles or rapists
- Poverty or hunger
- Funerals, cemeteries, or obituaries
- Drug addicts
- Bribes or backroom deals
- Pollution
- Broken marriages or single parent homes
- AIDS, cancer, or Alzheimers
- Mental illness
- Aging
- Deformities
- Death, grief, and mourning
- No synagogues, mosques, or temples, AND, believe it or not, no churches! The new heavens and new earth is the end of religion as

we know it. There will be no more temple (v. 22), for God will be with us, ending all religious systems and places, even that "old time religion."

John refers to the new Jerusalem as a bride, which tells us about God's personal relationship with His people. Contrast this with the Hindu, Buddhist or popular new age idea of heaven, where humans return to a state of impersonal nothingness, without identity, like a raindrop that returns to the ocean. Far beyond that, God is a personal being who desires to live together with us in an intimate, personal relationship—a community, the Holy City, for all eternity.

In verse six, Jesus tells John, "It is done! I am the Alpha and the Omega, the beginning and the end. To the thirsty I will give water as a gift from the spring of the water of life. Those who conquer will inherit these things, and I will be their God and they will be my children."

Is Jesus the only way to salvation? Here we see that Jesus alone owns the spring of eternal life. It can't be bought or earned. It is only given freely by Him. Those who conquer can only do so through Him. Salvation can only be given, not gained through effort. Salvation is only through the cross of Christ: where He did for us what we could not do for ourselves. Salvation is thus absolutely centered in the cross of Christ.

Jesus adds this warning for anyone who would presume that God's grace and the sacrifice of the Lamb of God means that we may live profanely: "But as for the cowardly, the faithless, the polluted, the murderers, the fornicators, the sorcerers, the idolaters, and all liars, their place will be in the lake that burns with fire and sulfur, which is the second death" (v. 8).

Once again, Revelation is without ambiguity. We either accept Jesus Christ or we don't. Beginning in verse 11, John gives a more detailed description of the new Jerusalem. Many have debated, and continue to do so, whether this is intended as a literal description of the city. Of course, it is impossible for us to comprehend what things look like in God's spiritual kingdom, since in this life we see things only through physical eyes. But in this description there is much that can be understood symbolically. The walls are made of transparent gold, symbolizing purity and holiness. The 12 foundations are of precious stone, named for each of the 12 apostles, symbolizing the foundation of the church. The 12 gates, named for each of the 12 tribes of Israel, symbolize the complete elect community of God, the church.

The city is described as a perfect cube, recalling the holy place in the temple, which was a perfect cube. The city has as its temple and as its light source the very presence of God. The city bustles with social activity, with people coming and going. The "kings of the earth" and the "nations" are no longer allied with the Antichrist as they were portrayed earlier in the book, but they are now the redeemed, the servants of Christ.

"Daily" Life in New Jerusalem

[1] Then the angel showed me the river of the water of life, bright as crystal, flowing from the throne of God and of the Lamb [2] through the middle of the street of the city. On either side of the river is the tree of life with its twelve kinds of fruit, producing its fruit each month; and the leaves of the tree are for the healing of the nations. [3] Nothing accursed will be found there any more. But the throne of God and of the Lamb will be in it, and his servants will worship him; [4] they will see his face, and his name will be on their foreheads. [5] And there will be no more night; they need no light of lamp or sun, for the Lord God will be their light, and they will reign forever and ever.

[6] And he said to me, "These words are trustworthy and true, for the Lord, the God of the spirits of the

prophets, has sent his angel to show his servants what must soon take place."

[7] "See, I am coming soon! Blessed is the one who keeps the words of the prophecy of this book."

[8] I, John, am the one who heard and saw these things. And when I heard and saw them, I fell down to worship at the feet of the angel who showed them to me; [9] but he said to me, "You must not do that! I am a fellow servant with you and your comrades the prophets, and with those who keep the words of this book. Worship God!"

[10] And he said to me, "Do not seal up the words of the prophecy of this book, for the time is near. [11] Let the evildoer still do evil, and the filthy still be filthy, and the righteous still do right, and the holy still be holy."

[12] "See, I am coming soon; my reward is with me, to repay according to everyone's work. [13] I am the Alpha and the Omega, the first and the last, the beginning and the end."

[14] Blessed are those who wash their robes, so that they will have the right to the tree of life and may enter the city by the gates. [15] Outside are the dogs and sorcerers and fornicators and murderers and idolaters, and everyone who loves and practices falsehood.

[16] "It is I, Jesus, who sent my angel to you with this testimony for the churches. I am the root and the descendant of David, the bright morning star."

[17] The Spirit and the bride say, "Come."

And let everyone who hears say, "Come."

And let everyone who is thirsty come.

Let anyone who wishes take the water of life as a gift.

[18] I warn everyone who hears the words of the prophecy of this book: if anyone adds to them, God will add to that person the plagues described in this book; [19] if anyone takes away from the words of the book of this prophecy, God will take away that person's share in the tree of life and in the holy city, which are described in this book.

[20] The one who testifies to these things says, "Surely I am coming soon."

Amen. Come, Lord Jesus!

[21] The grace of the Lord Jesus be with all the saints. Amen.

Revelation 22:1-21

Jesus directs John's attention to life inside the city. John reports that he saw a pure river of life, clear as crystal, flowing from the throne through the city, with trees bearing fruit on either side. The imagery of the river is similar to that of Ezekiel 47, a river flanked by trees that produce fruit and healing leaves, descriptive of the abundant and far-reaching effects of Jesus' work on the cross. There is no ill that cannot be cured and healed by God's grace. The city illuminated by the light of God echoes Isaiah 60:19 where the sun and moon are made obsolete by God's glory.

As we near the end of the book, we are reminded in verse six that the message of Revelation is trustworthy and that Jesus is coming soon. What did Jesus mean by "soon"? Is nineteen centuries from the time the book was written until this present day "soon"? Some say these prophecies have already been fulfilled; however, it seems obvious many of these prophecies have not, such as those of chapters twenty-one and twenty-two. Death is still with us, evil still exists in the world, the first heaven and the first earth are still here. Some believe these prophecies are being fulfilled in heaven, and there already is a new heaven and new earth that comes down to this earth and lives within the lives of those who accept Jesus Christ. Others point out that heaven is like this description; it is the eternity we enter when we die, and the eternity our resurrected bodies will inhabit forever and ever.

And while those viewpoints may be a part of what is meant here, we are still presented with the fact that the bodily second coming of Jesus has not yet taken place. Yet, in verses 7, 12, and 20 of this last chapter of Revelation and of the Bible, Jesus tells us He is coming soon. Perhaps the best way to deal with a word like *soon* in this context is to understand that by God's way of thinking, in any generation, "soon" could be when the believer dies and goes to be with God. "Soon" for all of us is just that; for we live, on average, no more than 70 or 80 years. Whether we live in the first century or the twenty-first century, Jesus is coming soon. The Revelation is never out of date.

He IS Coming!

Verses 11-17 begin the conclusion and call to action of Revelation, and again we are focused on the Lamb of God. Verses 11 and 15 warn that human deeds will never be enough to please God; only the imputed righteousness of Jesus Christ makes us pure and holy. Jesus assures us once more that He is indeed coming; and the only way into the Holy City, the new Jerusalem, is to have our robes washed in the blood of the Lamb, to believe in Jesus and accept Him as Lord. The invitation to accept His free gift is always there. The invitation to come to Jesus is always there; the door is always open.

"The Spirit and the bride say, 'Come!' And let everyone who hears say, 'Come!' And let everyone who is thirsty come. Let anyone who wishes take the water of life as a gift" (v. 17).

Verse 18 is a stern warning to all who would add to the gospel of Jesus Christ or take away from it—to all who misrepresent God, to all who add legalistic requirements to the gospel, to all who would turn the grace of our Lord Jesus Christ into the slavery of legalistic religion. There is no Christian life that is possible unless Jesus lives within us. If we replace Him, or we try to improve Him, then we do not have Him; we only have some cheapened counterfeit that leads to death.

There has never been a greater need for the Book of Revelation than there is right now. Seldom, if ever, have so many thought they understood exactly what the message of Revelation is while being so far from the truth of the gospel of Jesus Christ. Revelation is not primarily a precise prophecy of specific events, nor is it primarily a history. Far more than answering our questions about *when* events will happen, Revelation introduces us to the *who*, the "Lamb of God who takes away the sin of the world" (Jo 1:29).

And finally, for the third time in this last chapter of Revelation, in verse 20 Jesus tells us, "Surely I am coming soon."

And what a fitting conclusion to the powerful and meaningful book that we read in verse 21, "The grace of the Lord Jesus be with the saints. Amen."

There is no call here for futile human attempts to win God's favor by regulations, ritual, or regimentation. There is no call to improve upon what God has given us. We are not urged to make sure that we do everything we can because God helps those who help themselves.

Jesus concludes the Book of Revelation just as it began. In the beginning and at the end, as well as throughout all of its chapters and verses, the Revelation of Jesus Christ is all about God's amazing grace given freely because of the cross of Christ. Revelation concludes with a blessing and request that "the grace of the Lord Jesus be with the saints." There is no greater gift we could ask for or that we could expect. The grace of our Lord Jesus is what we need; and as He lives His life within us, what we want. Even so come, Lord Jesus.

If you haven't responded to Jesus' open invitation to turn from all of the isms, false religions, and religious legalisms that can only bring you misery and death, now is a good time to accept Him alone as your Savior. This book, the Revelation of Jesus Christ, is all about Him, the Lamb of God who alone can save you. It is truly the good news of Jesus Christ. May God open your eyes to know that more than you ever have before. Reject religion that enslaves, and embrace Jesus, who alone can liberate and save you. And may the grace of our Lord Jesus Christ be with you, now and forever.

Notes

CHAPTER ONE

1. Yancey, Philip. *The Jesus I Never Knew*
   (Grand Rapids: Zondervan, 1995), 239.

2. Ellul, Jacques. *Apocalypse: The Book of Revelation*
   (New York: Seabury Press, 1977), 10.

3. Lindsey, Hal. *The Terminal Generation*
   (Old Tappan, NJ: Fleming H. Revell, 1976), 44.

CHAPTER TWO

1. Jeske, Richard L. *Revelation for Today: Images of Hope*
   (Philadelphia: Fortress Press, 1983), 21.

2. Ibid, 23.

3. Minear, Paul S. *Christian Hope and the Second Coming*
   (Philadelphia: Westminster Press, 1954), 161.

4. Ibid, 169.

5. Moltmann, Jurgen. *Theology of Hope* (Trans. J.W. Leitch, New York:
   Harper & Row, 1967, Orig. pub. 1964), 17.

6. Ellul, Jacques. *Apocalypse: The Book of Revelation*, 30.

7. Mounce, Robert H. *The Book of Revelation*
   (Grand Rapids: Wm. B. Eerdmans, 1977), 19.

8. Ladd, George E. *A Commentary on the Revelation of John*
   (Grand Rapids: Eerdmans, 1972), 102.

9. Caird, G.B. *The Language and Imagery of the Bible*
   (Philadelphia: Westminster Press, 1980), 17.

10. Minear, Paul S. *Christian Hope and the Second Coming*, 175.

11. Wilcock, Michael. *The Message of Revelation: I Saw Heaven Opened* (Downers Grove: Inter-Varsity, 1975), 24.

12. Minear, Paul S. *Christian Hope and the Second Coming*, 166.

13. LaSor, William Sanford. *The Truth About Armageddon* (San Francisco: Harper & Row, 1982), 139-140.

14. Jeske, Richard L. *Revelation for Today: Images of Hope*, 54.

CHAPTER THREE

1. Jeske, Richard L. *Revelation for Today: Images of Hope*, 41.

2. Ibid, 42.

3. Moltmann, Jurgen. *Theology of Hope*, 18.

CHAPTER FOUR

1. Jeske, Richard L. *Revelation for Today: Images of Hope*, 12.

2. Caird, G. B. *The Language and Imagery of the Bible*, 61.

3. Fuller, Daniel P. *Gospel and Law: Contrast or Continuum?* (Grand Rapids: Wm. B. Eerdmans, 1980) xi.

4. Ellul. *Apocalypse: The Book of Revelation*, 128.

5. Jeske, Richard L. *Revelation for Today: Images of Hope*, 43.

CHAPTER FIVE

1. Ramsay, W. M. *The Letters to the Seven Churches of Asia* (Grand Rapids: Wm. B. Eerdmans, 1959), 44.

2. Wilcock, Michael. *The Message of Revelation: I Saw Heaven Opened*, 55.

3. Fuller, Daniel P. *Gospel and Law: Contrast or Continuum?*, 161.

4. Ladd, George E. *A Commentary on the Revelation of John*, 6 3.

5.   Ibid, 64.

6.   Ramsay, W. M. *The Letters to the Seven Churches of Asia*, 46.

7.   Ladd, George E. *The Gospel of the Kingdom*
     (Grand Rapids: Wm. B. Eerdmans, 1959), 101.

CHAPTER SIX

1.   Ladd, George E. *A Commentary on the Revelation of John*, 74.

2.   Caird, G. B. *The Language and Imagery of the Bible*, 18.

3.   Ladd, George E. *A Commentary on the Revelation of John*, 80.

4.   Torrance, Thomas F. *The Apocalypse Today*
     (Grand Rapids: Wm. B. Eerdmans, 1959), 38.

5.   Wilcock, Michael. *The Message of Revelation: I Saw Heaven Opened*, 69.

6.   Ibid, 77.

7.   Torrance, Thomas F. *The Apocalypse Today,* 44.

8.   Ibid, 45.

9.   Shea, Nina. *In the Lion's Den: A Shocking Account of Persecution and
     Martyrdom of Christians Today and How We Should Respond*,
     (Nashville: Broadman & Holman, 1997), 1.

10. Ladd, George E. *A Commentary on the Revelation of John*, 107.

11. Minear, Paul S. *Christian Hope and the Second Coming*, 162.

CHAPTER SEVEN

1.   Hiett, Peter. *Eternity Now!* (Nashville: Integrity Publishers, 2003), x.

2.   DeMar, Gary. *End Times Fiction* (Nashville: Thomas Nelson, 2001), 17.

3.   Ibid, 22-24.

4.   Lindsey, Hal. *The Terminal Generation*, 185.

5. Ladd, George E. *The Presence of the Future* (Grand Rapids: Wm. B. Eerdmans, 1974), 62.

6. Jeske, Richard L. *Revelation for Today: Images of Hope*, 14.

7. Minear, Paul S. *Christian Hope and the Second Coming*, 162.

CHAPTER EIGHT

1. Lindsey, Hal. *The Terminal Generation*, 50.

2. Wilcock, Michael. *The Message of Revelation: I Saw Heaven Opened*, 60.

3. Ladd, George E. *A Commentary on the Revelation of John*, 114.

4. Wilcock, Michael. *The Message of Revelation: I Saw Heaven Opened*, 83.

5. Ellul, Jacques. *Apocalypse: The Book of Revelation*, 168.

6. Ibid, 217.

CHAPTER NINE

1. Ellul, Jacques. *Apocalypse: The Book of Revelation*, 85.

2. Caird, G.B. *The Language and Imagery of the Bible*, 55.

3. Hiett, Peter. *Eternity Now!*, 159.

4. Torrance, Thomas F. *The Apocalypse Today*, 77.

5. Boyer, Paul. *When Time Shall Be No More—Prophecy Belief in Modern American Culture* (Cambridge, Massachusetts: Harvard University Press, 1992), 43.

6. Minear, Paul S. *Christian Hope and the Second Coming*, 156.

7. LaSor, William Sanford. *The Truth About Armageddon*, 114.

8. Ladd, George E. *A Commentary on the Revelation of John*, 114.

9. Torrance, Thomas F. *The Apocalypse Today*, 93.

CHAPTER TEN

1. Minear, Paul S. *Christian Hope and the Second Coming*, 172.

2. LaSor, William Sanford. *The Truth About Armageddon*, 146.

3. Morris, Leon. *Apocalyptic* (Grand Rapids: Wm. B. Eerdmans, 1972), 82.

4. Ellul, Jacques. *Apocalypse: The Book of Revelation*, 190-191.

5. Torrance, Thomas F. *The Apocalypse Today*, 119-120.

6. Ibid, 116.

7. Ibid, 121.

8. Ladd, George E. *The Gospel of the Kingdom*, 64.

CHAPTER ELEVEN

1. Gregg, Steve. *Revelation: Four Views, A Parallel Commentary* (Nashville: Thomas Nelson, 1997), 458.

2. Gregory of Nyssa in *The Nicene and Post-Nicene Fathers,* Second Series, Volume Five (Grand Rapids: Wm. B. Eerdmans, 1988), 544.

3. LaSor, William Sanford. *The Truth About Armageddon*, 139.

4. Ibid, 190.

5. Ladd, George E. *A Commentary on the Revelation of John*, 274.

CHAPTER TWELVE

1. Morris, Leon. *Apocalyptic*, 53.

2. LaSor, William Sanford. *The Truth About Armageddon*, 196.

Bibliography

Barclay, William. *The Revelation of John. The Daily Study Bible.* 2 volumes. Philadelphia: Westminster Press, 1960.

Berkhof, Louis. *The Second Coming of Christ.* Grand Rapids: Wm. B. Eerdmans, 1953.

Bock, Darrell. *Three Views on the Millennium and Beyond.* Grand Rapids, Zondervan, 1999.

Berkouwer, G. C. *The Return of Christ.* Grand Rapids: Wm. B. Eerdmans, 1972.

Boer, Harry R. *The Book of Revelation.* Grand Rapids: Wm. B. Eerdmans, 1979.

Boyer, Paul. *When Time Shall Be No More—Prophecy Belief in Modern American Culture.* Cambridge, Massachusetts: Harvard University Press, 1992.

Caird, G. B. *The Language and Imagery of the Bible.* Philadelphia: Westminster Press, 1980.

Clouse, Robert G. *The Meaning of the Millennium: Four Views.* Downers Grove, Illinois: Inter-Varsity Press, 1977.

DeMar, Gary. *End Times Fiction.* Nashville: Thomas Nelson, 2001.

Ellul, Jacques. *Apocalypse.* New York: Seabury Press Inc., 1977.

Fee, Gordon D. and Stuart, Douglas. *How to Read the Bible For All Its Worth.* Grand Rapids: Zondervan, 1993.

Fuller, Daniel P. *Gospel and Law: Contrast or Continuum?* Grand Rapids: Wm. B. Eerdmans, 1980.

Gregg, Steve. *Revelation: Four Views, A Parallel Commentary.* Nashville: Thomas Nelson, 1997.

Grenz, Stanley J. *The Millennial Maze: Sorting Out Evangelical Options.* Downers Grove, Illinois: Inter-Varsity Press, 1992.

Gundry, Robert H. *A Survey of the New Testament.* Grand Rapids: Zondervan, 1970.

Harrison, E. F. *Introduction to the New Testament.* Grand Rapids: Wm. B. Eerdmans, 1964.

Hendrikson, William. *More than Conquerors.* Grand Rapids: Baker Book House, 1944.

Hiett, Peter. *Eternity Now!* Nashville: Integrity Publishers, 2003.

Hubbard, David Allan. *The Second Coming.* Downers Grove, Ill.: Inter-Varsity Press, 1984.

Jeske, Richard L. *Revelation for Today: Images of Hope.* Philadelphia: Fortress Press, 1983.

Kyle, Richard. *The Last Days are Here Again.* Grand Rapids: Baker Book House, 1998.

Ladd, George E. *The Gospel of the Kingdom.* Grand Rapids: Wm. B. Eerdmans, 1959.

_____ *A Commentary on the Revelation of John.* Grand Rapids: Wm. B. Eerdmans, 1972.

_____ *The Presence of the Future.* Grand Rapids: Wm. B. Eerdmans, 1974.

Larkin, Clarence. *Dispensational Truth.* Philadelphia, by author, 1918.

LaSor, William Sanford. *The Truth About Armageddon.* San Francisco: Harper & Row, 1982.

Lindsey, Hal. *There's a New World Coming.* Santa Ana, Calif. Vision House, 1973.

Lindsey, Hal. *The Terminal Generation.* Old Tappan, NJ: Fleming H. Revell, 1976.

Mickelsen, A. Berkeley. *Interpreting the Bible.* Grand Rapids: Wm. B. Eerdmans, 1963.

Minear, Paul S. *Christian Hope and the Second Coming.* Philadelphia: Westminster Press, 1954.

Moltmann, Jurgen. *Theology of Hope.* Trans. J. W. Leitch, New York: Harper & Row, 1967 (Orig. pub. 1964).

Morris, Leon. *Apocalyptic.* Grand Rapids: Wm. B. Eerdmans, 1972.

_____ *The Revelation of St. John. The Tyndale New Testament Commentaries.* Grand Rapids: Wm. B. Eerdmans, 1969.

Newport, John P. *The Lion and the Lamb.* Nashville: Broadman Press, 1986.

Ramsay, W. M. *The Letters to the Seven Churches of Asia.* Grand Rapids: Baker Book House, 1963.

Sproul, R.C. *Knowing Scripture.* Downers Grove, Ill.: Inter-Varsity Press, 1977.

Shea, Nina. *In The Lion's Den.* Nashville: Holman & Broadman, 1997.

Torrance, Thomas F. *The Apocalypse Today.* Grand Rapids: Wm. B. Eerdmans, 1959.

Wall, Robert W. *Revelation. New International Critical Commentary.* Peabody, Massachusetts. Hendrikson Publishers, 1991.

Wilcock, Michael. *The Message of Revelation: I Saw Heaven Opened.* Downers Grove: Inter-Varsity, 1975.

A Call for Reformation

Almost 500 years after Martin Luther nailed his 95 theses to the Wittenberg church door, *Bad News Religion* identifies the most dangerous spiritual virus of the 21st century—a plague that can infect our hearts and minds, and finally control our souls—the deadly virus of religious legalism!
Bad News Religion can be purchased through your local bookstore or ordered through Plain Truth Ministries by calling **1-800-309-4466** or online at **www.ptm.org**.

CHRISTIANITY
——WITHOUT——
THE RELIGION

PLAIN TRUTH MINISTRIES